South Asia on the Move

 # Publications

The International Institute for Asian Studies (IIAS) is a research and exchange platform based in Leiden, the Netherlands. Its objective is to encourage the interdisciplinary and comparative study of Asia and to promote (inter)national cooperation. IIAS focuses on the humanities and social sciences and on their interaction with other sciences. It stimulates scholarship on Asia and is instrumental in forging research networks among Asia Scholars. Its main research interests are reflected in the four book series published with Amsterdam University Press: Global Asia, Asian Cities, Asian Heritages and Humanities *Across* Borders (HAB).

IIAS acts as an international mediator, bringing together various parties in Asia and other parts of clearinghouse of knowledge and information. This entails activities such as providing information services, the construction and support of international networks and cooperative projects, and the organization of seminars and conferences. In this way, IIAS functions as a window on Europe for non-European scholars and contributes to the cultural rapprochement between Europe and Asia.

IIAS Publications Officer: Mary Lynn van Dijk

Global Asia

Asia has a long history of transnational linkages with other parts of the world. Yet the contribution of Asian knowledge, values, and practices in the making of the modern world has largely been overlooked until recent years. The rise of Asia is often viewed as a challenge to the existing world order. Such a bifurcated view overlooks the fact that the global order has been shaped by Asian experiences as much as the global formation has shaped Asia. The Global Asia Series takes this understanding as the point of departure. It addresses contemporary issues related to transnational interactions within the Asian region, as well as Asia's projection into the world through the movement of goods, people, ideas, knowledge, ideologies, and so forth. The series aims to publish timely and well-researched books that will have the cumulative effect of developing new perspectives and theories about global Asia.

Series Editors
Tak-Wing Ngo, University of Macau, Macau

Editorial Board
Kevin Hewison, The University of North Carolina at Chapel Hill, USA
Hagen Koo, University of Hawaii, USA
Loraine Kennedy, École des Hautes Études en Sciences Sociales (EHESS), France
Guobin Yang, University of Pennsylvania, USA

South Asia on the Move

Mobilities, Mobilizations, Maneuvers

Edited by
Benjamin Linder and
Tarini Bedi

Amsterdam University Press

The publication of this book is made possible by the International Institute for Asian Studies.

Cover illustration: photo by Benjamin Linder
Cover design: Coördesign, Leiden
Lay-out: Crius Group, Hulshout

ISBN	978 94 6372 649 8
e-ISBN	978 90 4855 777 6 (pdf)
DOI	10.5117/9789463726498
NUR	906

Creative Commons License CC-BY NC ND (http://creativecommons.org/licenses/by-nc-nd/4.0)

Ⓒ Authors / Amsterdam University Press B.V., Amsterdam 2025

Some rights reserved. Without limiting the rights under copyright reserved above, any part of this book may be reproduced, stored in or introduced into a retrieval system, or transmitted, in any form or by any means (electronic, mechanical, photocopying, recording or otherwise).

Every effort has been made to obtain permission to use all copyrighted illustrations reproduced in this book. nonetheless, whosoever believes to have rights to this material is advised to contact the publisher.

Table of Contents

1 Introduction: South Asia on the Move　　　　　　　　　　7
　Benjamin Linder

2 Gendering Distance: Marriage and Mobility in Bangladesh's
　Riverine Borderlands　　　　　　　　　　　　　　　　35
　Malini Sur

3 At the Love Commandos: Narratives of Mobility Among
　Intercaste Couples in a Delhi Safe House　　　　　　　51
　Rashmi Sadana

4 Driving While Tamil: Policing as a Regime of Mobility in
　Postwar Jaffna, Sri Lanka　　　　　　　　　　　　　　67
　daniel dillon

5 Adventure Time: Adventure Tourism and the "Annihilation of
　Space by Time" in Nepal　　　　　　　　　　　　　　93
　Mark Liechty

6 After *Eat, Pray, Love*: Tourism, Orientalism, and Cartographies
　of Salvation　　　　　　　　　　　　　　　　　　　111
　Rumya S. Putcha

7 The Mobility of Regional Labor Hierarchies: Nepali
　Employment and Entrepreneurialism in the "South Asian" Gas
　Stations of North Texas　　　　　　　　　　　　　　129
　Andrew Nelson

8 Sometimes She Stands Like a Statue: Immobility in the
　Archives of Colonial Psychiatry　　　　　　　　　　　151
　Sarah Pinto

9 Disability on the Move: Disabled Mobilities in Contemporary
　India　　　　　　　　　　　　　　　　　　　　　　179
　Michele Friedner and James Staples

10 Conclusion: Thinking Theory, Pedagogy, Method   199
   Tarini Bedi

Index   215

1 Introduction: South Asia on the Move

Benjamin Linder

Abstract: The "new mobilities paradigm" (or "mobilities turn") has been one of the most fertile attempts at trans-/post-disciplinary scholarship in recent social theory. Yet notwithstanding its strides towards topical and geographical diversity, there remains a relative lacuna of studies about non-Western lifeworlds and contexts. South Asia—home to nearly one-fourth of the world's population, and with a diaspora spanning the entire world—has a particular experience of mobility that calls out for such a project. A special focus on mobilities, particularly from an ethnographic perspective, enables a more encompassing, intimate, and socially thick understanding of the region. Moreover, given the turn's roots, primarily in the United Kingdom and Northern Europe, a perspective on and from South Asia helps to provincialize Western approaches to (im)mobility. After briefly charting the rise of the mobilities turn, this introductory chapter makes the case for precisely this sort of regional approach to South Asian mobilities and briefly introduces the chapters that follow it.

Keywords: mobilities, South Asia, movement, postcolonialism

Locating: An Introduction

South Asia is on the move. The region moves and *is* moved, imaginatively and corporeally, territorially and technologically, culturally and geologically. Its tectonic movements drive the Himalayas to ever-greater heights but also generate devastating earthquake energies. The region houses rickshaws and metros, border-crossers and traders. It propels and attracts immigrants at multiple scales. Its varied cultural forms—from yoga to *samosa*, Ayurveda to Bollywood—traverse the globe. It is continually reshaped by political mobilizations and blockages, facilitations and frictions. South Asia itself emerged at the confluence of multi-scalar and multi-temporal

---

Linder, Benjamin, & Tarini Bedi (eds), *South Asia on the Move: Mobilities, Mobilizations, Maneuvers*. Amsterdam: Amsterdam University Press 2025
doi: 10.5117/9789463726498_CH01

(im)mobilities: ancient traders and religious pilgrims, imperial administrators and revolutionaries, Orientalist scholars and postcolonial theorists, Partition and refugees, diasporic migrants and their ambivalent returns, layered territories and patchy enclaves. The diversity of such movements is dizzying. We aim here to begin a conversation: one that grapples with the regional particularities of South Asian mobilities, one that situates them historically and ethnographically, and one that interrogates the territorial and disciplinary boundaries through which they are continually propelled, obstructed, and diverted.

In pursuit of such a conversation, this volume draws together diverse perspectives on mobilities in South Asia, that vast subcontinental region comprising Bangladesh, Bhutan, India, the Maldives, Nepal, Pakistan, and Sri Lanka. Depending on who does the tallying, we might also include Afghanistan, Tibet, and Myanmar in certain instances. Attunements to motion affect how we think not only of people and objects but also of regions and territories. The "new mobilities paradigm" (or "mobilities turn") has been one of the most fertile attempts at trans-/post-disciplinary scholarship in recent social theory. Yet notwithstanding its strides towards topical and geographical diversity, there remains a relative lacuna of studies about non-Western lifeworlds and contexts. South Asia—home to nearly one-fourth of the world's population, and with a diaspora spanning the entire world—has a particular experience of mobility that calls out for such a project. This is not to say that no work has been done in this vein—quite the contrary, in fact, as this introduction aims to demonstrate. Nevertheless, there have been surprisingly few attempts to gather and contrast such works under a regional umbrella. This introductory chapter makes the case for precisely this sort of regional approach to South Asian mobilities and briefly introduces the chapters that follow it. We ask what the mobilities paradigm can do for us when we look from and with South Asian lifeworlds, South Asian languages, and South Asian political relations. As all contributors to this volume suggest, these are inherently entangled with the world at large.

The "new mobilities paradigm" swept through the social sciences and humanities in the past two decades. Several reviews have charted this rise to prominence (e.g., Cresswell 2010, 2012, 2014; Merriman 2015, 2016, 2017; Adey et al. 2014a; Kwan and Schwanen 2016). Its commencement is difficult to date with any precision. The Centre for Mobilities Research (CeMoRe) at Lancaster University was established in 2003, though even their work built upon earlier theoretical strides in philosophy and social theory. For our purposes, 2006 is the most defensible year to begin. In 2006, two landmark articles set the stage, sketching the theoretical, methodological, and topical possibilities for this emergent perspective (Sheller and Urry 2006; Hannam, Sheller, and Urry 2006). These two publications articulated an emergent perspective, and, in so doing, gathered and focused its energies into a veritable agenda. Hannam, Sheller, and Urry's (2006) piece, moreover, was the editorial that inaugurated *Mobilities*, a journal that rapidly earned significant traction. Tim Cresswell's (2006a) *On the Move: Mobilities in the Modern Western World* appeared that year as well, followed by John Urry's (2007) *Mobilities* the following year. Taken together, this constellation of work coalesced into the backbone of mobilities research.

South Asia on the Move commemorates, sustains, and extends this tradition. Of course, South Asia has a long history of being analyzed and researched through other lenses and paradigms, and many of these were in some way concerned with movement. However, a special focus on mobilities, particularly from an ethnographic perspective, enables a more encompassing, intimate, and socially thick understanding of the region. The chapters that follow demonstrate the manifold possibilities of such an approach through their attention to diverse topics, from intercaste romance to disability, from medical immobilities to leisure tourism. If it has been almost twenty years since the initial mobilities turn, what new trajectories can South Asia open? What disruptions and productive challenges can it level towards a literature that remains disproportionately focused elsewhere? What would it mean to "re-Orient" (Frank 1998) mobilities studies, to thoroughly "provincialize" (Chakrabarty 2000) Western approaches to movement?

Mobilizing: The Mobilities Turn

At its core, the mobilities turn highlights the centrality, even ubiquity, of movement in the (re)constitution of social and political life. It redresses the pervasive "sedantarist metaphysics" (Malkki 1996) that assumes fixity, stasis, and enclosure as primary to movement, dynamism, and openness. Everything is mobile, in multiple ways and at multiple scales.

> Mobilities are centrally involved in reorganizing institutions, generating climate change, moving risks and illnesses across the globe, altering travel, tourism and migration patterns, producing a more distant family life, transforming the social and educational life of young people, connecting distant people through "weak ties" and so on. The human body and the home are transformed, as proximity and connectivity are imagined in new ways and often enhanced by communication devices

and likely to be "on the move." Changes also transform the nature, scale and temporalities of families, "local" communities, public and private spaces, and the commitments people may feel to the "nation." (Hannam, Sheller, and Urry 2006, 2)

Such an insight spread rapidly across the humanities and social sciences. Within geography, mobilities has joined other central concepts in the geographer's lexicon (e.g., space, place, territory, scale). This attests to the program's success (Kwan and Schwanen 2016), but also reflects the sense of intellectual promise and fertility with which it was greeted.

But, of course, the mobilities turn did not emerge in a vacuum. Its leading thinkers are quick to credit their diverse theoretical antecedents: Georg Simmel's (1997) urban sociology; science and technology studies; actor-network theory (Latour 2005); the spatial turn of earlier decades (see Sheller 2017); social network analysis; theoretical engagements with affect, sensation, and emotion; dynamic or complex systems analysis; Deleuze and Guattari's (1987) thinking on rhizomes, nomadology, and assemblages. To this hefty list, we might add other intellectual currents of the decades leading up to the mobilities turn: anthropologies of globalization (Appadurai 1996; Clifford 1997; Tsing 2005) and the progressive geographies of Doreen Massey (1994, 2005), as well as literatures on transport geography, tourism, migration, and borders, all of which have (im)mobilities baked into their respective objects. Mobilities work also deploys a wide array of research methodologies.[1] The new mobilities paradigm, in other words, is itself an assemblage, a patchwork of diverse provenance and composition. From the outset, it never aimed at total description; rather, it "suggests a set of questions, theories, and methodologies" (Sheller and Urry 2006, 210). It is a field characterized by "heterogeneity and continual development" (Faulconbridge and Hui 2016, 2). Indeed, its "multi-disciplinarity and plurality is an important hallmark of this rapidly expanding field" (Merriman 2015, 561; see also Adey et al. 2014b).

What, then, is the value of this paradigm? Given its refusal of disciplinary, regional, or even theoretical unity, is the mobilities turn too broad to have analytical traction? Since its inception, mobilities scholars have laid out several hallmarks that distinguish it from antecedent and related literatures. First, mobilities are fundamentally about meaning (Cresswell

---

[1] For discussions and examples of such diverse methods, see Fincham, McGuinness, and Murray (2009); Büscher, Urry, and Witchger (2010); and the chapters comprising Section 7 ("Methodologies") of Adey et al. (2014).

2006a). Moving beyond the rigid cartographies of transport geography or technocratic planning, mobilities research is far more concerned with the experiences, cultural mediations, and affective resonances that attend to movement. It links itself less with positivist spatial science than with critical and humanistic social science: "Mobility here is as much about meaning as it is about mappable and calculable movement" (Cresswell 2010, 552). Second, the mobilities turn is multi-scalar—or, even better, inter-scalar. It does not conceive of movement through hierarchies of discrete scalar levels (e.g., from the body to the planetary) but rather seeks to understand the entanglements of vectors as they traverse varied distances. Third, the mobilities perspective does not prize any particular mode or method of movement, enabling a linked analysis of everything from microbial spread to airplanes, from virtual information transfer to quotidian walking. Fourth, it takes mobility as the norm rather than the pathology, the rule rather than the exception. This works against the static ontologies of a sedantarist metaphysics. From a mobilities perspective, everything is necessarily, inevitably, constantly on the move—constituted, expressed, and assembled through overlapping routes. As outlined below, the authors in this volume explicitly attend to these dimensions of movement.

It is tempting to view this emphasis on dynamic movement with skepticism, to criticize it as a theoretical fad that is too romantic and Pollyannaish about mobility. To do so, however, ignores a set of core ideas that have been with the literature since its inception. The goal of the mobilities turn was never to replace a sedentarist metaphysics with a nomadic metaphysics. Even the earliest statements from within the literature are emphatic about this point. Mobilities must always be seen in relation to moorings (Sheller and Urry 2006), to frictions (Tsing 2005), to "place, stopping, stillness, and relative immobility" (Cresswell 2010, 552). In the very first issue of *Mobilities*, Peter Adey (2006) already observes that if everything is on the move, such a perspective will have little theoretical and explanatory purchase. As he puts it in that article's title, "If Mobility is Everything Then it is Nothing." This is the key to understanding the relational politics of mobilities *and* immobilities (Adey 2010). How are regimes of (im)mobility produced through legal, political, and cultural institutions (Cresswell 2006b, 2010b)? Who can move and who cannot? What are the qualities of these movements? How do mobilities depend on the relative immobility of infrastructure, political apparatuses, and populations? The mobilities perspective may begin with the foundational premise of a mobile universe, but it is a *differentially* mobile universe. It is a universe constituted by myriad movements that vary dramatically in terms of velocity, quality, direction, and duration.

One challenge, then, is to understand the breadth of (im)mobility experiences in diverse contexts. Ethnography remains particularly well-suited to capturing the diversity, nuance, and texture of lived experience, as this volume demonstrates. The chapters that follow are linked by a central concern for understanding the politics, cultural imaginaries, embodiments, and infrastructures of (im)mobility in South Asia. Put simply, this book examines varied experiences of movement (and stillness) as a means of better apprehending everyday life in and beyond the region.

Diverting: The Provinciality of Western Mobilities

Despite its far-reaching applications, the mobilities paradigm was spearheaded largely by a group of sociologists and geographers in the United Kingdom and Northern/Western Europe (Cresswell 2016). Especially in its early years, this created a series of (under)emphases and gaps. It was a body of work primarily practiced by Western scholars, trained and situated at Western academic institutions, and focused on Western contexts. Mobilities work did not actively exclude scholars, histories, and geographic contexts of the Global South. Quite the contrary, even the early works encourage and gesture towards these sorts of contributions. Even so, it is hard not to notice the disproportionate focus on Euro-American sites relative to those of Asia, Africa, South America, and elsewhere. Ten years into the mobilities turn, it could still be claimed that critical mobilities research was mostly "producing Northern-centric theorizations and marginalizing mobility articulations in global South contexts" (Cook and Butz 2015, 388). Asia, home to over half of the world's people, has received nowhere near its due proportion of mobilities coverage (Mom and Kim 2013; Lin and Yeoh 2016; Lin 2016).

Fortunately, this has progressively improved over the past ten years, and particularly in the past five. Five years into its run, *Mobilities* published a special issue devoted to Singapore. The launch of the journal *Transfers* in 2011 unleashed a welcome increase of non-Western perspectives, particularly with special issues and sections devoted to Asia and rickshaws. In 2016, *Environment and Planning A* devoted an issue to a series of papers on Asian mobilities originally delivered in 2013 at an Asia Research Institute conference at the National University of Singapore. Also in 2016, the *Annals of the Association of American Geographers* ran a special issue on mobilities, and the guest editors explicitly made decentering the literature a key theme, reflecting a "long overdue shift away from its conventional orientation toward the Global North" (Kwan and Schwanen, 2016, 249).[2] Between 2014 and 2018, the Centre d'Etudes de l'Inde et de l'Asie du Sud (Centre for South Asian Studies) in Paris organized a seminar/lecture series on South Asian mobilities. At the University of Chicago, the 2015 graduate student conference chose "South Asian Mobilities" as its theme. By 2017, Amsterdam University Press launched its "New Mobilities in Asia" book series. This is surely an incomplete list, but these are all promising signs that a reorientation of mobilities research is well underway.

South Asia is crucial to the project of reorienting mobilities research. In the late twentieth century, the region famously gave rise to some of the most trenchant, lasting, and intellectually engaging critiques of Eurocentrism, Orientalism, and the condition of postcoloniality. The nations of South Asia have a unique and particular relationship to imperial occupation and colonial violence, to postcolonial state formation and its contested frontiers. As it was for postcolonial theory, the goal is not only a matter of geographical and demographic representation, nor is it a matter of offering "alternative" historiographies, cartographies, and anthropologies. The project runs deeper than that. A radical decentering begs questions of ontology and the politics of knowledge production.

> It would also enable the generation of mobility theories that are no longer formulated predominantly in the West or on the basis of European-American ideas and practices regarding methods, data, and analysis. Also, Western theories would not simply be exported as if they were universal tools for making sense of other parts of the world that are taken to be little more than fields where materials can be harvested to test and refine theories formulated from a Western standpoint. (Kwan and Schwanen 2016, 251–52)

An excessive focus on Western/Northern mobilities not only yields explanations of questionable utility and applicability to the rest of the world. It also tends to position Western experiences, concepts, and formations as universal, despite being, in fact, particular and situated.

South Asian mobilities (and non-Western mobilities generally) deserve more attention, but a problem of definition immediately arises. As we have

---

2   Notwithstanding the admirable diversity of this special issue, it is worth noting that South Asia remains almost entirely absent, with the possible exception of Staeheli, Marshall, and Maynard's (2016) article on citizenship, which partially draws on a conference that took place in Sri Lanka.

seen, the mobilities turn encompasses a diversity of theoretical orientations, topical foci, academic disciplines, and research practitioners. To these, we want to add a sustained, deliberate diversification of geographic region and demography. What, then, constitutes "South Asian mobilities" as a research agenda? It cannot merely be a matter of studying things *that* move, since everything does at multiple scales; nor of studying movements bounded by territorial and regional geographies, since border crossings, immigration, and diaspora must also remain in our frame; nor of studying only South Asian bodies, lest we exclude the colonial authorities, tourists, expats, and development workers whose critical mobilities continue to shape life in the region. South Asian mobilities must include all of these while reducing to none of them. We advocate an expansive view. South Asian mobilities are diversely routed, weaving together multiple temporalities and scales. They are practiced by Americans in Bhutan and by Sri Lankans in Australia, Nepalis in Doha and rickshaw drivers in Delhi. They are imaginative and mediated as much as they are embodied and corporeal. They are also morethan-human and multinatural (Birtchnell 2016), including everything from timber (Grover 2000) to elephants (Shell 2015; Sohoni 2018). They intersect and move together. They diverge and obstruct. They encompass airline jets and lowland floods, *kora* and TikTok, trading and trekking, landslides and borders, metros and refugee camps.

"South Asian mobilities" marks an attunement and intellectual disposition. It names a way of seeing the region as always already on the move, and as braided into larger patterns of (im)mobility beyond. Even as we take such an expansive scope, the territoriality and geography of the region forges a common thread. South Asia—as a region or collection of states—is integral to all of the contributions in this book. It is a lived reality for those within its territories. For those who have moved abroad, it is variously an object of nostalgia, of belonging, of trauma. For outsiders, it has been (and remains) an object of desire, of alterity, of intervention. Concentrating on South Asia highlights mobilities in, to, and from a region in ways that enable us to think otherwise. Such mobilities destabilize the presumptions of Euro-American case studies. In short, they challenge prevailing pictures of how the world moves.

Advancing: South Asian Mobilities

Just as the mobilities turn built upon diverse antecedents and contemporary parallels, this volume on South Asian mobilities builds upon relevant studies scattered across different journals and books. Before undertaking a discussion of these works, it is worth reiterating that South Asian mobilities are nothing new (see, e.g., Ludden 1994). Mobilities, South Asian or otherwise, are not uniquely modern, nor are they a simple outcome of colonial encounter. Nevertheless, the last three centuries have certainly wrought accelerations and proliferations, as well as redirections and new blockages. Colonial encounters, technological developments, urban planning schemas, border contestations, new media, economic transformations, and multi-vector migrations have all (re)constituted the subcontinent. Part of the value of a regional mobilities approach is to understand the imbrications of these different sorts of movement—how they obstruct, propel, depend upon, or exclude. The contours are unwieldy, the concerns are varied. In this section, I briefly survey the work that has been done in this vein. It is not meant as a thorough or exhaustive review. Rather, the aim is to outline the literature's current topology and sketch how the contributors to this volume build upon and extend such work. The goal is to gather such work under a new banner of South Asian mobilities to advance the project outlined above. This requires sketching new fault lines that do not align with traditional disciplinary, topical, or theoretical boundaries.

We might reasonably begin such a sketch at the transnational, geopolitical scale—namely, the sphere of international borders and the sovereign territories they purportedly inscribe. Mobilities have a way of both fortifying and undermining territorial cartographies of the state and the sanctioned routes between them. Radicati (2019) shows how fishermen in Colombo, through their itineraries before and since the war, come to challenge and reinforce state narratives of Sri Lanka's ethnic, geographical, and socioeconomic composition. Transnationally, borders in South Asia are particularly contested, porous, militarized, and frayed (van Schendel 2013). Borderlands thus become ripe sites for mobilities researchers. Shneiderman (2013) discusses attempts to regulate and facilitate movement on the border separating Nepal from the Tibetan Autonomous Region in China, a region also traversed by traders whose diversions challenge modernist territorialities (Harris 2013). At the Pakistan-Iran border, Anwar (2016) examines the town of Taftan to explore the relationship between states and their socio-spatial margins. As she puts it, "Mobility in Asia's urbanizing margins presents not only opportunities to make money but is also a site where the conceptual boundaries of the economy and the post-colonial nation-state are continually being redrawn" (Anwar 2016, 1052).

The India-Bangladesh border marks a boundary at which different objects and bodies become subject to the interplay of violence and toleration from territorialized states (Cons 2016). It is a site of sovereign power, symbolism, and various sorts of resistance (e.g., Ferdoush 2019, 2021; Jones 2009a, 2009b, 2012; Shewly 2016).

The first contribution to this volume, by Malini Sur, explores the India-Bangladesh borderlands as well, drawing upon her longstanding ethnographic engagement with communities in the ecologically shifting riverine regions (Sur 2013, 2021). Exploring the lives of married women in Kurigram's borderland river islands in Bangladesh, Sur's chapter highlights how mobility intersects with histories of nation building, gendered identities, and anticipations of the future. Sur's sharp ethnographic analysis touches on many of the key themes that engage us in this collection, and her contribution foregrounds the intellectual throughlines woven within and between the chapters that follow. It is multi-scalar, simultaneously about international borders and intimate emotional lives, with a central concern for the gendering of distance. Rather than exploring movement for its own sake, Sur uses mobility as a lens to theorize the production of social life and the cultural and transnational meanings of marriage. This is what makes it a productive starting point from which to consider South Asian mobilities more broadly, as well as to kick off this volume.

If borders and borderlands are one locus to begin such analysis, we might just as well have started with another key theme of mobilities research: infrastructure. In one sense, infrastructures enable the myriad movements in South Asia. They are the moorings that channel and regulate all sorts of flows. At the same time, however, infrastructure is a site rife with meaning and contestation (Harvey and Knox 2012; Larkin 2013; Anand, Gupta, and Appel 2018). This is, perhaps, even more pronounced in South Asia, where waves of colonial and postcolonial developmental regimes render infrastructural projects particularly ambivalent: signs of modernity and progress, but also material drivers of inequality and uneven distribution. In colonial India, railways served as ideologically charged symbols of modern distinction, and more generally as a technology embroiled in varied economic and political projects (Aguiar 2011). Similarly, aviation was both a symbol and tool of British domination in the early twentieth century (George 2019). Still today, infrastructures reconfigure the continental geography of Asia, notably with the spree of Chinese-led infrastructure projects in the Himalayas (Rippa, Murton, and Rest 2020). At the national scale, roadbuilding reveals a set of shifting political justifications, socioeconomic promises, and cultural (dis)enchantments (Rankin et al. 2017). At the same time, Demenge's (2013) work in Ladakh shows that proximity to roads does not necessarily correlate with increased mobility.

Infrastructures of movement are always political. They are sites through which activists and researchers can glimpse the unequal distribution of resources and priorities, from transit access in Sri Lanka (Gunaruwan and Jayasekera 2015) to urban water networks in India (Anand 2017). They become screens upon which to project imaginaries of possible (trans)regional futures. The Delhi Metro promised cosmopolitan globality, but also led to new disciplining codes defining (un)acceptable norms of behavior and interaction (Butcher 2011). Rashmi Sadana (2022) has also conducted deep ethnography of the Delhi Metro, highlighting the social worlds embedded in (and constituted through) the urban transit system. That earlier work directly informs her contribution to this volume. In Chapter 3, Sadana recounts scenes from the Love Commandos, an organization offering safe haven (i.e., a safe house located near a Delhi Metro station) to couples facing ostracization and violence for their intercaste romances. The urban infrastructure of the Metro enables a certain sort of spatial mobility, and the safe house enables a certain sort of social mobility. Yet these are not discrete modes of movement. They are interwoven. As Sadana argues, the Metro and the safe house function as "two different kinds of urban institutions and platforms for mobility, both operating in conjunction with one another at specific moments" (Sadana, this volume). Modalities of movement create affordances for new modes of life, and vice versa.

The organization of mobility through urban infrastructures intervenes to direct and divert possible modes of moving through the city. Research on varied modes of urban movement highlights the importance of attending to the specific sociocultural contexts of urban transportation. Contrary to most Western cities, rickshaws remain a common, if contested, way of navigating South Asian streets (Tiwari 2014; Steele 2013). Prioritizing personal motorized vehicles in South Asia frequently causes congestion and pollution while also curbing prospects for more sustainable ways of traversing urban South Asia (Khanal, Gurung, and Chand 2017; Gopakumar 2015; Joshi and Joseph 2015). The hyper-affordable Tata Nano—touted as the "people's car" in India—failed to catch on not because it was a bad product but because it failed to adequately signify the class distinction aspired to by would-be buyers/drivers (Nielsen and Wilhite 2015). Similarly, everyday cycling once symbolized working-class heroism, but it now connotes an outmoded industrial poverty as pop culture prizes the automobile as the new marker of modernity in post-liberalization India (Joshi and Joseph 2015). Meanwhile, the Mumbai taxi system relies on a hereditary community of laborers (*chillia*) who are deeply invested in their sociohistorical and infrastructural role, even as this role gets disrupted and rendered precarious by the city's "modernization" agendas (Bedi 2016, 2022). Research in this vein amply demonstrates that modes of transportation are inextricably stitched into broader logics of social distinction and prestige.

(Im)mobilities index diverse experiences and cultural possibilities. They enable new socialities and foreclose others. In West Bengal, spatial and social mobility are intertwined: as rural youth migrate physically into Darjeeling, they become upwardly mobile socially, a process that yields emergent class antagonisms as urban youth become anxious about losing status or regressing away from their own class aspirations (Brown 2015). Mobilities reconstitute spatiality, as small towns become hubs for multi-scalar mobilities in Gujarat (Verstappen and Rutten 2015). Intersecting and interdependent mobilities—of tourists, laboring bodies, colonial authorities, commodities, refugees, and media—continually reproduce senses of place, from Darjeeling (Sharma 2016) to Dharamshala (Bloch 2018). In Kathmandu, new codifications of consumption—"Korean quality"—index the entangled trajectories of media, development aid, tourism, and migration that link Nepal and South Korea in the twenty-first century (Hindman and Oppenheim 2014). Mumbai trains differently interpellate intersectional subjects like deaf women through specialized carriages (Kusters 2019), and such trains themselves enable women vendors to carve out livelihoods and social networks (Aggarwal 2020). South Asian women have ambivalent experiences with mobility. Transport options can constrain women's participation in public activities (Adeel, Yeh, and Zhang 2016). On the other hand, women trekking guides in central Nepal fashion themselves as "modern" through their publicly mobile employment (Grossman-Thompson 2013, 2016a), and the availability of motorized scooters in Kathmandu has afforded Nepali women new degrees of privacy, intimacy, and freedom (Brunson 2014). Women must often perform a socially precarious balancing act, constantly weighing increased mobility and its attendant cultural possibilities against the demands of social honor and respectability (e.g., Mughal 2019; Kirmani 2020).

Mobilities, then, are never *merely* about physical displacement. They are bound up with cultural codes, sociopolitical hierarchies, and geographies of exclusion. In Chapter 4, daniel dillon discusses the dynamics of fear, policing, and violence facing Tamils in postwar Sri Lanka. Using the analytic "driving while Tamil," dillon highlights the continued tensions faced by intersectional bodies moving through the city of Jaffna. Based on careful and well-rendered ethnographic storytelling, dillon argues that mobilities in the region are "refracted and distorted through the ubiquitous presence of militarized policing, which I contend is the dominant mobility regime in the region" (dillon, this volume). In a very concrete sense, mobilities lay bare social categories, structuring who, why, and how people can (and cannot) move through space and society.

The case of foreign tourism in South Asia perhaps offers another vantage onto the imbrication of social categories and their attendant mobilities. It highlights the disparity in mobility access at the global scale, one structured by imperialism and maintained in contemporary "power-geometries" (Massey 1994) of the postcolonial world. New technologies have radically transformed foreign tourists' experience in/of the region, enabling an "interplacement" that keeps them connected to various elsewheres, plugged into other sociocultural worlds, and tethered to curatorial frames imposed by such mobile technologies (Howard and Küpers 2017). Other works have explored the interaction, or lack thereof, between foreign tourists and local South Asians, from the Taj Mahal (Edensor 1998) to the hippie haunts of 1960s and 1970s Kathmandu (Liechty 2017). Such encounters alter the contexts and relations within which they are enacted, as Ranasinghe and Cheng (2018) show in their study of the Vedda indigenous community in Sri Lanka. Tourists also enroll myriad objects in their travels. They bring luggage, goods, and currencies. They take souvenirs, photographs, and commodities. Norris (2008) highlights the journeys of Indian *sari*s as their cloth gets recycled and reincarnated into new garments—with new significations and expressions—for sale to tourists.

In Chapter 5, Mark Liechty links two aforementioned themes—temporality and infrastructure—with the development of tourism in Nepal. After "opening up" in the early 1950s, tourists began arriving in Nepal, and today foreign tourism is one of Nepal's key economic sectors. Liechty identifies three distinct phases in the development of tourism in the latter half of the twentieth century, each of which corresponds to transformations in technology and infrastructure, and therefore to different demographics of foreigners. Early on, slower and expensive technologies of mobility (e.g., ships and short-haul aircrafts) catered to wealthy travelers. By the 1960s, cheap oil and international road constructions rendered Nepal accessible to countercultural hippies (i.e., those with little money but lots of time) via famed and oft-mythologized overland bus routes. By the 1970s, the age of mass, middle-class tourism was underway, enabled by mass air travel and Nepal's strategic investments in branding itself as an "adventure" destination. As Liechty puts it, "At each stage in Nepal's tourism development story, new modes and means of transportation allowed people to use money to overcome the constraints of distance in new ways" (Liechty, this volume). Of course, foreign tourism is not wholly reducible to enabling infrastructures of physical movement. As Liechty's work (both in this volume and in his earlier work) also shows, tourists in Nepal are frequently driven by a particular set of images and imaginaries.

Here again, a mobilities perspective need not restrict itself to the physical mobility of bodies and objects. Westerners have a long history of projecting exotic fantasies onto South Asia, fantasies that induce a desire to travel and that also frame touristic journeys (e.g., Bishop 1989; Hutnyk 1996; Dodin and Räther 2001; Liechty 2017). These fantasies and images are themselves in constant motion, circulating and morphing in ways that transform widespread (mis)understandings of the region. These mobile images and imaginaries spur tourists to move, to be sure. But even for those who never visit, such representations continue to animate Orientalist fantasies of the region. In Chapter 6, Rumya S. Putcha explores this topic of representation precisely. Her chapter begins with John Chau—the ill-fated missionary and Christian influencer killed by the Sentinelese in 2018—and then proceeds to the global success of the literary and cinematic blockbuster *Eat, Pray, Love*. These two cases open a critical exploration of performative "Instagram tourism" and what Putcha calls "cartographies of salvation." Emphasizing both personal wellness and voluntouristic charity, this highly aestheticized mode of travel and its online representations echo—indeed, reinvigorate—well-worn Orientalist and imperialist antecedents, from the "White Man's Burden" to the perceived healing powers of the mythical East. Putcha's timely critique concludes that, in the popular Western imagination, through touristic journeys and the mediated mobile images they generate, "the Global South remains a spiritual oasis or a cautionary tale; a timeless, imagined place where one can either save or be saved" (Putcha, this volume).

Needless to say, despite ongoing inequality in global mobilities, it is not only foreign tourists that move. All of the issues raised above—the political, socioeconomic, infrastructural, and cultural dimensions of (im)mobilities— get foregrounded by the multiscalar migrations of South Asians themselves. Whether rural-to-urban, intraregional, or transnational, the movement of people has radically reshaped South Asian communities and, indeed, communities around the world. Of course, studies of migration from/within the region are nothing new (Gardner and Osella 2003), yet the mobilities approach offers a suite of theoretical tools to sharpen our understandings of where, why, and how migrants move. Most notably, it disrupts rational-choice models of movement that foreground political-economic push and pull factors, highlighting instead the diversely motivated and diversely meaningful experiences of lived migration. Movement *within* a country—from a countryside village to an urban core, for example—reshapes conceptions and definitions of home (Nelson 2013; Shneiderman 2015). South Asian countries in recent decades have seen pronounced spikes in the number of people going abroad. Bangladesh, for instance, has institutionalized transnational labor migration as a key part of development agendas (Crawford and Martin 2014). The quality, destination, and duration of such moves vary dramatically.

Such migrant mobilities are enabled and constricted by what Xiang and Lindquist (2014) call "migrant infrastructures." Thieme (2017) describes this phenomenon through a study of "educational consultants," the brokers and advisors who facilitate Nepali students wishing to study abroad. But such social (and material) infrastructures for migration are not equally accessible in the region. Based on religiously inflected concern for women's honor, an array of age- and gender-based policies lead Nepali women to migrate abroad via informal and illegal channels, greatly increasing the risk of violence and exploitation (Grossman-Thompson 2016b; Shivakoti 2020). Meanwhile, extant gender inequalities within Sri Lanka and Bangladesh drive large numbers of women to seek work abroad, leading to a feminization of migration that yields divergent experiences and multidimensional consequences (Afsar 2011). Migration also intersects with shifting ideas of masculinity through its association with sexuality, desire, and rites of passage (e.g., Ahmad 2009; Sharma 2013, 2018). The media representations of such mobile bodies are classed, too, as Mookherjee (2011) shows in relation to the forced migrants of the Bangladesh war in 1971.

An equally rich theme of mobilities work about migration is that of diasporic lifeworlds. Migrants exist in multiple social fields that must be negotiated in practice to navigate complex landscapes of power (Thieme 2006). These include everything from the gendered navigations of "going out" among Bhutanese teenagers in New Zealand (Basnet 2016) to the quotidian "detours" of Sri Lankan refugees in Sydney (Ratnam and Drozdzewski 2020). Sri Lankan maids in Lebanon forge emotional connections with their employers, unfolding still more complicated social terrains to navigate (Moukarbel 2009). Meanwhile, transnational migrants do not sever ties with their "home" country upon arrival in their destination. They maintain and reforge community relations through religious and cultural practice (e.g., Gellner 2015; Brown 2018; Pathirage 2018). New youth subcultures are ignited (van Ommen 2014). Pakistanis in the UK harbor "myths of return," though the precise meaning and experience of imagined homecomings shift across generations (Ali and Holden 2006). Similar dynamics characterize Sikh migrants straddling homes between the UK and East Punjab, who find myriad ways of signifying "belonging to, and inclusion within, not only Punjab as a region and India as a nation but also the NRI [nonresident Indian] community in Punjab/India and the global Punjabi village diaspora/transnational community" (Taylor 2015, 201). Considerations of prestige, consumption, and social location all transform the relations "back" in Punjab, yielding new ensembles of inclusion and exclusion. This raises the issue of economic ties and remittances, which are centrally important in places like Nepal (Seddon, Adhikari, and Gurung 2002; Seddon 2004; Endo and Afram 2011). Many migrants return, creating new registers of distinction and inequality, from India (Vakulabharanam and Motiram 2016) to Sri Lanka (Gerharz 2010). Finally, Baas (2016) problematizes the idea of neat migration circuits, arguing that Indian educational migration to Australia gives shape to new imaginaries of mobility as they come to pursue still new itineraries after "settling" in their destination.

In the case of Nepal, transnational migrants include students and Gurkha soldiers, tech workers and private security contractors, restaurant owners and construction workers, airport staff and housemaids. Their destinations are equally diverse, from Singapore to London, New York to the Persian Gulf (e.g., see Gellner and Hausner 2018; Toffin and Pfaff-Czarnecka 2014; Kiruppalini 2012; Malla and Rosenbaum 2017; Craig 2020). In Chapter 7, Andrew Nelson focuses on a lesser-examined community of immigrants: Nepali-speakers working at (and owning) gas stations in North Texas. As Nelson writes, the early occupational niche of "South Asian" gas stations in Texas was pioneered primarily by Pakistani and Indian immigrants, many of whom later sold their businesses to reinvest elsewhere. By the later 2000s, more recent Nepali immigrants had begun buying such gas stations. Nelson's analysis usefully undermines the regionalist tendency to treat "South Asians" with a broad brush, showing instead the nuanced, temporalized hierarchies through which distinct immigrant communities seek to make new lives and livelihoods abroad.

It is not difficult to see why some of the best work about mobilities in South Asia has dealt centrally with questions of borders and migration (e.g., Reece and Ferdoush 2018). In many ways, it is a natural fit. This section began its discussion at the scale of the geopolitical and gradually made its way back around to the question of transnational migration and diasporic lifeworlds. Indeed, these are critical issues to consider when it comes to movement in the region. At the same time, as the foregoing discussion also highlights, there are other sorts of movement at multiple other scales within, from, and into South Asia, from the global circulation of images to the everyday movements of racialized bodies across urban landscapes. Mobilities are always necessarily multiscalar.

The last two contributions of this volume show the importance of thinking beyond the urban and (trans)national scales in mobilities research. Both are concerned with questions of the body, "that scale which is closest in" (Dixon and Straughan 2010, 456). In Chapter 8, Sarah Pinto delves into the medical archives of colonial India to examine various modes of bodily stillness, from temporary paralysis to trance-like states. Particularly in the imperial context and its attendant processes of knowledge production, displacement, and violent rule, immobile bodies became vexing sites of medical and political import. Reflecting on the stakes of such cases in the medical archive, she writes,

> The still and mute patient draws attention to the stakes of repair—the violence of means, the ethics of returning people to damaged social worlds, the genealogies and implicit cartographies of critical strategies. Understood less as an auratic source of cultural or civilizational meaning than point of entry to the stakes of meaning-making, the still moment *opens up*, rather than forecloses, possibilities of making use of the body. It brings into clarity the way political projects are troubled by stillness. The call from the Indian medical archive of stillness is, then, not only to ask what patients are doing or demanding, or how their actions are managed or mistranslated, but to explore what is collectively enacted in the space of immobility. (Pinto, this volume)

In Chapter 9, Michele Friedner and James Staples explore bodily (im)mobilities through the lens of disability. While disability tends to be associated with restricted or obstructed movements, Friedner and Staples show how disability enables new sorts of socio-spatial mobilities around contemporary India. In both Chapter 8 and Chapter 9, common presumptions about the body vis-à-vis mobility are challenged, and in so doing, they each demonstrate the contextual, multiscalar, and often counterintuitive imbrications of different types of (im)mobility.

Proceeding: Next Steps, New Directions

For all its strengths, mobilities research remains over-focused on Western contexts and hypermodern modes of movements. As noted above, this has begun to shift in the last decade. However, South Asia, despite its geopolitical and demographic weight, remains underrepresented. The studies cited above are only a beginning, one which we hope to extend through the varied contributions in this volume.

The instantiation of the "new mobilities paradigm" nearly twenty years ago was a product of redrawing and transgressing such entrenched academic boundaries. It presented, in other words, not only a call to arms but a reevaluation of work already done, a fertile reassembling in pursuit of new angles and new conversations. To gather diverse works about (im)mobilities relative to South Asia is to make a similar move. A South Asian mobilities perspective is not merely about things *that* move but about centering movement in our framings and analyses. The diversity of our chapters, both in terms of their geographical sites and objects of study, is a core strength. The goal is to showcase the breadth of South Asian mobilities, not only as a particular set of research topics but as a conceptual attunement to the many ways in which movement—of bodies and images, of vehicles and ideas—continue to shape the region and its place in the world.

The possibilities for such an agenda are manifold. They build upon incipient trends in previous scholarship and chart new directions. The agenda is historical, seeking to understand the contingent production of (im)mobilities in different eras and epochs. It calls to rethink the regional coherence of South Asia itself as the contingent production of multiple intersecting mobilities: cartographies of empire, ancient trade networks, religious pilgrimage routes, mediated images, and more. The agenda is infrastructural, examining the channels and materialities through which circulation occurs: roads and bridges, trains and water pipes, dams and airports. The agenda is environmental and multispecies, attending to the particular animals and natural features that constitute a region of diverse ecologies: rivers and floodplains, street dogs and *yarsagumba*, rising mountain peaks and traffic-diverting cattle. The agenda is political and social, keeping a critical eye on how (im)mobility is constrained and expanded along registers of access and exclusion: gender, class, caste, age, ability, nationality, sexuality, ethnicity. The agenda is multiscalar: planetary and microbial, urban and atomic, transnational and tectonic. The agenda is economic, charting the multidirectional vectors of capital and resources: remittances and development aid, investments and gifts. Finally, the agenda is cultural, conceptualizing the radical new worlds that emerge from (im)mobilities in the region, across its far-flung diasporas, and along the routes that bind the two together.

This book advances an approach to South Asia that prizes mobilities and, conversely, an approach to the mobilities turn that diversifies its focus onto South Asia. Taken together, the chapters that follow highlight the importance of a mobilities perspective for South Asian studies and the importance of South Asia to a mobilities perspective. In Chapter 10, coeditor Tarini Bedi offers a conclusion in which she identifies further theoretical, methodological, and pedagogical directions.

South Asia is moving as never before. It has been mobile for quite some time, despite territorial, colonial, and nationalist claims that sought to fix it. Mobilities, then, deserve a central place in our empirical and theoretical treatments of the region. It is our hope that this volume marks the beginning of a larger conversation, that it initiates broader engagements with the themes and concerns raised in this introduction. Movements of all sorts traverse the region and beyond. South Asian mobilities offers a banner under which such diversity can unify, challenging existing approaches and coming to grips with a subcontinent ever on the move.

References

Adeel, Muhammad, Anthony Gar-On Yeh, and Feng Zhang. 2016. "Transportation Disadvantage and Activity Participation in the Cities of Rawalpindi and Islamabad, Pakistan." *Transport Policy* 47: 1–12.

Adey, Peter. 2006. "If Mobility Is Everything Then It Is Nothing: Towards a Relational Politics of (Im)mobilities." *Mobilities* 1 (1): 75–94.

Adey, Peter. 2010. *Mobility*. New York: Routledge.

Adey, Peter, David Bissell, Kevin Hannam, Peter Merriman, and Mimi Sheller. 2014a. "Introduction." In *The Routledge Handbook of Mobilities*, edited by Peter Adey, David Bissell, Kevin Hannam, Peter Merriman, and Mimi Sheller, 1–20. Abingdon: Routledge.

Adey, Peter, David Bissell, Kevin Hannam, Peter Merriman, and Mimi Sheller, eds. 2014b. *The Routledge Handbook of Mobilities*. Abingdon: Routledge.

Afsar, Rita. 2011. "Contextualizing Gender and Migration in South Asia: Critical Insights." *Gender, Technology and Development* 15 (3): 389–410.

Aggarwal, Aditi. 2020. "What's Urban Transport Planning Got to Do with Train Vendors?" *Economic & Political Weekly* 55 (16): 63–64. https://www.epw.in/journal/2020/16/postscript/whats-urban-transport-planning-got-do-train.html.

Aguiar, Marian. 2011. *Tracking Modernity: India's Railway and the Culture of Mobility*. Minneapolis: University of Minnesota Press.

Ahmad, Ali Nobil. 2009. "Bodies that (Don't) Matter: Desire, Eroticism and Melancholia in Pakistani Labour Migration." *Mobilities* 4 (3): 309–27.

Ali, Nazia, and Andrew Holden. 2006. "Post-Colonial Pakistani Mobilities: The Embodiment of the 'Myth of Return' in Tourism." *Mobilities* 1 (2): 217–42.

Anand, Nikhil. 2017. *Hydraulic City: Water and the Infrastructure of Citizenship in Mumbai*. Durham: Duke University Press.

Anand, Nikhil, Akhil Gupta, and Hannah Appel, eds. 2018. *The Promise of Infrastructure*. Durham: Duke University Press.

Anwar, Nausheen H. 2016. "Asian Mobilities and State Governance at the Geographic Margins: Geopolitics and Oil Tales from Karachi to Taftan." *Environment and Planning A* 48 (6): 1047–63.

Appadurai, Arjun. 1996. *Modernity at Large: Cultural Dimensions of Globalization.* Minneapolis: University of Minnesota Press.

Baas, Michiel. 2016. "Becoming Trans/Nationally Mobile: The Conflation of Internal and International Migration in the Trajectories of Indian Student-Migrants in Australia and Beyond." *South Asia: Journal of South Asian Studies* 39 (1): 14–28.

Basnet, Sunita. 2016. "Experiences and the Embodied Practices of Bhutanese-New Zealander Teenage Women: Young Bodies, Going Out and Sexual Practices." *New Zealand Geographer* 72 (3): 240–49.

Bedi, Tarini. 2016. "Taxi Drivers, Infrastructures, and Urban Change in Globalizing Mumbai." *City & Society* 28 (3): 387–410.

Bedi, Tarini. 2022. *Mumbai Taximen: Autobiographies and Automobilities in India.* Seattle: University of Washington Press.

Birtchnell, Thomas. 2016. "Mobilities and the Multinatural: A Test Case in India." *Transfers: Interdisciplinary Journal of Mobility Studies* 6 (2): 120–27.

Bishop, Peter. 1989. *The Myth of Shangri-La: Tibet, Travel Writing and the Western Creation of Sacred Landscape.* Los Angeles: University of California Press.

Bloch, Natalia. 2018. "Making a Community Embedded in Mobility: Refugees, Migrants, and Tourists in Dharamshala (India)." *Transfers: Interdisciplinary Journal of Mobility Studies* 8 (3): 36–54.

Brown, Bernardo E. 2018. "A Multicultural Church: Notes on Sri Lankan Transnational Workers and the Migrant Chaplaincy in Italy." In *Asian Migrants and Religious Experience: From Missionary Journeys to Labor Mobility*, edited by Bernardo E. Brown and Brenda S. A. Yeoh, 221–42. Amsterdam: Amsterdam University Press.

Brown, Trent. 2015. "Youth Mobilities and Rural-Urban Tensions in Darjeeling, India." *South Asia: Journal of South Asian Studies* 38 (2): 263–75.

Brunson, Jan. 2014. "'Scooty Girls': Mobility and Intimacy at the Margins of Kathmandu." *Ethnos* 79 (5): 610–29.

Büscher Monika, John Urry, and Katian Witchger, eds. 2010. *Mobile Methods.* Abingdon: Routledge.

Butcher, Melissa. 2011. "Cultures of Commuting: The Mobile Negotiation of Space and Subjectivity on Delhi's Metro." *Mobilities* 6 (2): 237–54.

Chakrabarty, Dipesh. 2000. *Provincializing Europe: Postcolonial Thought and Historical Difference.* Princeton: Princeton University Press.

Clifford, James. 1997. *Routes: Travel and Translation in the Late 20th Century.* Cambridge: Harvard University Press.

Cons, Jason. 2016. *Sensitive Space: Fragmented Territory at the India-Bangladesh Border.* Seattle: University of Washington Press.

Cook, Nancy, and David Butz. 2015. "The Dialectical Constitution of Mobility and Immobility: Recovering from the Attabad Landslide Disaster, Gojal, Gilgit-Baltistan, Pakistan." *Contemporary South Asia* 23 (4): 388–408.

Craig, Sienna R. 2020. *The Ends of Kinship: Connecting Himalayan Lives between Nepal and New York.* Seattle: University of Washington Press.

Crawford, David R., and Nina Martin. 2014. "The Transnational Project and Its Implications for Migrant Civil Society in Bangladesh." *Mobilities* 9 (2): 294–313.

Cresswell, Tim. 2006a. *On the Move: Mobility in the Modern Western World.* New York: Routledge.

Cresswell, Tim. 2006b. "The Right to Mobility: The Production of Mobility in the Courtroom." *Antipode,* 38 (4): 735–54.

Cresswell, Tim. 2010. "Mobilities I: Catching Up." *Progress in Human Geography* 35 (4): 550–58.

Cresswell, Tim. 2012. "Mobilities II: Still." *Progress in Human Geography* 36 (5): 645–53.

Cresswell, Tim. 2014. "Mobilities III: Moving on." *Progress in Human Geography* 38 (5): 712–21.

Cresswell, Tim. 2016. "Afterword: Asian Mobilities/Asian Frictions?" *Environment and Planning A* 48 (6): 1082–86.

Deleuze, Gilles, and Felix Guattari. 1987. *A Thousand Plateaus.* Minneapolis: University of Minnesota Press.

Demenge, Jonathan P. 2013. "The Road to Lingshed: Manufactured Isolation and Experienced Mobility in Ladakh." *Himalaya, the Journal of the Association for Nepal and Himalayan Studies* 32 (1): 51–60.

Dixon, Deborah P. and Elizabeth R. Straughan. 2010. "Geographies of Touch/Touched by Geography." *Geography Compass* 4 (5): 449–59.

Dodin, Thierry, and Heinz Räther, eds. 2001. *Imagining Tibet: Perceptions, Projections, and Fantasies.* Somerville, MA: Wisdom Publications.

Edensor, Tim. 1998. *Tourists at the Taj: Performance and Meaning at a Symbolic Site.* New York: Routledge.

Endo, Isaku, and Gabi G. Afram. 2011. *The Qatar-Nepal Remittance Corridor: Enhancing the Impact and Integrity of Remittance Flows by Reducing Inefficiencies in the Migration Process.* Washington, D.C.: The World Bank.

Faulconbridge, James, and Allison Hui. 2016. "Traces of a Mobile Field: Ten Years of Mobilities Research." *Mobilities* 11 (1): 1–14.

Ferdoush, Md Azmeary. 2019. "Symbolic Spaces: Nationalism and Compromise in the Former Border Enclaves of Bangladesh and India." *Area* 51 (4): 763–70.

Ferdoush, Md Azmeary. 2021. "Sovereign Atonement: (Non)citizenship, Territory, and State-Making in Post-Colonial South Asia." *Antipode* 53 (2): 546–66.

Fincham, Ben, Mark McGuinness, and Lesley Murray, eds. 2009. *Mobile Methodologies*. Basingstoke: Palgrave Macmillan.

Frank, Andre Gunder. 1998. *ReORIENT: Global Economy in the Asian Age*. Berkeley: University of California Press.

Gardner, Katy, and Filippo Osella. 2003. "Migration, Modernity and Social Transformation in South Asia: An Overview." *Contributions to Indian Sociology* 37 (1–2): v–xxviii.

Gellner, David, ed. 2013. *Borderland Lives in Northern South Asia*. Durham: Duke University Press.

Gellner, David. 2015. "Associational Profusion and Multiple Belonging: Diaspora Nepalis in the UK." In *Diasporas Reimagined: Spaces, Practices and Belonging*, edited by Nando Sigona, Alan Gamlen, Giulia Liberatore, and Hélène Nevea Kringelbach, 78–82. Oxford: Oxford Diasporas Programme.

Gellner, David N., and Sondra L. Hausner, eds. 2018. *Global Nepalis: Religion, Culture, and Community in a New and Old Diaspora*. Oxford: Oxford University Press.

George, Joppan. 2019. *Airborne Colony: Culture and Politics of Aviation in India, 1910–1939*. PhD Dissertation: Princeton University.

Gerharz, Eva. 2010. "When Migrants Travel Back Home: Changing Identities in Northern Sri Lanka after the Ceasefire of 2002." *Mobilities* 5 (1): 147–65.

Gopakumar, Govind. 2015. "Who Will Decongest Bengaluru? Politics, Infrastructures & Scapes." *Mobilities* 10 (2): 304–25.

Grossman-Thompson, Barbara. 2013. "Entering Public Space and Claiming Modern Identities: Female Trekking Guides and Wage Labor in Urban Nepal." *Studies in Nepali History and Society* 18 (2): 251–78.

Grossman-Thompson, Barbara. 2016a. "Gendered Narratives of Mobility: Spatial Discourse and Social Change in Nepal." *Sociology of Development* 2 (4): 323–41.

Grossman-Thompson, Barbara. 2016b. "Protection and Paternalism: Narratives of Nepali Women Migrants and the Gender Politics of Discriminatory Labour Migration Policy." *Refuge* 32 (3): 40–48.

Grover, Ruhi. 2000. "Rites of Passage: The Mobility of Timber in Colonial North India." *South Asia: Journal of South Asian Studies* 23 (1): 39–64.

Gunaruwan, T. Lalithasiri, and D. Harshanee W. Jayasekera. 2015. "Social Inclusivity Through Public Transportation: A Strategic Approach to Improve Quality of Life in Developing Countries." *Journal of Advanced Transportation* 49 (6): 738–51.

Hannam, Kevin, Mimi Sheller, and John Urry. 2006. "Editorial: Mobilities, Immobilities and Moorings." *Mobilities* 1 (1): 1–22.

Harris, Tina. 2013. *Geographical Diversions: Tibetan Trade, Global Transactions*. Athens: University of Georgia Press.

Harvey, Penny, and Hannah Knox. 2012. "The Enchantments of Infrastructure." *Mobilities* 7 (4): 521–36.

Hindman, Heather, and Robert Oppenheim. 2014. "Lines of Labor and Desire: 'Korean Quality' in Contemporary Kathmandu." *Anthropological Quarterly* 87 (2): 465–95.

Howard, Christopher. 2017. *Mobile Lifeworlds: An Ethnography of Tourism and Pilgrimage in the Himalayas.* New York: Routledge.

Howard, Christopher, and Wendelin Küpers. 2017. "Interplaced Mobility in the Age of 'Digital *Gestell.*'" *Transfers: Interdisciplinary Journal of Mobility Studies* 7 (1): 4–25.

Hutnyk, John. 1996. *The Rumour of Calcutta: Tourism, Charity, and the Poverty of Representation.* London: Zed Books.

Jones, Reece. 2009a. "Agents of Exception: Border Security and the Marginalization of Muslims in India." *Environment and Planning D: Society and Space* 27 (5): 879–97.

Jones, Reece. 2009b. "Sovereignty and Statelessness in the Border Enclaves of India and Bangladesh." *Political Geography* 28 (6): 373–81.

Jones, Reece. 2021. "Spaces of Refusal: Rethinking Sovereign Power and Resistance at the Border." *Annals of the Association of American Geographers* 102 (3): 658–99.

Jones, Reece and Md Azmeary Ferdoush, eds. 2018. *Borders and Mobility in South Asia and Beyond.* Amsterdam: Amsterdam University Press.

Joshi, Rutul, and Yogi Joseph. 2015. "Invisible Cyclists and Disappearing Cycles: The Challenges of Cycling Policies in Indian Cities." *Transfers: Interdisciplinary Journal of Mobility Studies* 5 (3): 23–40.

Khanal, Prashanta, Anobha Gurung, and Priyanka Bahadur Chand. 2017. "Road Expansion and Urban Highways: Consequences Outweigh Benefits in Kathmandu." *Himalaya, the Journal of the Association for Nepal and Himalayan Studies* 37 (1): 107–16.

Kirmani, Nida. 2020. "Can Fun Be Feminist? Gender, Space and Mobility in Lyari, Karachi." *South Asia: Journal of South Asian Studies* 43 (2): 319–31.

Kiruppalini, Hema. 2012. "From Sentries to Skilled Migrants: The Transitory Residence of the Nepali Community in Singapore." *European Bulletin of Himalayan Research* 40: 59–82.

Kusters, Annelies. 2019. "Boarding Mumbai Trains: The Mutual Shaping of Intersectionality and Mobility." *Mobilities* 14 (6): 841–58.

Kwan, Mei-Po, and Tim Schwanen. 2016. "Geographies of Mobility." *Annals of the American Association of Geographers* 106 (2): 243–56.

Lagji, Amanda. 2019. "Waiting in Motion: Mapping Postcolonial Fiction, New Mobilities, and Migration through Mohsin Hamid's *Exit West.*" *Mobilities* 14 (2): 218–32.

Larkin, Brian. 2013. "The Politics and Poetics of Infrastructure." *Annual Review of Anthropology* 42: 327–43.

Latour, Bruno. 2005. *Reassembling the Social: An Introduction to Actor-Network Theory.* Oxford: Oxford University Press.

Liechty, Mark. 2017. *Far Out: Countercultural Seekers and the Tourist Encounter in Nepal.* Chicago: University of Chicago Press.

Lin Weiqiang. 2016. "Re-Assembling (Aero)mobilities: Perspectives beyond the West." *Mobilities* 11 (1): 49–65.

Lin Weiqiang, and Brenda SA Yeoh. 2016. "Moving in Relations to Asia: The Politics and Practices of Mobility." *Environment and Planning A* 48 (6): 1004–11.

Ludden, David. 1994. "History outside Civilisation and the Mobility of South Asia." *South Asia: Journal of South Asian Studies* 17 (1): 1–23.

Malkki, Liisa H. 1997. "National Geographic: The Rooting of Peoples and the Territorialization of National Identity Among Scholars and Refugees." In *Culture Power Place: Explorations in Critical Anthropology,* edited by Akhil Gupta and James Ferguson, 52–74. Durham: Duke University Press.

Malla, Binayak, and Mark S. Rosenbaum. 2017. "Understanding Nepalese Labor Migration to Gulf Countries." *Journal of Poverty* 21 (5): 411–33.

Massey, Doreen. 1994. *Space, Place, and Gender.* Minneapolis: University of Minnesota Press.

Massey, Doreen. 2005. *For Space.* London: Sage.

Merriman, Peter. 2015. "Mobilities I: Departures." *Progress in Human Geography* 39 (1): 87–95.

Merriman, Peter. 2016. "Mobilities II: Cruising." *Progress in Human Geography* 40 (4): 555–64.

Merriman, Peter. 2017. "Mobilities III: Arrivals." *Progress in Human Geography* 41 (3): 375–81.

Merriman, Peter, and Lynne Pearce. 2017. "Mobility and the Humanities." *Mobilities* 12 (4): 493–508.

Mom, Gijs, and Nanny Kim. 2013. "Editorial." *Transfers: Interdisciplinary Journal of Mobility Studies* 3 (3): 1–5.

Mookherjee, Nayanika. 2011. "Mobilising Images: Encounters of 'Forced' Migrants and the Bangladesh War of 1971." *Mobilities* 6 (3): 399–414.

Moukarbel, Nayla. 2009. "Not Allowed to Love? Sri Lankan Maids in Lebanon." *Mobilities* 4 (3): 329–47.

Mughal, Muhammad A.Z. 2019. "From Sickle to Pen: Women's Education and Everyday Mobility in Rural Pakistan." *Transfers: Interdisciplinary Journal of Mobility Studies* 9 (2): 82–100.

Nelson, Andrew. 2013. "The Mobility of Permanence: The Process of Relocating to Kathmandu." Working Paper II. Kathmandu, Nepal: Centre for the Study of Labour and Mobility.

Nielsen, Kenneth Bo, and Harold Wilhite. 2015. "The Rise and Fall of the 'People's Car': Middle-Class Aspirations, Status and Mobile Symbolism in 'New India'." *Contemporary South Asia* 23 (4): 371–87.

Norris, Lucy. 2008. "Recycling and Reincarnation: The Journeys of Indian Saris." *Mobilities* 3 (3): 415–36.

Pariyar, Mitra. 2020. "Caste, Military, Migration: Nepali Gurkha Communities in Britain." *Ethnicities* 20 (3): 608–27.

Pathirage, Jagath Bandara. 2018. "Liberalizing the Boundaries: Reconfiguration of Religious Beliefs and Practice amongst Sri Lankan Immigrants in Australia." In *Asian Migrants and Religious Experience: From Missionary Journeys to Labor Mobility*, edited by Bernardo E. Brown and Brenda S. A. Yeoh, 101–28. Amsterdam: Amsterdam University Press.

Radicati, Alessandra. 2019. "Island Journeys: Fisher Itineraries and National Imaginaries in Colombo." *Contemporary South Asia* 27 (3): 330–31.

Ranasinghe, Ruwan, and Li Cheng. 2018. "Tourism-Induced Mobilities and Transformation of Indigenous Cultures: Where Is the Vedda Community in Sri Lanka Heading to?" *Journal of Tourism and Cultural Change* 16 (5): 521–38.

Rankin, Katharine N., Tulasi S. Sigdel, Lagan Rai, Shyam Kunwar, and Pushpa Hamal. 2017. "Political Economies and Political Rationalities of Road Building in Nepal." *Studies in Nepali History and Society* 22 (1): 43–84.

Ratnam, Charishma, and Danielle Drozdzewski. 2020. "Detour: Bodies, Memories, and Mobilities in and around the Home." *Mobilities* 15 (6): 757–75.

Rippa, Alessandro, Galen Murton, and Matthäus Rest. 2020. "Building Highland Asia in the Twenty-First Century." *Verge: Studies in Global Asias* 6 (2): 83–111.

Sadana, Rashmi. 2022. *The Moving City: Scenes from the Delhi Metro and the Social Life of Infrastructure*. Oakland: University of California Press.

Seddon, David. 2004. "South Asian Remittances: Implications for Development." *Contemporary South Asia* 13 (4): 403–20.

Seddon, David, Jagannath Adhikari, and Ganesh Gurung. 2002. "Foreign Labor Migration and the Remittance Economy of Nepal." *Critical Asian Studies* 34 (1): 19–40.

Sharma, Jayeeta. 2016. "Producing Himalayan Darjeeling: Mobile People and Mountain Encounters." *Himalaya, the Journal of the Association for Nepal and Himalayan Studies* 35 (2): 87–101.

Sharma, Jeevan Raj. 2013. "Marginal but Modern: Young Nepali Labour Migrants in India." *Young* 21 (4): 347–62.

Sharma, Jeevan Raj. 2018. *Crossing the Border to India: Youth, Migration and Masculinities in Nepal*. Philadelphia: Temple University Press.

Shell, Jacob. 2015. "When Roads Cannot Be Used: The Use of Trained Elephants for Emergency Logistics, Off-Road Conveyance, and Political Revolt in South and Southeast Asia." *Transfers: Interdisciplinary Journal of Mobility Studies* 5 (2): 62–80.

Sheller, Mimi. 2017. "From Spatial Turn to Mobilities Turn." *Current Sociology Monograph* 65 (4): 623–39.

Sheller, Mimi, and John Urry. 2006. "The New Mobilities Paradigm." *Environment and Planning A* 38 (2): 207–26.

Shewly, Hosna J. 2016. "Survival Mobilities: Tactics, Legality and Mobility of Undocumented Borderland Citizens in India and Bangladesh." *Mobilities* 11 (3): 464–84.

Shivakoti, Richa. 2020. "Protection or Discrimination? The Case of Nepal's Policy Banning Female Migrant Workers." In *Urban Spaces and Gender in Asia*, edited by Divya Upadhyaya Joshi and Caroline Brassard, 17–34. Cham: Springer.

Shneiderman, Sara B. 2013. "Himalayan Border Citizens: Sovereignty and Mobility in the Nepal-Tibetan Autonomous Region (TAR) of China Border Zone." *Political Geography* 35 (1): 25–36.

Shneiderman, Sara. 2015. "Regionalism, Mobility, and 'The Village' as a Set of Social Relations: Himalayan Reflections on a South Asian Theme." *Critique of Anthropology* 35 (3): 318–37.

Simmel, Georg. 1997. *Simmel on Culture*, edited by David Frisby and Mike Featherstone. London: Sage.

Sohoni, Pushkar. 2018. "Translocated Colonial Subjects in Collaboration: Animals and Human Knowledge." *Transfers: Interdisciplinary Journal of Mobility Studies* 8 (1): 1–14.

Staeheli, Lynn A., David J. Marshall, and Naomi Maynard. 2016. "Circulations and the Entanglements of Citizenship Formation." *Annals of the American Association of Geographers* 102 (6): 377–84.

Steele, M. William. 2013. "Rickshaws in South Asia: Introduction to the Special Section." *Transfers: Interdisciplinary Journal of Mobility Studies* 3 (3): 56–61.

Steele, M. William, and Weiqiang Lin. 2014. "History, Historiography, and Be(com)ing on the Move: Introduction to the Special Section." *Transfers: Interdisciplinary Journal of Mobility Studies* 4 (3): 43–48.

Sur, Malini. 2013. "Through Metal Fences: Material Mobility and the Politics of Transnationality at Borders." *Mobilities* 8 (1): 70–89.

Sur, Malini. 2021. *Jungle Passports: Fences, Mobility, and Citizenship at the Northeast India-Bangladesh Border*. Philadelphia: University of Pennsylvania Press.

Taylor, Steve. 2015. "'Home is Never Fully Achieved ... Even When We Are in It': Migration, Belonging and Social Exclusion within Punjabi Transnational Mobility." *Mobility* 10 (2): 193–210.

Thieme, Susan. 2008. "Sustaining Livelihoods in Multi-Local Settings: Possible Theoretical Linkages Between Transnational Migration and Livelihood Studies." *Mobilities* 3 (1): 51–71.

Thieme, Susan. 2017. "Educational Consultants in Nepal: Professionalization of Services for Students Who Want to Study Abroad." *Mobilities* 12 (2): 243–58.

Tiwari, Geetam. 2014. "The Role of Cycle Rickshaws in Urban Transport: Today and Tomorrow." *Transfers: Interdisciplinary Journal of Mobility Studies* 4 (1): 83–96.

Toffin, Gérard, and Joanna Pfaff-Czarnecka, eds. 2014. *Facing Globalization in the Himalayas: Belonging and the Politics of Self.* New Delhi: SAGE.

Tsing, Anna. 2005. *Friction: An Ethnography of Global Connection.* Princeton: Princeton University Press.

Urry, John. 2007. *Mobilities.* Malden, MA: Polity Press.

Vakulabharanam, Vamsi, and Sripad Motiram. 2016. "Mobility and Inequality in Neoliberal India." *Contemporary South Asia* 24 (3): 257–70.

van Ommen, Premila. 2014. "Himalayan Melodies and Heavy Metal." *HIMAL Southasian* 27 (4): 130–45.

van Schendel, Willem. 2002. "Stateless in South Asia: The Making of the India-Bangladesh Enclaves." *Journal of Asian Studies* 61 (1): 115–47.

van Schendel, Willem. 2013. "Afterword: Making the Most of 'Sensitive' Borders." In *Borderland Lives in Northern South Asia*, edited by David Gellner, 266–71. Durham: Duke University Press.

Verstappen, Sanderien, and Mario Rutten. 2015. "A Global Town in Central Gujarat, India: Rural-Urban Connections and International Migration." *South Asia: Journal of South Asian Studies* 38 (2): 230–45.

About the author

Benjamin Linder is an anthropologist and cultural geographer with interests in transnational mobilities, cultural transformation, and urban place-making in Nepal. He serves as the Coordinator for Public and Engaged Scholarship at the International Institute for Asian Studies (IIAS) at Leiden University, the Netherlands.

2 Gendering Distance: Marriage and Mobility in Bangladesh's Riverine Borderlands

Malini Sur

Abstract: This chapter explores how marital life worlds and the anticipation of new conjugal futures unevenly gather circuits of mobility and exchange in Bangladesh. The diverse relationships that marriage has with mobility open new lines of enquiry for probing borderlands as sites of negotiations and belongings amidst nation-building and the force of transnational imaginaries. As containers of culture and mobility, marriages realign questions of distance in territorial and emotional terms. This chapter casts historical and ethnographic attention to marriage and conjugality from the borderland *chars* of Kurigram district in Bangladesh, which adjoin India.

Keywords: marriage, mobility, displacement, borders, gender, nations, transnationalism, Bangladesh

Within the first month of my arrival in a remote village in Kurigram district of Bangladesh to conduct fieldwork—about a mile away from the Bangladesh-India border—rumors had circulated that an Indian researcher was trying to locate her lost relatives. The sounds of motorcycle engines interrupted our winter morning in an otherwise sleepy village located in a shifting landscape of *chars* (river islands). The motorcycles circled into the courtyard of the house where I was residing, and the men who alighted conveyed that their mother Rupaiya Begum had summoned me. Rupaiya had family in India who she had not seen since her abduction and marriage in Bangladesh. While Rupaiya's sons mistook me for their niece, others demanded that as an Indian citizen, I needed to document their displacements from India.

Linder, Benjamin, & Tarini Bedi (eds), *South Asia on the Move: Mobilities, Mobilizations, Maneuvers*.
Amsterdam: Amsterdam University Press 2025
doi: 10.5117/9789463726498_CH02

From the initial days of my fieldwork in Kurigram, I was made aware of the imminent flooding that defined land loss and low agricultural returns. Ecological changes and economic hardships compelled men to undertake employment in Dhaka's garments factories, start small businesses in local markets, and smuggle goods and seasonally migrate to India for work. Some families had mortgaged their land, taken loans, and funded their sons to migrate to Europe and the United States. While the men had migrated abroad, they had left behind their recently wedded spouses. These marital life worlds unevenly gathered borders, nations and global circuits of mobility and exchange, laying bare the anticipations and anxieties that surround conjugal futures in this ecologically shifting borderland. The relationships that mobility has with marriage open new lines of enquiry for probing the creation and maintenance of borders, nation-states, and transnationality. In thinking along with my colleagues in the spirit of this collection, I cast attention to married women's accounts of the divergent scales at which conjugal futures are imagined and lived. The locus of my investigation is remote border chars located in Bangladesh's Kurigram district. These chars adjoin a similar riverine landscape in the Indian state of Assam and comprise a borderland where I conducted fieldwork from 2007 to 2015. Here, married women's accounts of relationality and distance blur the neat scholarly classifications of migration within and beyond national boundaries.

In her study of Bangladeshi brides moving within the district of Sylhet in Bangladesh and from Sylhet to London, Katy Gardner has powerfully shown how marriages function as a threshold and social institution that significantly alter prior roles and relationships. For Gardner, anthropology's attention to life courses foregrounds life events and the expectations that surround their unfolding (Gardner 2009, 248). Gardner opens diverse kinds of movements through which people's life courses unfold and the cultural and gendered expectations that reorder these to close ethnographic scrutiny. She shows how people's lives are simultaneously shaped by the forces of history, global structures, and place-making. By analysing the temporal and spatial possibilities that surround movement, Gardner expands the intellectual horizons of migration studies (Gardner 2009, 229–32, 247). More recently, Siddharthan Maunaguru (2019), in the light of wars and violent displacements, has offered a new conceptual apparatus to study marriage as an evolving social process rather than as a static social institution. In his work on wartime Sri Lanka and among the Tamil diaspora in Canada, and through his engagement with Janet Cartsen's call to explore 'marriage processes' (Cartsen 2000), Maunaguru shows how Tamil marriages came to be modified and transnationally readapted to account for the insecurities and uncertainties that the war in Sri Lanka had generated. For Maunanguru, transnational marriages that are contingent upon mobility are as much about brokerage that happens in Sri Lankan villages as about the bureaucracies that play out in Canada's immigrant courtrooms; marriage alliances and mobilities help people to reimagine and articulate expectations and fears that surround conjugal unions. As he suggests, violent political events impinge upon people's experiences of marriages, and their pasts and futures (Maunaguru 2019, 13–17, 157). Nitya Rao has shown how marriage is not only fundamental to being a good Muslim in Bangladesh but also supports migration; it is a means to negotiate desirable marital alliances. Marriage alliances reveal the intersections of labor flexibility in global markets and notions of social status and prestige in Bangladesh (Rao 2012, 26). Read together, these valuable insights on migration, gender, and marriage challenge the sedentary overtones that define scholarly engagements with social structures, and demonstrate how distinct regimes of globalization, violence, and mobility in turn reorder marriage.

Unlike Sylhet, a prosperous Bangladeshi district that has been well studied for international migration, marriage, and gendered roles (Gardner 1992, 2008, 2009), Kurigram, being the most poverty-stricken district of Bangladesh, features in studies on climate change, food insecurity, and seasonal migration within Bangladesh (Khandakar 2012; Eztold et al. 2016; Karim and Muhammad 2016; Guha et al. 2023). Yet, my fieldwork in Kurigram's borderland chars makes evident how women's borderworlds have always extended beyond Bangladesh's territorial margins into India and, more recently, Europe and the United States. Marriages anchor long and contentious histories of movement and displacements; married women narrate their material and emotional gains and burdens in everyday life and mobility. In opening women's marital borderworlds to close ethnographic scrutiny, I demonstrate the intersecting territories and timescales at which social life operates and is regulated at the India-Bangladesh borderlands (Sammadar 1999; van Schendel 2005; Hussain 2012; Alexander et al. 2015; Cons 2016; Ghosh 2017; Sur 2019, 2021). In fact, as I propose to show, marriages realign questions of distance territorially and emotionally. Marriages and the ensuing mobilities and immobilities attest to how communities, nations, and transnational forces regulate and gender border lives.

Marriage, Mobility, and Nation-Building

In the 1990s, a proliferation of scholarly engagements on globalization generated rich insights on the complex flows of peoples, ideas, and cultures and on the interlocking webs of relationships (Appadurai 1996; Portes et al. 1999). The euphoria surrounding the fall of the Berlin Wall inspired scholars to study global flows, cultural transmissions, and aspirations for the future (Appadurai 1996). In comparison to old forms of globalization, these developments generated a transnational field that was defined by new demographic and technological complexities (Portes et al. 1999, 217; Appadurai 1996). At the turn of the twenty-first century, a 'movement-driven' social science that encompassed all forms of mobility and practices of living and place-making gained momentum (Urry 2000; Büscher and Urry 2009, 100). The mobile turn foregrounded movement and its accompanying social imaginaries, and it opened the social relationships that underlined the politics of movement to scrutiny (Cresswell 2006; Cresswell 2010, 21).

Scholars of transnational mobility unsettled the 'methodological nationalism' that had shaped the study of societies and cultures in the social sciences (Wimmer and Glick Schiller 2003). This displaced a singular focus on nation-states as the predominant locale of scholarly engagement in migration studies. Yet, if reterritorialized identities generated new scholarly directions (Gupta and Fergusson 2008), this progressed alongside concerns that modernity and globalization were placing societies in differential positions of power and access. Not only flows but the hindrances to movement provided critical tools to understand the 'interplay of power, resources and ideology in the contemporary world' (Heyman and Cunningham 2004, 293). Scholars demonstrated how diverse temporalities, histories, and gendered roles informed migratory pathways (King et al. 2006; Pratt and Yeoh 2003), producing "temporal baggage" (Crewer 2001), "liminal times" (Kirk et al. 2017) and "contingent temporality" (Robertson 2019). Since migration encompassed life courses, biographic sequences, and imaginaries of pasts, presents, and futures (Crewer 2001; Gardner 2009; Robertson 2019, 170, 174; Sur 2020), it also related fundamentally to marriage as a social process (Maunaguru 2019).

In South Asia, scholars investigating borderlands offered important departures to the state-led, sedentary, and security-centric analysis of movement and mobility with state subversion and illegality (Samaddar 1999; Van Schendel 2005; Hussain 2013; Cons 2016; Ibrahim 2018; Sur 2021). These studies show the limitations of national citizenship and identities in regulating social life and mobilities across borders. Today, as borderland societies continue to live in the shadows of the COVID-19 pandemic and have experienced severe border closures and restraints on movement, scholars are once again reminded about the centrality of nations, nationalism, exclusions, and indeed the nation-state's regulation of families and sexualities (Chatterjee 1993; Uberoi 1996; Kaur 2012). Farhana Ibrahim's rich exploration of nineteenth-century marriage mobility from Kutch attends both to the transnational circuits these unions generated, as well as the suspicions that surround contemporary marriages. Ibrahim demonstrates the centrality of national identities and the role of border enforcement in policing national territory and citizenship. She shows how complex webs of mobilities in border regions underline marriages, and how such unions are not only situated in societal structures but also exemplify people's aspirations (Ibrahim 2018). Marriage mobilities and aspirations relate fundamentally to how women experience contrasting notions of home and foreign lands. As Katy Gardner (1993) importantly reminds us in the context of Sylheti transnational migration, and with close attention to those unable to migrate, *desh* (home) has multiple valences and sentiments associated with locality, sacredness, and fertility. Equally, Bangladeshis express concerns about desh where prosperity is not possible due to economic distress and political instability. Given Sylhet's long history of migration and dependence on remittances, the importance of *bidesh* (foreign land) holds relevance as a site of material power and propensity (Gardner 1993). From Kurigram's borderland chars, the region's contentious histories of regional mobility to India and new and emergent migration pathways to Europe and the United States are apparent.

Kurigram's contentious histories with Assam first as a neighboring province in British India, and after August 1947 as a state in independent India, the emergence of Bangladesh as an independent nation-state in 1971, Bangladesh's status as a leading garment exporter, and the new force of international migration invite a reconsideration of the scales at which desh and bidesh are reconfigured. In what follows, I cast attention to women's abductions and displacements across the Kurigram-Assam borderland, drawing briefly on a long history of territorial politics and mobility that lasted from the late 1930s until 1971 and on women's marital experiences of immobility and loss in the light of global migration from Kurigram to Dhaka in the 1990s and, more recently, to Europe and the United States. Historical and contemporary mobilities have reordered marriages and impinged upon women's experiences of relationality and distance.

Banditry and Borders

One early winter morning in 2007, six men circled the courtyard of the house where I was living in Kurigram, leaving a trail of spiralling dust. More than my identity as an Indian Bengali, my connections to the state of Assam in India located just across Bangladesh's Kurigram district where I had been conducting fieldwork led to rumors that I was searching for lost relatives in the chars. The news of my arrival had reached Rupaiya Begum, the wife of the deceased bandit Atabor. Rupaiya Begum was born and raised in Assam, India, just across the Bangladesh-India border. Her neighbors arrived at her house insisting that I was likely to be her granddaughter. Rupaiya had not seen her daughter after marriage. She was guilt ridden due to her absence in her daughter's life. Ashamed and distressed, Rupaiya sent her sons to locate me. On that morning, hearing a man loudly screaming at Khairun, my host, that she was insulting him and his mother by sheltering me, I hurriedly rushed out. Khairun and I faced Rupaiya's tall and muscular sons who towered over us. After an angry exchange, when we all agreed that I was not related to Atabor and Rupaiya, and was not their niece, we all drank tea. Amicable conversations ensued (Sur 2018).

A few weeks later, I arrived in Rupaiya Begum's house. It was dusk and the winter mist had set in. Across their house, we could see India's new barbed wire border fence cutting across the rice fields. Her son waited impatiently for his consignment of smuggled cows to arrive from Assam. As I sat down with Rupaiya, she looked at me. She was happy that I had come to see her but sad that we were not related. She was married to the bandit Atabor, whose exploits were legendary in the chars. Known for his extraordinary bravery, he was infamous for regularly crossing the border from Kurigram and raiding villages in Assam. In one such raid, he not only returned with a large consignment of cows but also with Rupaiya Begum. Rupaiya's beauty had garnered her fame. This happened in the mid-1950s, a period when the river islands were known for banditry and territorial incursions. From 1947 until 1971, the chars interspersed East Pakistan and India's borderlands, and presented a fluid and dangerous space.

Despite the partition of the Indian subcontinent in 1947, which created a newly independent India and Pakistan, with Pakistan's territory split into East Pakistan and West Pakistan, the border was hardly settled. In fact, in these shifting chars, peasant migration to and settlements in Assam dated back to contentious border-making in British India. This zone had been a site of territorial anxieties that were especially evident in the late 1930s in British India. On the eve of the partition of the Indian subcontinent, British intelligence agents had marked it as a camp from where Assam's territory would be claimed for Pakistan. Territorial anxieties surrounded the political mobilization of the opposing meanings of religious identities (i.e., Hindu and Muslim) and of ethnic and linguistic identities (i.e., Bengali and Assamese). Some feared—and others anticipated—that Muslim political parties would make claims for Assam's territories and incorporate them into a Muslim dominated Pakistan. Meanwhile, the movement of peasants and their families from Kurigram for reclaiming wetlands and marshes was seen as a Muslim Bengali territorial takeover of Assam's land for Pakistan (Sur 2021). Even after 1947, peasants and cattle raiders crossed the border and made claims on each other's territories and produce (Van Schendel 2005; Sur 2021). The unstable nature of the riverine land provided passage not only for the movement of goods, like cattle, but also for the abduction of women and cross border marriages.

Despite the violent connotations of her abduction, Rupaiya had settled into conjugal life, domesticity, and motherhood in East Pakistan. Her new responsibilities as Atabor's second and younger wife gave her legitimacy, and her abduction and resettlement were well within acceptable moral and sexual codes that were then prevalent in riverine societies. Such unions were neither regarded to be illegitimate nor forced and were located within established codes of conjugality and sanctioned religiously. In Rupaiya Begum's village, she had two contemporaries who had similar life paths as hers; upon their abduction they had also married and resettled into conjugality.

Rupaiya's abduction, marriage, and her subsequent resettlement in East Pakistan did not challenge conventional nationalist notions of honor and shame that related to Hindu Indian women. Scholars have shown how India forcibly reclaimed Hindu women who were abducted on the eve of the partition of the Indian subcontinent (Menon and Bhasin 1998; Das 2006). The dust from the violent displacements during the partition of the Indian subcontinent had hardly subsided when India sought to forcibly recover Hindu women who had by then resettled into conjugal relationships in West Pakistan. Forced to return to India against their will, these women were separated from their husbands and children; some were remarried by their families, while others were sheltered in state-run rehabilitation homes. Women's bodies and sexualities functioned as sites for establishing Indian nationalism and citizenship (Menon and Bhasin 1998; Das 2006). Yet, in the fluid and shifting riverine borders abductions and marriages created new families; Indian Muslim women slid into Pakistani and later Bangladeshi citizenship. Rupaiya accepted her role as Atabor's second wife as she would have in a marriage negotiated by her family. Atabor and his family were apprehensive that if they allowed her to go to Assam, her family would not permit her to return. She resigned to their wishes; she also had no other means to travel to India. She was unaware of her family sending people to look for her. Atabor was also feared in India for his exploits and raids.

When I met Rupaiya, she had retired from the routines of domesticity, including cooking and caring for household animals, activities that took up most of her daytime since her husband's demise. Her daughters-in-law conveyed that, after the family meal at sunset, she would spend evenings talking about her life and childhood in Assam, and about her daughter. When Rupaiya's daughter turned sixteen, Rupaiya insisted that she should be married in Assam. They arranged her marriage through a broker. She hoped that her daughter's relocation would revive her contacts with her estranged family. Instead, Rupaiya's daughter completely disappeared from their lives. By this time, the Assam Movement (1979-1985) against Bangladeshi undocumented foreigners had taken place, leading to stronger border enforcement (Sur 2014). Even today, many continue to travel from Kurigram to Assam for wage work and seasonal migration taking risks to life and crossing a heavily militarized border.

Rupaiya's daughter's marriage and migration to Assam did not yield the desired outcomes. The alliance she had requested her sons to negotiate in Assam did not ensure that she could cross the Bangladesh-India border, and neither did her daughter cross the border to visit her. This marriage alliance did not enable Rupaiya to reestablish contact with her family. Her son's arrival at our doorstep was a testament to her guilt surrounding her daughter's marriage and her inability to participate in her daughter's life. At the India-Bangladesh borderland, emotional belongings and the 'moral force of kinship,' as Sahana Ghosh reminds us, animate women's lives and desires to perform their roles as transborder families and kins. Transborder kinship entails border-crossings, and the differential regimes of border management that prevent Bangladeshi citizens from crossing the border without passports and visas to see their relatives causes them anguish (Ghosh 2017, 47–49). In Rupaiya's case, her immobility—initially on account of her marriage but more recently on account of her age—generated maternal guilt.

On another winter day, two young men arrived on a motorcycle and alighted in our courtyard. Their mother, Dina Begum, had sent them to fetch me after hearing that a researcher from India had arrived from across the border. They left our house only after I had given my word that I would visit their mother. Within an hour and half of their departure, Dina called me. The phone calls continued until we decided on a day that I would visit her. A few days later, when I reached Dina's house, she narrated in detail her life in Assam. In 1969, Dina's father was displaced from Kurigram and compelled to relocate across the border to Assam, along with many other Muslim and Hindu families. During the Liberation War of Bangladesh, residents from the river islands that were proximate to India were displaced and sheltered in the state of Assam. Dina and her family resided in a relief camp in Assam, about five miles from their village in Kurigram. During the two years that they resided there, Dina's father, who was a tailor by profession, set up a profitable business. Dina recalled how, unlike other families in the camp who struggled, their family experienced prosperity for the first time in many years. Although they were displaced due to state violence and the large-scale scarcities that the war generated, their relocation in Assam provided them with hope for a good future.

Yet, this proved short lived. Once Bangladesh became an independent nation in 1971, Indian border guards arrived at the refugee camps and segregated Hindu and Muslim refugees. While the Hindu families were allowed to resettle in Assam and subsequently gain Indian citizenship, the border troops informed the Muslim refugees that, since Bangladesh was now an independent Bengali and Muslim nation, they needed to return. When her father protested and agreed to relocate from the camp to a rented accommodation, pointing towards the Hindus who were being allowed to stay back, his pleas fell on deaf ears. The Indian troops argued that they had strict orders to send Muslim refugees back. Much against their will, and with reluctance, Dina Begum and her family returned to the newly independent Bangladesh and to their village in Kurigram. Subsequently, she married an agriculturalist and businessman in Kurigram and resettled into a relatively prosperous domesticity. Yet, despite her marriage and social mobility and the new house extension that she was constructing when I visited her, their humiliating return continued to haunt Dina Begum. Her conjugal life and relative prosperity could not take away her stigma of not having an option to resettle across the border in India.

Rupaiya and Dina's marriages demonstrate how border territorialities and nation-building distinctly impinged upon their lives. For Rupaiya Begum, Assam remains her natal home, which she was compelled to leave behind and could never visit even after her daughter relocated. In her mental map, the Kurigram-Assam borderland is a part of the same riverine space—desh—or homeland which has seen movement and settlement for many generations. In her case, marriage by abduction imposed a new context for settlement in which her husband regulated her mobilities fearing that she would not return. For her, returning home implied travelling to Assam rather than India. By the time she arranged an alliance for her daughter, in her imagination, Assam was still a neighboring district. But borders had hardened, and moving from Kurigram to Assam was seen as unauthorized movement between India and Bangladesh. For Dina Begun, on the other hand, the emergence of Bangladesh as an independent nation where Muslims like her were the majority community necessitated her exit from her short-lived camp life in Assam. Even though she desired to live in Assam, by then the demarcations between India and Bangladesh—despite cordial diplomatic relations—were firmly etched on religious divisions. Their departure from Assam, and despite their return to a newly independent Bangladesh implied dishonor. Rather than thinking about her life in Assam as temporary shelter in the face of violent displacement, she conveyed that returning to Bangladesh was an act of displacement. She insisted that they would have been more prosperous had she had a chance to resettle in Assam. Although both Rupaiya and Dina live in border chars from where Assam is visible across the rice fields, as married Muslim women, their families, communities, and Bangladeshi border troops prevent them from crossing the Bangladesh-India border.

Separations and Immobility

Although their husbands had migrated to Italy, Mina and Naher remained behind in Kurigram's border villages. Both were parents of toddlers and had not seen their husbands for over three years. Their husbands' remittances ensured that Mina and Naher had the money to hire domestic helpers to assist with childcare and household chores. Their gold earnings and bangles emphasized their high status as compared with their co-sisters, who wore cheaper brass jewellery. Their husbands' families had repaid the loans that they had taken for migration with the remittances within a year and a half. The remittances not only ensured regular money for household repairs and groceries but also paid for festive clothes and feasts. A portion of the remittances were provided to Mina and Naher, according to their husbands' instructions. International migration from Bangladesh results in substantial increases in household incomes due to remittances, and wives of emigrants are also able to claim a portion of this and start banking (Luna and Rahman 2019). Mina and Naher's husbands had used their foreign migrant status not only to ensure the well-being of their families but also to ensure that their wives had access to money. Mina and Naher's families had spent relatively large amounts of money for their marriages, taking into account their prospects of international migration. Even as they desired to be reunited with their husbands, the women themselves did not complain about their separation or status in their marital homes. They anticipated that their husbands would eventually arrange for their European visas. They lived in the hope that their husbands would visit them and take them and their children to Italy. They regarded their separation from their husbands as temporary, and they understood this to be a womanly sacrifice for the greater good of the entire family.

In Kurigram, relatively recent possibilities for international migration have generated new expectations and disappointments from marriage alliances. These were evident in Khairun's narrations relating to her eldest daughter Moutushi's marriage alliance. Khairun headed a household comprising her daughter and two sons, while her husband, Kamal, worked as a supervisor in a garment factory near Dhaka. Khairun's father, a retired clergyman, and Khairun's younger brother resided very nearby and visited them every day to enquire about their wellbeing (Sur 2021). Her brother arrived with provisions from the market and farm produce, and he helped Khairun manage the small patch of land adjoining the house where they cultivated vegetables. In Kamal's absence, Khairun made all the decisions and turned to her father and brother for assistance. When her husband Kamal returned home, in anticipation of which she dyed her hair and took out a set of bright sarees, her relationships with her natal family would completely change. Kamal was dominant and asserted his opinion ostensibly on all matters relating to their lives. Although Khairun never disagreed with her husband she nevertheless played a central role in taking decisions on household matters, including taking initiative and seeking out suitable grooms for arranging her daughter Moutushi's marriage.

Moutushi was married to a college lecturer and resided at her husband's residence in a char twenty kilometers away. She regularly visited and stayed with Khairun along with their two-month-old daughter. Khairun initially conveyed that Rezaul was an excellent choice for a groom. His family had agricultural and homestead land, and he was well respected. In addition to his salary as a lecturer, he had an income from a shop that he had set up in the local market, where he sold seeds and other agricultural products. Khairun's sense of wellbeing at having successfully negotiated her daughter's marriage was short-lived. Within a year, when an overseas marriage alliance was fixed for her brother-in-law's daughter with a groom twenty years older than the girl, Khairun felt a deep sense of disappointment. Her feelings intensified when the girl, related to Khairun through her husband's elder brother, migrated to New York a few months following the marriage. Soon after, their remittances ensured her family was able to construct a new house.

Khairun felt that she had been cheated in the marriage alliance for Moutushi. She blamed her neighbor, who had brokered both of the marriages, and alleged that she tricked her into a lesser deal for the more beautiful Moutushi. In comparison with the groom in New York, who worked as a janitor, Rezaul's profession was highly regarded, but his income and his life in a nearby village were not. Although everyone in Khairun's family liked

Rezaul for his gentle and respectful demeanor, the fact that Moutushi's cousin could marry and migrate to bidesh shattered all of their hopes.

Khairun moved between the routines of domesticity, from her early morning bath to lighting the oven, from cooking the first rice meal for the family to caring for her goats and poultry in melancholia. Although she was involved in all family decisions and had access to additional money from her husband's remittances every month, she despaired for Moutushi's future. Moutushi herself had absorbed her mother's sorrow. Instead of showing me her marriage album, she spoke to me in sad tones as she displayed an album containing her cousin's marriage photographs. She had received these photographs from New York by post, along with a photograph of the new house that her uncle and aunt had constructed.

In between chasing transborder cattle trails, and during the time that I resided with Khairun and Moutushi, their lamentations dominated our conversations. Despite the financial security and prestige of being married to men who were educated and had a stable income, they continued to live with a deep sense of loss and despair that was completely shaped by their relative's relocation to bidesh. While Rupaiya desired a match for her daughter in Assam and in retrospect continued to doubt her decision, Khairun was convinced that fixing a marriage within Kurigram had impaired her daughter's life chances and future. Khairun and Moutushi, despite their spatial proximity, appeared to be emotionally distant—each enveloped and preoccupied with their own thoughts and silences.

Conclusion

Marriages in Kurigram's char borderlands reposition the concepts of desh and bidesh spatially, culturally, economically, and politically. Spatially, Kurigram is a borderland zone with a long history of contentious movements and settlements. Today, it is a location from where men not only travel to Dhaka to cope with economic uncertainties but also configure new futures in Italy and New York. It simultaneously operates as a borderland that shares complicated boundaries with India and where people move across the border with increasing risks to life. These intersecting scales shape women's experiences of marriage and displacement. As containers of culture and mobility, marriages in Kurigram's borderlands generate new gendered logics of distance. Married women continue to live divided lives across spatial and material boundaries; they carry burdens of borders and nations. National and transnational forces collapse in remote border chars as women come to terms with their marriages, contribute to and gain emotional and material benefits, exercise power and authority, and experience immobility and disappointments.

In Kurigram's chars, territorial animosities and movements follow women's lives like shadows. Located in a borderland and in an ecologically shifting landscape of chars, marriages and movements reconfigure notions of desh and bidesh. Some women still imagine movement between Bangladesh and India in terms of locality and community; even though the restraints of conjugality and a hardened border have ensured immobility. Others continue to nurture a sense of deep dishonor and dislocation despite material prosperity and the legitimacy of national citizenship in Bangladesh. Others, though only separated by an eight-hour bus ride, continue to live apart for most of the year; in such instances remittances from Dhaka offer prospects of material wellbeing without easing the pain of marital separation. Yet, in other instances, couples endure the long labors of separations when men migrate alone to bidesh. Like Kurigram's moving chars, where river waters erode settlements and lives are exacerbated by climate uncertainties, married women are constantly drawn into movements that have crafted contentious territorial and identity politics. Here, the power of borders, the force of nations, and transnational circuits converge. Movement happens through marital and maternal separations and material prosperities, bringing with it new expectations and despairs.

Acknowledgments

I thank Sidharthan Maunaguru, Rakesh Kumar, Benjamin Linder, and Tarini Bedi for their generous suggestions during an intense period of long Covid.

References

Alexander, Calire, Joya Chatterji, and Annu Jalais. 2015. *The Bengal Diaspora: Rethinking Muslim Migration*. London: Routledge.
Büscher, Melissa, and John Urry. 2009. "Mobile Methods and the Empirical." *European Journal of Social Theory* 12 (1): 99–116.
Cons, Jason. 2016. *Sensitive Space: Fragmented Territory at the India-Bangladesh Border*. Seattle: University of Washington Press.
Cresswell, Tim. 2010. "Towards a Politics of Mobility." *Environment and Planning D: Society and Space* 28 (1): 17–31.

Das, Veena. 2006. *Life and Words: Violence and the Descent into the Ordinary.* Berkeley: University of California Press.

Etzold, Benjamin, Ahsan Uddin Ahmen, Selim Reza Hassan, and Sharmind Neelormi. 2014. "'Clouds Gather in the Sky, but No Rain Falls': Vulnerability to Rainfall Variability and Food Insecurity in Northern Bangladesh and Its Effects on Migration." *Climate and Development* 6 (1): 18–27.

Gardner, Katy. 1993. "Desh-Bidesh: Sylheti Images of Home and Away." *Man* 28 (1): 1–15.

Gardner, Katy. 1995. *Global Migrants, Local Lives: Travel and Transformation in Rural Bangladesh.* Oxford: Oxford University Press.

Gardner, Katy. 2009. "Lives in Motion: The Life-Course, Movement and Migration in Bangladesh." *Journal of South Asian Development* 4 (2): 229–51.

Ghosh, Sahana. 2017. "Relative Intimacies: Belonging and Difference in Transnational Families." *Economic and Political Weekly* 52 (15): 45–52.

Guha, Bishal, Md. Alif-Al-Maruf, Anutosh Das, and Dulal Sarker. 2023. "Assessing the Internal Out-Migration on Basis of Influence Area: A Case Study of Kurigram, Rangpur and Gaibandha Districts, Bangladesh." *GeoJournal* 88 (5): 5511–36.

Gupta, Akhil, and James Ferguson. 2008. "Beyond 'Culture': Space, Identity, and the Politics of Difference." *The Cultural Geography Reader.* London: Routledge, 72–79.

Heyman, Josiah McC., and Hilary Cunningham, eds. 2004. "Movement on the Margins: Mobilities and Enclosures at Borders." Special issue of *Identities: Global Studies in Culture and Power* 11 (3).

Hussain, Delwar. 2013. *Boundaries Undermined: The Ruins of Progress on the Bangladesh/India Border.* London: Hurst & Co.

King, Russell, Mark Thomson, Tony Fielding, and Tony Wanes. 2006. "Time, Generations and Gender in Migration and Settlement." In *The Dynamics of International Migration and Settlement in Europe,* edited by Rinus Penninx, Maria Berger, and Karen Kraal, 233–67. Amsterdam: Amsterdam University Press.

Ludden, David. 2003. "Presidential Address: Maps in the Mind and the Mobility of Asia." *Journal of Asian Studies* 62 (4): 1057–78.

Maunaguru, Sidharthan. 2019. *Marrying for a Future: Transnational Sri Lankan Tamil Marriages in the Shadow of War.* Seattle: University of Washington Press.

Menon, Ritu, and Kamla Bhasin. 1998. *Borders & Boundaries: Women in India's Partition.* New Brunswick: Rutgers University Press.

Portes, Alejandro, Luis E. Guarnizo, and Patricia Landolt. 1999. "The Study of Transnationalism: Pitfalls and Promise of an Emergent Research Field." *Ethnic and Racial Studies* 22 (2): 217–37.

Pratt, Geraldine, and Brenda Yeoh. 2003. "Transnational (Counter) Topographies." *Gender, Place and Culture: A Journal of Feminist Geography* 10 (2): 159–66.

Luna, Sabnam Sarmin, and Md Mizanur Rahman. 2019. "Migrant Wives: Dynamics of the Empowerment Process." *Migration and Development* 8 (3): 320–37.

Rao, Nitya. 2013. "Breadwinners and Homemakers: Migration and Changing Conjugal Expectations in Rural Bangladesh." *Journal of Development Studies* 48 (1): 26–40.

Rashid, Syeda Rozana. 2013. "Bangladeshi Women's Experiences of Their Men's Migration: Rethinking Power, Agency, and Subordination." *Asian Survey* 53 (5): 883–908.

Robertson, Shanthi. 2019. "Migrant, Interrupted: The Temporalities of 'Staggered' Migration from Asia to Australia." *Current sociology* 67 (2): 169–85.

Samaddar, Ranabir. 1999. *The Marginal Nation: Transborder Migration from Bangladesh to West Bengal.* New Delhi: Sage.

Schiller, Nina Glick, Linda Basch, and Cristina Szanton Blanc. 1995. "From Immigrant to Transmigrant: Theorizing Transnational Migration." *Anthropological Quarterly* 68 (1): 48–63.

Sur, Malini. 2014. "Divided Bodies: Crossing the India-Bangladesh Border." *Economic & Political Weekly* 49 (13): 31–35.

Sur, Malini. 2018. "The Story of Atabor the Bandit, or How the NRC Reinforces Divisive Narratives." *The Wire*, August 2. Available at: https://thewire.in/rights/assam-nrc-bangladesh-border

Sur, Malini. 2019. "Danger and Difference: Teatime at the Bortheast India-Bangladesh Border." *Modern Asian Studies* 53 (3): 846-873.

Sur, Malini. 2020. "Time at Its Margins: Cattle Smuggling across the India-Bangladesh Border." *Cultural Anthropology* 35 (4): 546–74.

Sur, Malini. 2021. *Jungle Passports: Fences, Mobility, and Citizenship at the Northeast India-Bangladesh Border.* Philadelphia: University of Pennsylvania Press.

Urry, John. 2007. *Mobilities.* Malden, MA: Polity Press.

van Schendel, Willem. 2005. *The Bengal Borderland: Beyond State and Nation in South Asia.* London: Anthem Press.

van Schendel, Willem. 2009. *A History of Bangladesh.* Cambridge: Cambridge University Press.

van Schendel, Willem and Itty Abraham, eds. *Illicit Flows and Criminal Things: States, Borders, and the Other Side of Globalization.* Bloomington: Indiana University Press.

Wimmer, Andreas, and Nina Glick Schiller. 2003. "Methodological Nationalism, the Social Sciences, and the Study of Migration: An Essay in Historical Epistemology." *International Migration Review* 37 (3): 576–610.

About the author

Malini Sur is an Associate Professor of Anthropology at Western Sydney University and serves as the President of Australian Anthropological

Society. Her book *Jungle Passports: Fences, Mobility, and Citizenship at the Northeast India-Bangladesh Border* (University of Pennsylvania Press, 2021) was awarded the President's Book Prize from the South Asian Studies Association of Australia, Bernard S. Cohen Prize (honourable mention), and Choice Outstanding Academic Title (2022).

3 At the Love Commandos: Narratives of Mobility Among Intercaste Couples in a Delhi Safe House

Rashmi Sadana

Abstract: Marriage as being about family rather than individuals is a common South Asian trope, and while there is truth to it, it is one that is continually being negotiated by families and couples alike. Meeting runaway intercaste couples hiding in a safe house in Delhi led me to reflect on a new geography of love at work in their lives and in the city today, especially in relation to caste, which is always imbricated with class and gender in urban India. By mapping the social and physical parameters of runaway couples' mobility in a single ethnographic context, I argue that it is the quest for mobility rather than an expression of individual choice that is most significant about their flouting of social norms.

Keywords: caste and class, India, marriage and family, mobility, urbanism

In 2010, a Delhi-based organization named "Love Commandos," with the tag "No More Honour Killings," created a new political platform and course of action for addressing an age-old phenomenon: Indians attempting to cross lines of caste or community to marry someone of their choosing.[1] Part vigilante group, part nongovernmental organization, the group has

---

1   See Inderpal Grewal's (2013) analysis of how the idea of honor killing—which hinges on racial and religious difference and "the crime of culture"—gets produced in Euro-American contexts and projected back onto Eastern contexts as a kind of "outsourced patriarchy." I see the Love Commandos' own use of the term as evidence of that transnational feedback loop as honor killing has become a catch-all term even for Indians.

Linder, Benjamin, & Tarini Bedi (eds), *South Asia on the Move: Mobilities, Mobilizations, Maneuvers*. Amsterdam: Amsterdam University Press 2025
doi: 10.5117/9789463726498_CH03

garnered significant attention in both Indian and foreign media.[2] The Love Commandos' method—as epitomized by the image on their website of five burly men with arms folded across their chests—is to extract and provide a safe haven for couples who are in imminent danger. However, their larger goal is to highlight the social attitudes and circumstances that lead to conflict within families and communities.[3] They, in fact, do not see the one-thousand-plus murders within families each year—a United Nations estimate considered to be on the low side—as being about "honor," but rather about issues of prestige, money, and familial power plays, often sanctioned by the police and community leaders. The organization wants to square India's anti-caste discrimination laws with social practice, and to do it on a mass scale, one couple at a time.

The appearance of the Love Commandos on the Indian social and political scene dovetails with a larger Dalit rights movement and a rising incidence of so-called "love marriages" in Indian society. The Love Commandos brandish the concept of love as a way toward a more equal and just society while also subversively questioning the love that families actually have for their children. When I was living in India from 2007 to 2012, the incidence of couples in crisis, as reported in the news, was sometimes presented as a social epidemic. These often sensational accounts were partly due to instances of extreme violence, referred to in the mainstream press as "honor killings," but they also had to do with the sheer numbers of couples on the run, so many that the Delhi government created its own hotline to help couples. Marriage and love relationships are continually evolving but perhaps never more so than in a digitally enabled, economically liberalized society, whereby young people from all social strata have more access to information and to each other. At the time, I was researching the social impact of Delhi's new Metro rail system (see Sadana 2022), and in the course of that research, I came to know about the Love Commandos, whose office was near a metro station I frequented. I saw the Metro and the Love Commandos as two different

---

2   See, for instance, Gethin Chamberlain, "Honour Killings: How the Love Commandos Rescue India's Young Lovers," 36; Pallavi Pundir, "Romeo and Juliet in Delhi"; Ben Doherty, "Rescued by the Love Commandos," 9; Martin Gilmour, "Rescued by the Love Commandos," *Examiner*, 13 January 2013, 30; Jane Mulkerrins, "A Matter of Love or Death," *Irish Daily Mail*, 9 February 2013, 37–41; "The World's Only Army for Love," *Pretoria News*, 28 February 2013, 37; Tanul Thakur, "In the Name of Honour," *Man's World India*, 9 April 2015, http://www.mansworldindia.com/people/in-the-name-of-honour/

3   The prime example of the Love Commandos being recognized for its social change platform was when it was featured on the popular issues-oriented Indian talk show *Satyamev Jayante*, hosted by Bollywood superstar Aamir Khan. See Season 1, Episode 5, "Is Love a Crime?" (3 June 2012).

kinds of urban institutions and platforms for mobility, both operating in conjunction with one another at specific moments. This conjunction resulted from my own "patchwork composition" of the mobilities I saw and intersected with (Linder, this volume). The stories of mobility presented here do not focus on marriage itself as a vehicle for a change in social status, but rather the stories show the ways in which intersecting mobilities are socially produced and in flux. The couples are on the move, but so are ideas about family, caste, and class, their own desires, and their own ways of navigating urban and periurban spaces.

Intercaste couples who I interviewed at a Love Commandos' safe house (a converted two-bedroom apartment in a ramshackle building on a narrow lane near one of the city's main markets) were not so much acting on the newfound freedoms of a more globalized consumer- and urban-oriented culture in India's era of economic liberalization; rather, they were uncovering for themselves the ways in which the ruse over caste identities is a foil for issues of social status and economic mobility.[4] The narratives I present and analyze here—in the form of two extended case studies extracted from a range of in-depth interviews with couples at the safe house—primarily concern the relationships of two intercaste couples and how they fortify their own love arrangements, even if, as we will see, their futures are uncertain. What might the "old" issue of intercaste marriage tell us about the changing social experience of mobility in urban India, particularly when placed within the frame of the Love Commandos' activism and the kinds of couples that end up there?

In talking to couples, I found their stories of love and crossing caste boundaries to be tales of economic insecurity, status, and power relations within the family, often leading to coercion and fear of violence. Furthermore, I came to see how the politics of the Love Commandos organization, with their larger platform for social change, intersected with the narratives of mobility relayed by the couples themselves. These narratives—of individuals within family and community contexts, living between notions of urban and

---

4   An intercaste relationship or marriage is one between individuals from two different subcastes, or *jatis*, which are the interstitial caste groupings—of which there are hundreds—that vary by region. Over ninety percent of Indians marry within their subcaste, although intercaste marriages are becoming more common. Intercaste marriage in most communities carries the taint of having had a marriage by choice (rather than formal or informal arrangement by one's parents), or "love marriage." See Donner (2002) for an ethnographic example of how choosing one's own marriage partner *within* one's subcaste is becoming more acceptable. The cases I explore here are of couples who not only choose their own marriage partner but also cross caste lines while doing so; both issues are central to their stories.

periurban lifestyles, and amid shifting ideas of class, caste, and status—were about their ideas of mobility as much as about love, marriage, or family. The "answer" for couples was not to disengage with family—despite being holed-up in a safe house—but rather to eventually reform their families so they fit with their own expectations of their futures. I came to see the safe house not as an end point for lovers but rather as part of an affective urban landscape that mediated their understanding of love, aspiration, and caste. The safe house symbolized a dramatic shift in their own temporal and spatial coordinates—at once a space of waiting and part of a new urban social network. Mobility in this framing is a form of embodiment, a physical movement that leads the couples to a new environment that they then inhabit and adapt to; and mobility is an analytic, a way to understand the spatial relationships between couples' parental homes versus a safe house, and being stuck at home versus being on the move.

Intercaste relationships challenge and disturb affective ties, as will be illustrated below, but they are also part of a newer, more trenchant critique of caste society amid dramatic changes in urban lifestyles and attitudes. Such changes include, for instance, the slow but steady empowerment of Dalit voices.[5] In my ethnography, this critique comes through the couples themselves, who are more aware—due to digital media technologies and greater access to education—of how their stories fit into the larger social scene. In this regard, the Love Commandos organization is emblematic of a larger trend whereby individual stories of couples get channeled into a broader social cause. At the same time, the couples' narratives of mobility give meaning and nuance to the mission of the Love Commandos.

Methods and Context

Marriage and love relationships are continually evolving but perhaps never more so than in a digitally enabled, economically liberalized society, wherein young people from all social strata have more access to information and to each other. When I was researching the social impact of Delhi's new metro rail system in the 2010s, I came to know about the Love Commandos, whose office was near a Metro station I frequented. I saw the Metro and the Love Commandos as two different examples of mobility operating, in specific moments, in conjunction with one another. The narratives I present and

---

5   See Rao (2009) for a full examination of the rise of Dalits as political subjects in contemporary India.

analyze here—in the form of two extended case studies extracted from a range of in-depth interviews with couples in a Love Commandos' safe house as well as interviews with the cofounder of the organization—primarily concern the relationships of two intercaste couples and how they fortify their own love arrangements, even if, as we will see, their futures are uncertain.

In the ethnographic case I explore here, love is a vehicle towards marriage, family, and social acceptance; but most significantly, it is part and parcel of young people's making their way in the world and defining their aspirations. "Aspirational" has become a catch-all term in India (and many other places) to describe a cross-class striving, usually toward a globally recognized middle-class status, but in fact, as the recent anthropological literature shows, it takes quite different forms and meanings (Schielke 2009; Heiman, Freeman, and Liechty 2012; Chua 2014). Jocelyn Chua (2014, 40) writes of "intemperate aspiration"—that is, wanting too much, especially consumer goods and the new lifestyles they make possible—in relation to how people in Kerala view the increasing incidence of suicide among young people. There is a similar moral quality put onto young couples seeking a love marriage: not that they want too much materially but rather that they want too much *for themselves*, a marriage partner that suits their needs rather than their family's. By seeking escape—not in the form of suicide but in the form of running away from their families, at least temporarily—intercaste couples who go to Love Commandos' safe houses are able to recast their love in terms of broader *societal* aspirations.

Unlike other couples in the National Capital Region who flee (see Mody 2008),[6] the couples at a safe house are not alone and instead find themselves in an instant, if ephemeral, community, one defined by a political objective: the upholding of India's secular marriage laws.[7] Being at a Love Commandos' safe house helps couples take control of the moral narrative of their stories and thereby encourages the social transformations that are at the heart of their stories. At the same time, it is important to understand the nature of each couple's "escape," since while they have come to the safe house and are at an impasse with their families, they desire to reintegrate with their families as long as their partners are accepted by them. Their aspirations are meant to lead to a kind of moral and practical reform within

---

6   "National Capital Region" is the term for Delhi and its environs, extending to neighboring cities in the states of Uttar Pradesh, Haryana, and Rajasthan.
7   Specifically, the Special Marriages Act of 1954, which allows a civil contract between a man of at least twenty-one years of age and a woman of at least eighteen years of age. Most significantly, the act enables couples to be married without religious rites or any other ceremonial requirements.

the family, and their own reintegration is imagined as part of that reform and, indeed, as part of their social mobility. This understanding—their understanding—reveals the precise limits and possibilities of the couples' own aspirations. In this respect, my ethnography shows how relationships forged outside the norms of caste create new forms of subjectivity (Das 2010, 376). By casting the couples' stories as narratives of mobility, I mean to highlight the issues of status, economic insecurity, and familial power relationships that underlie the prevalent and often deterministic discourses on caste violence, love versus arranged marriage, and urban-rural divides. As the term "narratives" implies, these are stories with temporal beginnings, middles, and ends, and yet they are also stories of spatial mobility, of particular intersections and correspondences. In this spatial frame, mobility is not a progression but rather a set of variables that represent social conflict and struggle.

The personal conversations I had with the couples (which were all in Hindi and are represented here by my translations) about self, family, and caste, and inevitably about politics and society, created camaraderie and a level of trust between us. My time with them was intense, mostly because the couples' circumstances and their unknowable futures always hung in the air. Our conversations, not surprisingly, focused mostly on their relationships, families, jobs, prospects, and stories of how they ended up at the safe house. They were often linear narratives, and I have presented the two case studies here in that manner. Their narratives of love and aspiration—interlaced with a seesaw of class and caste expectations their families had of them—were also undeniably part of a larger financial calculus of marriage, kin-making, and social mobility. Their physical and social mobilities—mostly accessed through jobs, education, and transport—were continually balanced by what they saw as the immobilities of social and familial obligation.

Once in the safe house, at an undisclosed location not far from Connaught Place in central Delhi, I go into a larger bedroom off the other side of the sitting room and meet three couples chatting softly as they sit or recline on thin mattresses lined up on the floor.[8] At first, the couples keep talking over each other and their stories get intertwined, when in real life they were

---

8   My interviews with the couples at the Love Commandos safe house took place between March and May of 2015 and July of 2016, when I made a number of visits to talk to couples. I chose the couples to write about in this article based on my analysis of how typical their narratives were. I have disguised the names of the young people I interviewed, as well as some of their identifying details, in order to protect their privacy and whereabouts.

not, at least not until they reached the safe house. The young women sit braiding each other's hair, the young men massage each other's heads. It is a very typical kind of homosociality of everyday life, and it also counters the Westernized image of the heterosexual couple in love, impervious to the world around them (Osella 2012). This talking and interacting between the couples and between the young men and young women is a kind of communion of its own, even if a rather unstable "community" per se. The Love Commandos organization frames love as an ideology, as a stand-in for secularism, human rights, and choice. But for the couples at their shelters, love understandably has more fine-grained meanings. These meanings involve intimate feelings, but they also have to do with the precise contexts within which their relationships arose. In their descriptions of their lives and families, the couples' ideas of "love," "caste," and "marriage" get broken down into hopes and fears about status (a mix of class and caste expectations), money, and acceptance. The moral hierarchy between class and caste flips back and forth in the course of the narratives, as the couples assert in different moments that it is caste (not class) or class (not caste) that is the root of the problem.[9]

Love's Logic

Ajay and Gita are hiding out at a Love Commandos safe house for intercaste couples on the run. Ajay is a compact and energetic twenty-five-year-old, clean-shaven and earnest. Gita, who is twenty-one, seems shy at first, with a slight, sweet voice, but this comportment changes once she, too, begins to animatedly describe their predicament. Theirs was a "caste problem," Ajay explains. They come from the same district in Haryana, but he is from a lower caste, she from a higher one. The way he describes it, his voice low and intent, Gita is a Jat, a dominant caste in the Punjabi sub-caste schema, while he comes from a lower caste that works with wood, *lakri ka kam*. Gita chimes in using the English word, "carpenter."

These words and designations are meant to create a distance between them, but they seem to have the opposite effect. They seem to be part of the couple's intimacy, of their acceptance of each other. Ajay and Gita met at a government polytechnic college in Haryana. They were classmates, "sitting

---

9   Mark Liechty (2003, 8) describes this dynamic well in relation to youth and consumerism in Kathmandu, where the social imperative of money and the market economy make the moral logic of caste subordinate to the economic logic of class.

on the same bench," studying for a diploma in electronics and communications. They were friends and then their friendship became love (*pyar hua*).

Ajay says, "I don't know exactly when our friendship got converted to love and went to a higher level. There was no scope for any physical relationship. It was a matter of the heart. Our families do not understand that love is something that happens in the heart, they think it is only physical love." Gita jumps in, "First we tried so hard to get our families to accept us. 'Just accept us, accept us,' we said, 'Let us get married in a good way.'"

Ajay's plan had been to wait two years, so he could secure a good job before getting married to Gita. "But her people," Ajay explains, "once they came to know about us, they had another idea." This other idea was to get her married to another boy.

Ajay: "They wanted to push her out of the house. They found someone else for her in a matter of ten days—not even. In that many days they found a boy whose background they did not even know, and whether he is good or bad, they were ready to send her away with him." Ajay emphasizes the "ten days" again and again. Now, he is indignant. In love's computations, time equals familiarity: this other boy equals ten days, while Ajay and Gita equal four years.

"He was someone my father met, but I did not meet him," explains Gita about the boy her family wants her to marry. "You see, he had a government job and some land." Was this boy also a Jat, like Gita? Ajay interjects, "Yes, same caste, meaning a mentality that he has land, money, that he's rich, even if he has committed four murders or some other crimes. That's the mentality."

Where caste was a problem in relation to Ajay marrying Gita, it was now a "mentality" that enabled Gita's parents to foist this other boy on their daughter. What is essentially a financial deficit in Ajay's profile becomes understood as a "caste mentality."

Gita: "My parents did my engagement with this other boy and printed marriage cards, without asking me, for the same day as my older sister was to get married. They trashed the old cards and just printed both our names together on new cards."

Now, it is Gita's turn to be indignant. Her future seems to hinge on the phrasing of a wedding card, and it is the manner in which her parents quite literally wrest control over her life's narrative. It is at this point that Ajay obtains information on the internet ("*net pe*") about the Love Commandos. He gets in touch with them and describes his and Gita's predicament of (1) being locked up by their families, (2) having their cell phones taken away, and (3) being threatened physically.

Days before the wedding, Gita goes with her mother to get fitted for her wedding clothes at a market in Bahadurgarh where they are supposed to meet her aunt.

"Once there," she explains, "I took my mother's phone and pretended to call my aunt." She then gets out of her mother's sight on the pretense of looking for her aunt. Following Ajay's instructions, she makes her way to the Mundka Metro station, the last stop on the Green Line. An array of jeeps, vans, and buses wait outside the station, ferrying passengers to and from the Haryana border. Gita meets Ajay at Mundka as planned, and they buy tokens and get on the train. Ajay is familiar with the Metro, but it is Gita's first time, though she is too worried about being followed to notice it much. She speaks to her father on the mobile, saying she cannot find her mother and so she is coming home, when she is actually on the Metro with Ajay, going away and not coming home.

"We first go to Inderlok," Ajay explains, "and then change lines and go to Rajiv Chowk." He pauses for a bit, and then admits, "It didn't leave us with a good feeling to have left our families in this way. But their mentality is a little different. Here we have made a new family, found new brothers and sisters."

At the safe house, they are not alone. They have support and even camaraderie, but it is a temporary situation. Without jobs and money, they cannot forge a future, and the Love Commandos can only help them so much, though for couples who do not get reintegrated with their families, the organization does help to settle them and arrange for "furniture and pots and pans."

Thinking about the future, Ajay tells me that he has to get back on his feet again, and this means getting a job. He had received a diploma in junior engineering from the polytechnic college. He also wants to try again to convince their families, even though Gita's family has, in the meantime, filed a kidnapping case against him. On a more somber note, he adds, "If they don't accept us, we will start our life separate from them."

Love's (Im)mobilities

Renu and Shiv got married under duress. I met them in the same Love Commandos safe house where I had met Ajay and Gita. Shiv explains how the couple managed to be together, even when they knew their parents didn't approve of their relationship.

"We began to talk and meet often. We went all over Delhi by Metro—Old Fort, Red Fort, movies, and lots of times at New Delhi Railway Station."

It was during this period that "friendship *ho gai*"—the friendship happened—and then, Shiv says, "I slowly realized she is the perfect girl to get married to."

"I am from the lower schedule caste, *chamar*," Shiv says carefully, "Here, actually, the whole country has a problem with my caste." There is a problem with Renu's profile too. She is a higher caste than Shiv, but is originally from Bihar, which, as Shiv remarks, is seen as "a poor and backward state."

Shiv: "We heard relatives asking things behind our backs. 'Where is the girl from? What does her father do?' they asked, and I told them she is from Bihar. They said, 'Our son won't marry someone from there, we have a problem with that.' My problem is that I am going to marry someone who I want to live with."

Theirs was a relationship that began at home, Renu explains. Her family had rented a room out to him at their place in Gurgaon. Shiv used to come over and talk, mostly to Renu's mother. Her mother liked him, his good manners, and the fact that he was educated. Renu had noticed him too. She had not been looking for a boyfriend but became familiar with him during his visits to talk to her mother.

Shiv believes his parents should be the ones to select a girl for him, that it is their right because they have "taken care of us all our lives." But once Renu makes her feelings known to him, he quickly falls for her.

The problem with telling the family was that the question of marriage was immediately put on the table. Shiv was not ready to get married. He is still studying and does not have a job. He not only cannot support Renu, but he is being supported by his family and is living with his aunt.

The breach in trust with the couple and their families occurs at this juncture: the families are hurt and upset by the not knowing, and everyone has a hard time getting over this fact. It is not that they do not try; they do, and like Renu, Shiv does not give up on trying to convince his parents. "My father was so mad," Shiv says, "He wanted to hear the news from me directly, not through my aunts. He came to see me and beat me up. He stopped giving me money and told me to move back home."

"Our own planning failed," Shiv continues. "I had to go home, stop my studies, and work in a call center to support myself while we kept trying to convince both sides." This retreat into the family becomes the first step towards their social disconnection.

Both Shiv and Renu tell their parents that they cannot marry anyone else. After a lot of convincing, Renu's family agrees to meet with Shiv. Of course, they already know him and have met him many times before, but this is the first time since the revelation of his relationship with their daughter.

Shiv admits he was afraid at the prospect of meeting with them. "Parents can kill children over this in Haryana," he says.[10]

Renu interjects, "My papa is good; they only talked."

Shiv continues, "I told them, 'I'm from a lower caste, and that can't be changed. But please tell me what I can do? Do I need to earn 15,000 or 50,000 or 70,000 rupees? Do I need to get a government job to come take your daughter's hand?' But all her father said was that I should have taken his permission before starting to go out."

Renu's mother softens and admits that Shiv is a sincere and "good boy" from a "good family." But she still does not agree to them marrying due to caste and the pressures from family and society. Shiv said,

> My mother suggested to my father to let me marry Renu, then my uncle came and said that the family will disown us if they let me marry her. Growing up we always heard about our family, that elders know better, that they will match you to the right family, a good home with good values, and that relatives will be the backbone of your life, that they will secure your future, like social security. If you marry by choice, we were told, you will be all alone. I said to my parents, "Okay, I will not marry Renu if you can give me on stamp paper that the girl I marry will make us all happy."

Shiv's father eventually tells the couple to do what they want, but it is clear that his words act as more of a dismissal than a show of support. The couple is back to square one, and each is becoming more isolated. Shiv struggles with his call center job because he has to walk four miles to get there each day. Renu's parents threaten her, make her stop working, and take away her phone, restricting her physical and social mobility at once. Shiv now feels compelled to have an exit strategy. He is afraid that Renu's parents could send her to Bihar, where she would be out of his reach. He is also resigned to society's "false standards," according to which, he says, "respect is given only to anyone who is financially well off."

---

10 Haryana has the lowest ratio of women to men, according to the 2011 Census of India. There are 877 females to every 1,000 males in the state, whereas the all-India rate is 940 females to 1,000 males. See the Government of India 2011 census website: http://www.census2011.co.in/sexratio.php. Delhi sociologist Ravinder Kaur (2004) has analyzed the relationship between North India's skewed sex ratio and the "importing" of girls across state borders within India to make up for the gap in the number of marriageable girls. She shows that these cross-border alliances not only cross regional and linguistic barriers, but also those of religion and even caste. For a historical and anthropological perspective on cross-region marriages in North India, also see Chowdhry (2007).

By this time, Shiv has also been reading posts on the Love Commandos' website and chats with one of their volunteers online. Moving forward means getting married. A lawyer friend of Shiv's advises him not to go in for a court marriage because, in Haryana, word can get around, "people talk and relatives have resources." These "resources," several couples in the room pipe up to explain, are nothing less than *goondas* (thugs) dispatched by the family.

When some more of Shiv's relatives show up at the house to pressure his parents, Shiv abandons his plan to wait for his next paycheck from the call center and leaves the house. He travels ticketless on a train the ninety kilometers to Gurgaon. He then contacts one of Renu's friends to relay a message to Renu. The friend arranges for the two to meet.

Renu: "I left the house with no phone, no money, and no idea that by 5 p.m. that day I would be married."

Shiv: "We don't have our school certificates or documents since they are with our parents at home. We want to study, to go back to work, to eventually live with my parents."

Love, Marriage, and Family

Parents, the couples tell me, are actually ready to support their children. It is the relatives that pose the problem and the societal pressure, which is so intense that parents become willing to lock up their kids or disown them, or even to threaten violence to relieve this pressure.

The families, for their part, see their children in more and more contexts in which making choices and being independent become important—in college, in the workplace, and even navigating the city. These are all spaces in which people from lower-middle-class and lower-caste backgrounds in particular have the possibility of blending in to some extent, places where their own aspirations can be lived and felt. In this case, greater freedom and mobility actually means assimilating ("sitting on the same bench," whether it be in a college or on the Metro), at least up to a point. Families know that giving their children certain freedoms might lead to others, which has generally been the excuse for monitoring the behavior and whereabouts of young women in particular.

It should be noted that most young people seek out their parents' approval in their marriages and often expect their parents to help them find a suitable match. Young people can be as concerned about social status, wealth, and occupation as their parents are. Marriages arranged by parents are regarded as being more morally correct on several counts. Allowing your parents to arrange your marriage, or at the very least have a say in it, shows that you have respect for them and the larger kin network. This respect, in practical terms, means that you are not thinking solely of your desires and personal preferences but rather are concerned with how your spouse will fit into your immediate family as well as your larger kin network. The individual choice that is assumed to be at the heart of love marriages, then, is seen as selfish. This dynamic, depending on the degrees of arranged-ness in a marriage, can play out in numerous ways, from outright violence to quiet acceptance, whereby norms are reconfigured. Nevertheless, Shiv's critique is one you hear more and more, one that questions the moral superiority of arranged marriages.

The Love Commandos' safe house offers an escape, and yet the couples that end up there experience a new form of physical confinement and immobility; put another way, their current "invisibility" to their families is informed by the visibilities of caste and class at the heart of their stories. For the couples I met, the process of waiting in the safe house comes to bear on the meaning and experience of love and the caste politics that undergird their situation. They wait for legal redress, which makes their long days at the safe house inherently meaningful, but they also wait, in a sense, for social change. Each person I talked to at the safe house cared deeply for their family, and lamented the turn of events that had led them to the safe house. At the same time, the details of the couples' stories illustrate their own critiques of society and of how their own families are enmeshed in what they see as hypocritical and outmoded views. Their disappointment was also palpable. In the ethnographic cases I have explored, the temporal and anticipatory nature of the couples' confinement colors their entire narratives, since their aim is not individual liberation—their escape not an end-point—but rather, it is to align familial interests and networks with urban ones. This alignment is in fact essential to their mobility in a neoliberal economy and globalized cultural realm.

Conclusion

Meeting runaway intercaste couples hiding in a safe house in Delhi led me to reflect on the kinds of mobility at work in their lives and in the city today. Mobility is embodied through their movements in the city, and mobility is also an analytic used to understand the particularities of caste, class, and gender identities in and around Delhi. By highlighting the social and physical parameters of their mobility in a single ethnographic frame, I show the ways in which they overlap and connect to each other, an experience of urban life made concrete in the narratives of the two couples. The narratives also reveal that it is the quest for mobility rather than an expression of individual choice that is most significant about the couples' flouting of social norms. By tying together different kinds of mobility—social and physical—I have highlighted how mobility functions in the lives of the couples, as a way to think through and concretize the "mobility paradigm," and to reveal how mobility and immobility play out in a discrete ethnographic context (Urry and Sheller 2006; Salazar and Smart 2011; Cresswell 2012).

Marriage has long been a key index of social mobility, a way to move up in life, confirm the status quo, and socially reproduce. Seeing these couples' quest for the conformity of marriage without the social certainty that surrounds marriages that are accepted by families can be jarring. The couples' cases in and of themselves, as sedentary tales of people sitting and waiting in a safe house, help us understand how some young people in India are redefining what "moving up" in life may mean. However, when we map aspects of these couples' lives onto the urban landscape—to see their social trajectories as including pivotal metro rides or the relationships between government colleges they attended, markets visited, and rooms hiding out in—mobility is revealed to be not as linear as the word "trajectory" might suggest. Mobility itself is made of stops and starts, as well as "entanglements of vectors" (Linder, this volume). These entanglements become the very coordinates of these couples' lives; they may be mapped out but are difficult to unravel. The couples' social mobility—fueled by aspirations for education, living with the person of their choice, and moving around the city in a way that enables caste invisibility and social confidence—has altered each of their senses of belonging to places where they are "from," whether Haryana or Rajasthan or Bihar. As a result, they must forge new senses of belonging, bridging urban and familial networks and attitudes. Their experiences of escape and confinement, physical release and constriction, are not isolated acts but rather attempts to dislodge the social order and challenge their own social designations. Marriage and love relationships in these narratives have been lifted from the realm of the family and taken into unfamiliar and unknown spaces. Family gets dispersed and reconfigured in the process. At stake are certainly the lives of the couples but also the social and political meanings of love and caste.

"Mobility," then, is not merely being on the move, nor is it only about what impedes or enables movement, but rather it is a complex of institutions that bear on the social and affective relations between individuals, and, as we have seen here, on the very notions of self, family, and caste. Loving someone across a caste boundary, while questioning and reinterpreting the meaning of that boundary and the mobilities it impedes and enables, as Ajay, Gita, Shiv, and Renu do, is, in fact, the work of social change. Mobility, in my rendering, is not unmoored from place, nor is it unmappable; it is more precisely a set of mechanisms rooted in the city, its environs, and its connections to elsewhere.

Acknowledgments

This essay is a condensed and revised version of an article of the same name that appeared in *Anthropology and Humanism* 43 (1): 39–57.

References

Chamberlain, Gethin. 2010. "Honour Killings: How the Love Commandos Rescue India's Young Lovers." *Observer*, 11 October.

Chowdhry, Prem. 2007. *Contentious Marriages, Eloping Couples: Gender, Caste and Patriarchy in North India*. Delhi: Oxford University Press.

Chua, Jocelyn Lim. 2014. *In Pursuit of the Good Life: Aspiration and Suicide in Globalizing South India*. Berkeley: University of California Press.

Cresswell, Tim. 2010. "Towards a Politics of Mobility." *Environment and Planning D: Society and Space* 28 (1): 17–31.

Doherty, Ben. 2013. "Rescued by the Love Commandos." *Sydney Morning Herald*, 5 January.

Donner, Henrike. 2002. "'One's Own Marriage': Love Marriages in a Calcutta Neighborhood." *South Asia Research* 22 (1): 79–94.

Gilmour, Martin. 2013. "Rescued by the Love Commandos." *Examiner*, 13 January.

Grewal, Inderpal. 2013. "Outsourcing Patriarchy: Feminist Encounters, Transnational Mediations and the Crime of 'Honour Killings.'" *International Feminist Journal of Politics* 15, no. 1: 1–19.

Heiman, Rachel, Mark Liechty, and Carla Freeman. 2012. "Charting an Anthropology of the Middle Classes." In *The Global Middle Classes: Theorizing Through Ethnography*, edited by Rachel Heiman, Carla Freeman, and Mark Liechty, 3–29. Santa Fe: School for Advanced Research Press.

Kaur, Ravinder. 2004. "Across-Region Marriages: Poverty, Female Migration, and the Sex Ratio." *Economic and Political Weekly* 39 (25): 2595–603.

Liechty, Mark. 2003. *Suitably Modern: Making Middle-Class Culture in a New Consumer Society*. Princeton: Princeton University Press.

Mody, Perveez. 2008. *The Intimate State: Love-Marriage and the Law in Delhi.* New Delhi: Routledge.
Mulkerrins, Jane. 2013. "A Matter of Love or Death." *Irish Daily Mail*, 9 February.
Pretoria News. 2013. "The World's Only Army for Love." 28 February.
Pundir, Pallavi. 2012. "Romeo and Juliet in Delhi." *Indian Express*, 7 November 7.
Rao, Anupama. 2009. *The Caste Question: Dalits and the Politics of Modern India.* Berkeley: University of California Press.
Osella, Caroline. 2012. "Desires Under Reform: Contemporary Reconfigurations of Family, Marriage, Love and Gendering in a Transnational South Indian Matrilineal Muslim Community." *Culture and Religion* 13 (2): 241–64.
Sadana, Rashmi. 2022. *The Moving City: Scenes from the Delhi Metro and the Social Life of Infrastructure.* Oakland: University of California Press.
Salazar, Noel B., and Alan Smart. 2011. "Anthropological Takes on (Im)Mobility." *Identities* 18 (6): i–ix.
Schielke, Samuli. 2009. Ambivalent Commitments: Troubles of Morality, Religiosity and Aspiration among Young Egyptians." *Journal of Religion in Africa* 39: 158–85.
Thakur, Tanul. 2015. "In the Name of Honour." *Man's World India*, 9 April. http://www.mansworldindia.com/people/in-the-name-of-honour/.
Urry, John, and Mimi Sheller. 2006. "The New Mobilities Paradigm." *Environment and Planning A* 38 (2): 207–26.

About the author

Rashmi Sadana is the author of *The Moving City: Scenes from the Delhi Metro and the Social Life of Infrastructure* and *English Heart, Hindi Heartland: The Political Life of Literature in India.* She coedited *The Cambridge Companion to Modern Indian Culture.* She teaches at George Mason University.

4 Driving While Tamil: Policing as a Regime of Mobility in Postwar Jaffna, Sri Lanka

daniel dillon

Abstract: Despite over a decade of ostensible peace, the island of Sri Lanka has yet to experience a shift into genuine peace. Rather, various government institutions have extended the ethos of militarization and counter-terrorism into the daily lives of Sri Lankans in ways that are felt disproportionately by members of low-caste, low-class, and minority communities (ethnic, religious, and sexual). This chapter focuses on how this manifests in Jaffna Town, in northern Sri Lanka, with attention to policing as a regime of mobility. Drawing on ethnographic research with rickshaw drivers and a well-documented police shooting, this chapter argues for "driving while Tamil" as a heuristic that highlights the assemblage of forces that structure mobilities in the region, particularly for young Tamil men.

Keywords: militarization, mobilities, policing, Sri Lanka

October 20, 2016 was a Thursday. The University of Jaffna was in session. In fact, the first-years started their holiday the very next day; the upper classes were rapidly approaching final exams. As is customary, it was a time of high stress for most students, and house parties were being hosted all over the peninsula to celebrate the end of term. Sundaraj Sulakshan and Nadarasa Gajan, both third-year students studying at the university, were returning home from one such party in Kankasethurai, at the far north of the peninsula, around 11:00 pm that night. Gajan was staying at the university hostel back in Jaffna Town, and so Sulakshan gave him a ride back into town on his motorbike. Neither made it home that night.

Police reports claim that at around 11:30 pm the pair attempted to run through a checkpoint at Kokkuvil, about 5 kilometers north of Jaffna Town. Police also alleged the pair were drunk, though what evidence they used to reach that conclusion is unclear. As the official story goes, the pair ran the checkpoint somehow avoiding the police but promptly running into a wall. Postmortem reports by the medical examiner based out of Jaffna Teaching Hospital soon revealed that both young men had been shot multiple times, casting doubt on the claim they were intoxicated. Sulakshan, the driver, had been struck in the head, likely dying instantly. Gajan, however, died the next day from the combination of gunshot wounds and crash-related injuries. Many locals quickly deduced an alternative narrative in which the police opened fire on the youth, killing Sulakshan and thus causing the crash that also killed Gajan. They then attempted a cover-up to obfuscate their role, slandered the dead to further cast doubt, and repeatedly denied wrongdoing and any empirical facts that suggested it.

As in so many cases, the accounts of this incident are incomplete and heavily biased. It is impossible to know precisely what did and did not happen on that night, and what I have already sketched here is near the limit of what can be known for certain. I cannot say, then, whether Sulakshan and Gajan were drunk, or if they stopped at the checkpoint, or if they sped through but had good reason for doing so. What dialogue may have occurred between them and the police on duty is likely lost to the unknowable past. I am quite certain that one thing can be known, however; regardless of whether they were guilty of anything else, Sulakshan and Gajan were guilty of the crime of "driving while Tamil" in a highly militarized and anxious postwar Sri Lanka. This phrase, a play on the popular notion of "driving while Black" (see Gilroy 2001), is meant here to draw attention to the specific nexus of history and power that underscores any analysis of postwar northeast Sri Lanka.

Many know at least the broad strokes of the island's turbulent postcolonial transition, but it would be worth mentioning a few important details. Since well before independence, there was an ongoing debate about the rights of minorities on what was then known as Ceylon. A series of proposals and counterproposals wrestled with the expectations of a Sinhala majority and the demands for protections and representation of various minority groups, most notably Tamils but also Muslims and Burghers. A satisfactory resolution was not found, and over time a nationalistic and fundamentalist coalition led the island to recast itself as an explicitly Buddhist nation, Sri Lanka, whose only official language was Sinhalese. Fast forwarding a bit, tensions erupted into full-blown war between Tamil separatist groups and the central government in Colombo, a conflict that lasted decades, killed tens of thousands, and scarred the land and psyche of the nation.

The dramatic conclusion of that conflict is perhaps the best-known part. For my purposes, it is enough to note that the war was won by the central government under the banner of president Mahinda Rajapaksa (and at the hands of minister of defense Gotabaya Rajapaksa) through a move to total war. Though the government continues to deny these "allegations," the United Nations, numerous INGOs, and scores of scholars have documented the dramatic increase in broadscale, indiscriminate bombing by government forces, as well as compelling evidence of extensive crimes against humanity in the last years of the conflict and after. It is also worth noting that the Tamil Tigers (aka the LTTE) were not blameless, having their own track record of civilian (suicide) bombings, evidence of forced recruitment (including of children), and other war crimes. Once the Sri Lankan military brutally crushed the LTTE, open conflict ended and peace was declared with much fanfare.

The absence of conflict is not the same as the emergence of peace, however. The end of the war in Sri Lanka might best be understood, as historian Nira Wickramasinghe (2014) characterizes it, as an "oppressive stability" of highly militarized and centralized power, rather than the development of a positive peace (Galtung 1969). By which I mean to say, these violent forces left their marks well beyond the simple fact of the conflict, with widespread trauma (Somasundaram 2013; Subramaniam 2017), displacement (De Alwis 2009; Thiranagama 2013b), and continuing social tensions (Thiranagama 2018). Sri Lanka remains an island still struggling for peace well after the end of the war (Amarasingam and Bass 2016). This opening vignette is thus not just a tragedy that struck a chord; it is indicative of the broader setting in which the legacies of decades of violence continue to echo into the everyday lives of generations who were promised new opportunities for peace and prosperity in the postwar era.

Returning to the argument, "driving while Tamil" is meant to evoke a number of overlapping insights drawn from cultural geography, mobilities studies, Black and Queer feminisms, and broader studies of surveillance and policing. In mobilizing this admittedly charged heuristic, I aim to draw focus to the problem in a new way so that we might see it more clearly. To foreshadow my conclusions a little, the police shooting already outlined above and the ethnographic narratives below,[1] drawn from my research

---

1   I am inclined to think of these ethnographic fragments as "geographic stories," drawing on the remarkable work of Black feminist geographer Katherine McKittrick. I am fond of her

alongside rickshaw drivers in Jaffna Town, show how viscerally incomplete the island's conflict and reconciliation remains. Despite the prioritization of infrastructural reconstruction and various development initiatives, mobility in the northeast must be viewed as refracted and distorted through the ubiquitous presence of militarized policing, which I contend is the dominant mobility regime in the region.

Though centering ethnicity in its wording, in thinking with the term "driving while Tamil," I also mean to evoke the assemblage of hierarchies at work in the encounters found in this chapter, which also invoke gender, class, and caste in policing, literally, who is permitted—privileged, we might say—to move freely and whose movements are deemed suspect or even dangerous. These varied hierarchies, structured as they are around a host of social differences, cohere and contract situationally. Hence, my preference is to think of them as an assemblage, a sticky, messy concept for a disordered world (Puar 2007; see also Manalansan 2014), over the mobility-themed intersection (Crenshaw 1991). By extension, my use of "driving while Tamil" echoes the recent surge in attention to and activism against anti-Black racism and police violence to highlight the consequences of resistance, even if only perceived. Unfortunately, these too are unequally felt.

On the Difference between Military and Militarization

I was surprised to ride up to the stand one weekday afternoon to find Pradeepan and Sandeep chatting with a couple of uniformed army guys. I walked over and hovered around the edges of the conversation for about fifteen minutes before the Yarl Devi pulled in and everyone scattered into hurried activity. The army guys waved goodbye as they walked over and started up their bus. The drivers and I took up positions to land hires. Everyone rushed about to work, giving me a few moments to write up some quick notes. Thirty minutes later the stand was quiet, calm, and sparse. I joined Sandeep in the back of Pradeepan's auto and struck up a conversation. I was surprised they were so friendly with the army guys given what I knew about their experiences during the war. "Sandeep, how can you be so nice

---

observation, quite early in *Demonic Grounds* that "technologies of transportation... while materially and ideologically enclosing black subjects... also contribute to the formation of an oppositional geography" (McKittrick 2006: ix). Rickshaws are many things: capacious, open objects subjected to close scrutiny; substantial economic investments that sometimes become fiscal anchors; and engines of vehicular and bodily autonomy (Featherstone 2004).

to army people when the army killed your parents?" I asked. It would be so easy for him to blame the military, but he didn't, not really.

"No, no, my friend," he said in English. He always uses English when he wants to make sure I understand. "They only doing job. They fighting… protecting. Good people. Only police I don't like." I waited. This was not an answer I expected. "Why don't you like the police?" I prompted. Here Pradeepan joined in, also in English, "Us army, no problems. Us police, many problems." I had noticed how frequently the police drove by, slowly watching us from inside their AC-ed cars. At the time I had paid more attention to the vehicles, all '80s models, clearly heavily used. Nothing like the beefy SUVs and muscle cars many US police drive. But I could see it now. The soldiers would walk up and down the lane, chat and drink tea, smoke cigarettes at the small shop. The police kept to themselves, they mostly drove their cars, and when they spoke to any of us it was inquisitorial. I remember how uncomfortable I felt when the police first noticed my presence and started asking about me. This always in Sinhala, a language rarely understood in Jaffna, where over ninety-eight percent of residents are native Tamil-speakers.

That was the day I knew I needed to pay attention to the police. While there is a huge presence of military personnel in the region, they largely remain in their bases. An army or navy bus comes to the station almost daily to transport troops traveling via the railway system, so soldiers do not even need to arrange local transportation. Despite being less than a kilometer from an important army installation, drivers encountered soldiers primarily while driving back and forth on hires, zipping past bases as the soldiers played volleyball. A more common occurrence was uniformed police officers responding to accidents, issuing traffic citations on the side of roads, or, more often, surveilling the streets, especially Station Road.

The military occupies space by maintaining a presence at formal installations. The police do this as well, but they frequently also, like drivers, spread out from one or more nodes and move through the spaces of the street. This is, in part, a difference in function. I'll have more to say about this in a moment, but for now I wish to highlight this: the role of the military presence in the north/east is to *hold* territory, the role of the police is to *discipline* it. A large military presence means the central government can respond to any emerging threats that might challenge its sovereignty, none of which have materialized in the years since the violent and dramatic close of the war in 2009. A large police presence allows the state to enforce its will upon the residents, who are still viewed with a skeptical eye by the central government and even many average Sinhalese living throughout the island.

Sandeep could see me thinking all this as he sat beside me. "The police are no good," he said, switching back to Tamil. "They harass people, *bothering no helping*. They don't even speak Tamil. How can I ask them to help if they cannot understand my words?"[2] These guys knew what was going on. The police were there to watch for trouble, not prevent it. And people like my friends were prime suspects for future trouble. There is no shortage of rumors or misperceptions about rickshaw drivers. Such rampant distrust of the profession obviously makes drivers subject to greater scrutiny, but here I want to trace out the connection from rumors and suspicion of criminality and terrorism to implications in policing practices and the pervasive feeling of oppression that I am trying to document. That is, in a phrase, the problem of "driving while Tamil," which is the problem especially felt by young Tamil men while moving through public space as they are implicitly, and sometimes overtly, targeted for surveillance, harassment, and enforcement by police, the everyday manifestation of state power and authority.

Anthropologist Beatrice Jauregui approaches a similar problem from within different contexts. She has written extensively on the anthropology of policing, much of which is beyond my scope here but is certainly worth engaging, with an emphasis on the importance of culturally and historically nuanced analyses of police powers and cultures. To wit, the police and the state are not equivalent, the police authority to use violence is not total, nor are police the only facet of the state with authority to use violence (Jauregui 2013). In her book *Provisional Authority*, she offers a rich accounting of the development of a police culture in northern India in which the police are compelled to accept bribes and participate in other forms of corruption due to the force of various social relations. In this case, the police in the region rely on the good will of the communities over which they have authority to surveil and discipline; without acceding to the will of the people the police are unable to carry out their most basic functions (Jauregui 2016).

Crucially, the context in Sri Lanka is one marked by decades of conflict and militarization, as I noted earlier. The anecdote at the beginning of this section helps to show how militarization does not necessarily imply active participation of the military but is rather a more pervasive cultural and institutional response to the island's multiple, brutal postcolonial conflicts. Sri Lankan feminist scholar Neloufer de Mel describes militarization as a set of ideological processes and material practices that center aggressive and violent solutions to social and political problems (2007, 12–13). This

---

2   Italics within a quote indicate code switching. In this case, an English phrase used within a Tamil sentence.

happens not only when a military tries to gain political dominance, as in Myanmar, but also when civilian leaders mobilize military power to resolve their own conflicts, which is the case in Sri Lanka.[3] In leaning so heavily on violent solutions to conflict and dissent, militarization seeps into a society's cultures and values in ways that align with various forms of extremism like religious and ethnic nationalism (de Mel 2007, 23–30).

To see how this has played out in Sri Lanka, one need look no further than the rise of the Rajapaksa family, particularly brothers Mahinda and Gotabaya, who have led the central government and military hand-in-hand for much of the last twenty years. Under their leadership, political power and authority was heavily centralized (despite multiple agreements to create a more decentralized form of government, a frequent demand of Tamil political leaders), a virulent strain of Sinhala Buddhist nationalism was promoted as official state ideology, and widespread human rights violations were carried out in the name of military victory and postwar security. The brothers Rajapaksa and their political allies created and remade many institutions to codify these priorities, ensuring their influence even during the leadership of comparably political moderates from 2015 to 2020.

The Special Task Force (STF), an elite paramilitary police unit imbued with counterterror authority, was initially created in 1983, for example, but became a favorite tool used against political opponents, journalists, and human rights activists.[4] It is notable that the Aragalaya of 2022, Sinhalese for "struggle," were protests that initially grew out of criticism of high-level government financial mismanagement. Rather quickly, however, the "GotaGoGama" encampment near Galle Face Green,[5] the social and commercial heart of Colombo, grew to include protests against militarization and disappearances, the weaponization of the STF for political purposes,

---

3   It can also emerge from processes such as "military fiscalism," which can be seen in both Myanmar and Sri Lanka and in which various sectors of the economy become dominated by or dependent upon the military for capital and/or labor (Venugopal 2011). In Sri Lanka's case, several tourist resorts were seized during the end of the war while other destinations were constructed on seized property, with the military now comprising nearly a third of the island's entire tourism revenue (see Perera 2016).

4   The STF features prominently in many accounts of state violence during and after the war, for example in Rohini Mohan's graphic accounts of Tamil men and women who were tortured or disappeared (2014).

5   "Go Home Gota" was the go-to protest chant of the time, using the commonplace shorthand for Gotabaya. Meanwhile, "gama" is a common naming convention for Sinhalese towns, making the encampment something akin to 'The Town of Go Home Gotabaya.' One might note that all of these are based on Sinhalese (and English) language conventions, helping to indicate the movement's largely middle-class Sinhalese priorities and population.

and other scars on Sri Lankan democracy. Also worth noting, the official response by the brothers Rajapaksa was to mobilize the police to break up the protests/encampment as terrorist activity, resulting in an immediate groundswell of increased protests. Ultimately, the police stood down after widespread criticism, and the protests successfully pushed for the resignation of both Mahinda and Gotabaya Rajapaksa, who were succeeded by more centrist members of the ruling coalition. One of newly empowered President Ranil Wickremasinghe's first acts was to redeploy military and STF personnel to clear the Presidential Palace, which had been occupied by protesters in the last days before Gotabaya Rajapaksa's ouster.

The provisional authority of policing thus morphs into something far more ominous when it encounters a culture of robust militarization and powerful ethnic nationalism. It is still attentive to the needs and desires of citizens and communities, but instead of creating a space for dialogue or agency, it amplifies postwar traumas and anxieties in ways that are easily weaponized against minority communities. The Aragalaya, for all its pro-democracy rhetoric, was still a largely Sinhalese movement, with Tamil organizations and activists frequently criticized for trying to use the historic moment to ask for redress of their own longstanding grievances (see Satkunanathan 2022). My argument throughout this chapter is that not only is postwar policing weaponized (most dramatically through the STF, but also through mundane policing activities), it is weaponized in ways that specifically target people like the rickshaw drivers with whom I worked to understand contemporary Sri Lankan Tamil masculinity. Frankly, it is weaponized in a way that makes it dangerous for anyone to be caught "driving while Tamil," but especially for young men like Sulakshan and Gajan. Or, for that matter, for my friend Sandeep.

The Logics of Policing

I will turn now to an analysis of how the logics of policing and counterterrorism, which are sometimes separate but increasingly the same, converge to target these young men.

A key distinction in police studies is between high and low policing. High policing refers to practices in the service of specific purposes, usually in service to state and civil society elites. Take, for example, the extraordinary procedures for protecting a president or VIP. Low policing is the set of practices aimed at maintaining order or other nonspecific ends. This can include everything from routine patrols to more targeted campaigns like "stop and frisk" (Brodeur 1983). This is a broad mandate, and arguably grants police the world over more authority and fewer limitations than any other part of their respective states (Dubber 2005, introductory chapter).[6]

The global "war on terror" exacerbated this, greatly augmenting the sphere of established policing theory and practice (Deflem 2010). The critical change was to add counterterrorism to the mandate of ordinary police forces as part of a broader effort to scale up the forces able to respond to terrorist threats, reshaping low policing from the maintenance of order to the prevention of terrorism as terrorism itself became a loosely defined threat of disorder. A move that is often heralded, even demanded by civil society (Silver 1967), such that, in some contexts, counterterrorism becomes the guiding logic of entire state institutions. This perfectly conforms to the logic of a "risk society," in which police (and other state agencies) recalibrate their efforts toward increased information gathering and brokering with the aim of risk management akin to the work of insurance agencies (Ericson and Haggerty 1997). Unfortunately, there is good reason to believe such efforts are merely performative, doing little or nothing to prevent terrorism while harming marginalized communities (Davis 2003; Kaba and Ritchie 2022; Parmar 2011).

As Walter Lacquer (1999) has noted, however, the conception of terrorism is often capacious and implicit; a guiding principle akin to "you'll know it when you see it." Such an ill-defined mandate radically expands the authority of the state to police all manner of perceived risks. This empowerment tends to result in the reallocation of resources for police action against "suspicious" populations and a heightened concern over spaces and practices of mobility (Bowling and Sheptycki 2012, 114–17), already suspect for their potential to allow "geographical deviance" (Cresswell 1996).[7] Within the logic of terrorism/counterterrorism these spaces of potential transgression become perpetual *potential* targets of future terrorist attacks or "breeding grounds" of discontent that could lead to terrorist sympathies in the local population.[8]

---

6   An important insight coming from the ethnographic study of policing has shown that police authority in practice is often dependent upon the wider network of social relations at play in a given context (e.g., Jauregui 2016; Martin 2013). This softens the theory a bit and reminds us that policing tends to be done with a certain degree of consent from the policed, or at least some segments of society that are able to claim they represent larger communities.

7   In identifying certain people or practices as "out of place," and therefore suspicious, the underlying logic is revealed in its transgression (Douglass 1984 [1966]). Consider the frequent association of crime and dirt, like referring to criminals as filth or trash.

8   A similar process can be seen in the response to the 2004 tsunami, when fear of another crisis spurred massive securitization to restrict movement in the name of protection and risk reduction (Hyndman 2007). As is often the case, these security regulations were especially

This itself is often premised on the "broken windows" theory of policing, a rather dubious theory that assumes that minor crimes like vandalism beget larger and more violent crimes, thus broken windows on an abandoned car can be taken as an indication an area will be rife with other criminal acts and should therefore be subject to increased police surveillance and actions (Camp and Heatherton 2016). The conceptual leap from minor infractions like breaking a window on a clearly abandoned car to serious ones like assault and murder is obviously a large one, and itself presumes a disposition to criminality wholly separate from structural factors like poverty, a disposition that is not supported by research. All the same, the approach is extremely popular, becoming the basis for such policies as New York's "stop and frisk," which codified harassment of Black and brown communities as legitimate police activity. Stuart Schrader's *Badges Without Borders* offers a very compelling analysis linking global counterinsurgency initiatives. His book focuses on the mid-twentieth century (that is, before "terror" was the enemy), exploring concrete and detrimental effects on US police cultures, especially noting how race and racism become interwoven with globalized notions of threat assessment (Schrader 2019).[9]

Sri Lankan state and civil society responses to the Tamil Tigers are rife with principles of racialized counterterrorism.[10] These are augmented with concerns about "the underworld," a common expression that evokes organized crime, youth criminality that is widely believed to be tied to wartime traumas, and perpetual fear among the Sinhala majority that their culture and religion are under siege.[11] Invocations of the underworld often lump together under one banner everything from petty criminals to street gangs, drug smugglers, and terrorist agents, setting them apart

disruptive for poor and ethnic-minority Sri Lankans, while wealthier islanders and tourism developers were more likely to be granted exceptions or privileged access to at-risk areas.

9   The interlinkage of racism and US policing has a long and graphic history long before the events that Schrader analyzes, of course. The logic of counterinsurgency simply allows police to deflect accusations of racism by arguing that their activities are motivated by outside considerations, which has in several cases allowed even greater violations of human rights under the guise of legitimate police work (e.g., Ralph 2020).

10   Arguably, this is part of how the Sri Lankan state won in their struggle against the Liberation Tigers of Tamil Eelam. In successfully branding the Tamil Tigers' de facto state a terrorist organization, the Sri Lankan government was able to garner material support and impunity from international human rights enforcement. To this day, the Sri Lankan government continues to deflect serious sanctions by packaging its efforts as counterterrorism.

11   Fears of Sinhala minoritization are well documented and much analyzed in the course of the war. While the Sri Lankan context is not specifically analyzed in the text, I would point readers toward the essays in *Fear of Small Numbers*, which I believe best theorize the roots of these anxieties (Appadurai 2006).

from an implicitly moral society.[12] It is not uncommon for references to the underworld to implicitly, if not explicitly, include rickshaw drivers, who are widely suspected of criminal activity or worse. Capacious categories like terrorism and the underworld, make it easy to criminalize what before might have been nuisance or a social eyesore, and to intensify disciplinary severity against previously minor offenses. And thus, drivers and other street workers can be subjected to increased police surveillance (and enforcement) for all manner of crimes real and imagined (see Browne 2015).[13]

In Jaffna, this is reinforced by a prevalent sense of danger, which leads the local elite to demand greater state intervention. As Daniel Bass has noted, the circulation of rumors of violence and danger is often an act by those who feel they lack recognition, especially among local elites or other semi-privileged social positions who are accustomed to wielding considerable agency (Bass 2008). In this case, local elites and civil society in the periphery, exasperated at being ignored by their counterparts in Colombo, the center of state and economic power, are inclined to petition for action against an alleged threat.[14] By demanding an increased police presence to combat the danger, local elites assert their power to sway the state and thereby receive recognition as representatives of their community. I felt this directly during my research residence; reliably, any mention of my work among rickshaw drivers would elicit unsolicited stories of bad actors (drunkards, smugglers, and thugs) who prowled the road as tuk tuk operators. It became so much a focus of conversations within certain segments of society that I began to avoid those social circles all together.

What I quickly realized, however, was that the reality of danger is far less important than the perceived *potential*. Anthropologist Jason Cons illustrates the power of such potential in the complex border between India and Bangladesh. There, the notion of "sensitivity" is so powerful and

---

12   This mimics the problematic bifurcation between state and society by extending it to an amorphous and other "uncivil" society, which stands even further apart (Jauregui 2016, Chapter 1).

13   This relationship of mobile labor with policing is pivotal. As Romit Chowdury writes, "transport workers cannot take for granted a right to labor in the city; instead, they have to seize that right through repeated encounters with" the state, traffic police being the subject of his particular concern (2023, 121). One can see how this would be an issue in a context in which "claiming the state" is a deeply contested process that has consistently resisted calls for recognition by ethnic, religious, and sexual minorities (Thiranagama 2013a; see also Ellawala 2019).

14   The panic around crime in Jaffna is not founded on empirical evidence. After a fierce period of concern in the middle of 2018, the government released a statement pointing to its latest crime statistics which showed a progressive decrease. Nonetheless, a pledge was made to increase police activities in the Northern Province.

pervasive that, he argues, it remakes the space of the border itself into anxiety-driven assertions of state sovereignty which lay bare the reality of the state-in-formation (Cons 2016). One can see a parallel with the case of postwar Sri Lanka, where the state is concertedly asserting its power and authority after decades during which those claims were highly contestable.[15] Despite the war being over for a decade now, the reality of the government's victory is less important than the worry that the Tamil Tigers might return. Or, more to my point, the end of open conflict and emergence of relative safety is less important than pervasive anxieties that violence could erupt again at any moment.

This anxiety is often associated with the Sri Lankan Tamil diaspora, especially the community in Toronto, which is easily portrayed as "Tiger sympathizers" after years of activism attempting to memorialize wartime atrocities and to hold the Sri Lankan government accountable. The picture is far more complex than a case of "long-distance nationalism," however, as Sharika Thiranagama (2014) has shown through ethnographic work (2014). Toronto Tamils' expressions of support for the Tamil Tigers are more often about rallying the community to push back against local ethnic prejudices, or are caught up in struggles between leaders of community factions, than an attempt to intervene in Sri Lankan or international politics. Solidarity is certainly still strongly and passionately felt by many and itself can form a key aspect of orienting frameworks of history and geography (Fuglerud 1999). However, the expression of that allegiance is so varied and diverse that it becomes nonsensical to view the diaspora as any kind of cohesive entity acting to revive the Tigers or even carry on its vision in any meaningful way.[16]

That the diaspora is far from thinking and moving, as one has not stopped social and political leaders in Colombo or Jaffna from using the alleged threat of diasporic nationalists as a pretense for increased militarization and securitization of the peninsula. Not only did police regularly monitor diasporic Tamils visiting on holiday or service trips, they often went directly to the source of their movements through the area, the rickshaw drivers they hired. I knew one such diasporic activist who had a longstanding arrangement with two of the drivers from Station Road, where I did my

---

15   Coincidentally, the Indian and Bangladeshi governments also justify their actions with reference to preventing terrorism and human smuggling, couching their acts in humanitarian, if paternalistic, terms (Cons 2016).
16   Even beginning to explain the scale and scope of this is an enormous task. Thankfully, Amarnath Amarasingam has been researching Sri Lankan Tamil diaspora politics for years. Those interested should read his book *Pain, Pride, and Politics* or his more recent chapter (Amarasingam 2015; 2018).

research. Whenever she or a close associate published an article, held an event, or went on weekend trips out of town, the local police invariably would come to the rickshaw stand and inquire about her whereabouts, placing drivers in a difficult position between protecting a regular client's privacy and avoiding further attention or coercion from police.

The Force of Policing

Here, I think it would be useful to consider Jeffrey Martin's work with police in Taiwan where, to sum up his argument, "legible affect *is* the 'force' in Taiwanese policing" (2017, 91). In Martin's view, which is well supported by ethnography of, and in close collaboration with, a diverse range of police units, *qing*, which he glosses as "affect," is the substance of much police work in Taiwan. A looser, but more generalizable gloss might be "connected feeling," where the feeling is both derived from and produces social connections. This emphasis would seem to muddy analytic distinctions between civil and political power as well as between low and high policing (Martin 2017, 96). Put simply, the centering of "*qing*-work" in Taiwanese policing manifests a vastly different kind of force than analyses centered on Weberian or Foucaultian notions of state authority and power tend to emphasize. Rather than wielding the ominous disciplinary rod that threatens violence if people resist, the police, Martin shows us, pluck at threads of social ties with threats of stigma or bureaucratic difficulties to compel cooperation.[17]

This is not to say, of course, that Taiwanese police do not have the same legal access to violence afforded to police in other societies and cultures. Rather, it suggests that policing ought to be understood as far more than governmentality made manifest or the exertion of biopower. Policing is not simply war or politics by other means; it may be that in some cases, but it is often more, and sometimes less. Most importantly, it is a process, one that is deeply structured by a host of factors that are both internal and external to its operations. These factors necessarily influence the manifestation of this process, and in the context of postwar Jaffna, at least two factors are of particular concern in explaining how policing manifests as a regime

---

17   I think here of Sara Ahmed's meditations on will and willfulness, which so elegantly demonstrate how different times and places present their own definitions of social order and those who refuse to abide by it. Though compelled by different kinds of threats, in both dynamics presented here the police exert force to impose their will on citizens whose actions may be perfectly legal but resist official desires (Ahmed 2014).

of mobility. First, a culture of militarization and securitization that is a direct result of the island's postcolonial history of conflict and disaster. Second, a social environment of suspicion and tension that exacerbates communal traumas, fears, and anxieties rather than allowing for meaningful reconciliation.

As many have noted, one power of the state is that it can mitigate its own fear by instilling anxiety, even terror, in its subjects (Aretxaga 2003; Green 1999; Taussig 1992).[18] Few would object that Sri Lanka continues to be an anxious state in anticipation of further natural and human crises (Choi 2015). Many analysts agree; Gotabaya Rajapaksa's 2020 presidential election can be directly traced to the Easter Bombings of 2019, in which a small number of Tamil-speaking Muslims bombed churches and tourist sites. Gotabaya's reputation, as former defense minister under his older brother and former president, Mahinda Rajapaksa, was seen by many voters as the kind of strong leadership needed to prevent future attacks. He took that mandate and ran with it, immediately ramping up policing operations, mobilizing elite military units, and cracking down on journalists, activists, and even dissenters from within his own political party.

In a context in which both the government and the public hold a great deal of anxiety about the moral and material wellbeing of the nation (Venugopal 2015; see also Davis 2005, 47–50)—before the pandemic and mismanagement-induced financial crises of 2022—the promise of law and order through *preventing disorder* created a vast and powerful consensus that something needed to be done about those believed to be criminally inclined. Aggressive policing to prevent terrorism and organized crime emerged as a reasonable response to mitigate these powerful societal anxieties, thereby legitimating practices of harassment and surveillance of the marginal, such as drivers, who are viewed as always almost terrorists/criminals.

I make this digression not to intervene in the field of police studies but to demonstrate that the feeling of being watched and harassed by the police, a feeling that is widespread among drivers, is more than misperception or paranoia. Indeed, it begins to seem like a nearly inevitable product of the nature of the state, made even more certain and ominous by the long history of conflict in northern Sri Lanka. The pervasive sense of unease

---

18   The use of "subjects" is intentional. Discussions of citizenship make clear that citizens of a liberal democracy have rights by nature of their membership. This is not the experience of Sri Lankan Tamils, who are subject to a Sinhala majority prone to ethnonationalism and illiberal democracy (Devotta 2002; Ismail 2018). Nor, it could be added, is this the case for racial minorities in the United States, past or present (see Lowe 1996; Rudrappa 2004)

that permeates Sri Lankan social space has already produced panics that have "required" intervention. Rajesh Venugopal (2015) captured one such moment in 2012, when mysterious "attacks" were reported across the island. The culprits, grease devils. These spectral creatures were blamed for several assaults, but no corporeal attackers were ever found, suggesting that it was not a simple case of deflected agency. Though some in positions of authority dismissed it as rural superstition, ultimately the decision was made to increase policing and security initiatives in areas that reported an attack to address the concern.

This was not the only moral panic to lead to increased surveillance of local populations. A small series of attacks on local officials in the north were highly publicized, though credible evidence of the attackers' political backing was frequently ignored in favor of headlines that emphasized wild and uncivilized youth gangs.[19] It is thus no coincidence that during May of 2018, in the grips of another moral panic, the police reacted with such severity when they received a call about a street fight at the railway station. I was not there that day, but saw some of the drivers later that day. They explained that it was mostly some local teens who had gotten into a squabble and began pushing and shoving; a few drivers attempted to break it up and keep the young men apart when the police arrived on the scene.

The way it was told to me, by many people then and after, was that the police came and immediately started swinging their batons. By the time they had "de-escalated" the situation, one young man had to be taken to the hospital for his injuries and twelve were arrested, including a few of the Station Road rickshaw drivers. Several chose to avoid the station, the only place they were permitted to make money from driving, for days. At least one for over two weeks, afraid that further events would get out of hand and see him arrested as well. There are still men who I cannot account for after that day. For all intents and purposes, they disappeared. Perhaps alive, perhaps not; and nearly impossible to say which. But I do know one of my closest friends was caught up in the activity and jailed for a month. The conditions he described were deeply inhumane, and his treatment likely meets international legal standards for torture.

This was the most palpable manifestation of the police force, and its potency should absolutely not be underestimated in a region in which trauma is rife. However, the police were able to exert their force over everyone in the

---

19 See the situation brief outlining increased police presence in response to an alleged resurgence of the politically backed Aava gang, which they connect to a highly publicized shooting of two local students (Adayaalam 2016).

community, even people who were not present at the time, for months after that incident, by compelling the local union to ban games of cards, carrom board, and other "unprofessional activities" at stands all across Jaffna. It is hard to express in such a short space the significance of these timepass activities (Jeffrey 2010), but I have discussed elsewhere the central role of play, carrom board in this case, in creating and maintaining bonds in the community attached to one of the town's most important rickshaw stands (dillon 2019; 2021). On the premise of a fight breaking out between groups of youth unaffiliated with that stand, the police compelled the union to ban such activities for more than a month at every stand in town, a ban that was actively enforced through patrols, surveillance, and pressure from a union leadership looking to avoid any further consequences.

A Story about a Checkpoint

As discussed earlier, Station Road is a community that likes to share in the suffering and windfalls of its members. The key word here is "share." When a few guys have a great day or when several are struggling, the rented storefront often transforms into an unofficial party room and everyone is invited. It is not uncommon for the "work" of the afternoon, even sometimes the day, to turn into a drinking party. Typically, a small group each contributes a few hundred rupees to buy beer or arrack, which is shared with all present regardless of who paid.[20] Most commonly, a one-liter bottle of arrack is purchased collectively and shared among five or six men. Spirits are downed *and* lifted in an informal ritual of solidarity and support.[21]

Everyone is his own man (as it is always a homosocial affair), but for brief moments in time, every man is bonded and beholden to the others. When Lathan, as he tends to, drank too much one Saturday evening, the group set about arranging for him to get home safely, despite his insistence that he could do it himself. The catch that day was that we had heard from drivers arriving for the evening train that the police had set up security

---

20   The process is communal but not entirely equal. I was obligated by my status to contribute more and others were sometimes refused from contributing at all out of respect for their financial difficulty. Crucially, these sorts of determinations were not communal, but are made by the instigator or one of the de facto leaders of the stand.

21   For an analysis of Sri Lankan drinking rituals, see Gamburd 2008. While Gamburd's study focuses on *kasippu*, the local moonshine, many of her observations relate to legal drinking as well. In particular, she notes that drinking imported alcohol is seen as moral and acceptable in part due to its status implications.

checkpoints in several locations around town. It was likely anyone leaving from the station would be stopped, and anyone smelling of alcohol, as many of us no doubt did, risked immediate arrest. Lathan, obviously, could not be allowed to drive. Nor could most of the rest of us.

Pradeepan, ever the leader, devised a plan. Siddarth would drive Lathan's rickshaw with Lathan in the back, taking a circuitous route to avoid a common checkpoint location. Pradeepan and I would first take a quick detour to get some petrol before taking a second route along pot-holed secondary streets to pick up Siddarth and bring him back to the station. In that moment, it was unclear if my involvement was assumed—I had bought the guilty bottle and commiserated as part of the group—or strategic, as my presence offered the plausible deniability of a hire and, if necessary, the social capital necessary to try to talk ourselves out of trouble.

However, as Pradeepan pulled out from the petrol station and turned down an alley the stakes were clarified a little. "Police," I said, pointing to the lights at the end of the alley. He immediately gripped the brake and whipped us around to find another route. I might be able to get us out of trouble, but apparently neither of us wanted to risk it. This was, I came to understand, a common practice among drivers. Since the police generally spoke little to no Tamil and most of the drivers spoke only rudimentary Sinhala, chances of miscommunication were high. Rather than submit to police surveillance and take their chances, many drivers would rely on shared information and intuition to avoid checkpoints altogether. Flouting, in the process, the state's gaze, manifested in the checkpoint (Jeganathan 2004). This sometimes required multiple and major detours, such as that night, when a two-kilometer trip usually done in under five minutes doubled back and stretched around the surveillance zones for over fifteen minutes.

The irony is that by flouting the checkpoint the drivers play into the state's rationale for establishing checkpoints in the first place. In escaping the encounter, drivers do not challenge the state's narrative, and, in this instance give credence to the state's logic of necessary surveillance (Visweswaran 1994, Chapter 4).[22] We see then the contest of state "strategy" and resistant "tactics" played out in mundane geographies (de Certeau 2002), but in a context that makes clear that resistance comes at a cost. Of course, the state only knows, empirically, that drivers are flouting the mobility regime

---

22   Readers familiar with Visweswaran's argument will realize I am implying a parallel between police and ethnographic forms of knowledge production. Researchers, myself included, are almost always complicit in state projects of knowledge/power to some degree. For an insightful discussion of this dilemma, see Jauregui 2013.

if they fail in their efforts not to be seen. But direct observation is not the only way the police are able to surveil the drivers of Jaffna, nor would I add, is empirical proof often expected to justify mobility restrictions. Perhaps the most nefarious aspect of the police's mobility regime strategy is their association with the local rickshaw owners' association. Though glossed as the English "union," the *sangham*, as it's also called, functions more as a form of management over the registered drivers in the province.

Contrary to the notions of autonomy and freedom that many young drivers are fond of discussing, drivers are legally required to register with the Ministry of Transportation and the police as rickshaw owners/drivers. In Jaffna, though I cannot attest to other districts, they were also required to join the union. This was non-negotiable. Indeed, one of the most frequent topics of conversation when I interviewed the *sangham* leaders was a series of cases in which unregistered drivers were court ordered to join the union and abide by its professional regulations. According to the union president, the union had proven to the court its effectiveness at regulating drivers and its willingness to cooperate with police in criminal matters. This is where it is worth remembering that policing is not synonymous with police officers and instead extends through multiple spaces and social spheres as a disposition to surveillance and enforcement, in this case much more akin to the relational, affective force mentioned in the work of Jeffrey Martin above.

Thinking there must have been a miscommunication, I asked for clarification. The secretary, who was sitting with his back to the side wall, stood up and pointed to three newspaper articles that had been clipped and pinned to a bulletin board. These, he said, were proof. Each article recounted a case in which the police received a complaint about a driver. The one they were most proud of, understandably, involved a tourist who had left 400,000 rupees in an auto by mistake. She had quickly contacted the police to report the money missing, who inquired with the union. Through their records, they were able to contact and track down the driver within minutes. He was called to the *sangham* office, where the lost money was found in the back of his rickshaw, the driver completely unaware it had even been there. The leaders were quite proud of their intervention in this case, but it is easy to see how this close relationship could take on more ominous tones for the union's members.[23]

---

23 It was later alleged to me, but I could never confirm, that the union had been responsible for calling the police about the fight at the station. The man who told me this claimed the union leaders had come to intervene thinking it was a dispute between drivers, but then called the police when they realized non-members were the instigators.

There was certainly no love lost between the station drivers and the union leadership. Whenever I asked drivers about the union, most would list a series of complaints, prime among them that they were not really interested in helping or protecting drivers. Only Robin, himself a past president of the organization, spoke in the *sangham's* defense. He rattled off the financial benefits available to members such as low-interest, low-payment loans, death benefits, and the occasional gift at significant life events like a child's puberty ceremony or a wedding. The leadership's opinion of the station drivers was even more harsh. "Those guys are all a bunch of *rowdies* and thugs," the president told me during one interview. "They smoke and drink, listen to loud music. They wear shorts. And when we try to punish them, they come in here making threats and causing trouble. You shouldn't work with them. They are not good men."

I did not recognize (most of) the drivers in his description, but I did recognize the remarks of many local elites. Most crucially, I noticed the quick association of unprofessionalism or allegedly low morals (e.g., smoking, drinking, wearing shorts) with outright criminality (i.e., rowdies and thugs) (see Miller 2011). The moral valence of deviance, of difference, in Jaffna, and possibly Sri Lanka at large, is intense and easily weaponized to discipline those deemed improper citizens (Foucault 1995). While I witnessed my fair share of what Romit Chowdury (2023) describes as the relational bonds of "everyday morality" and homosocial trust among men in South Asian public space, the rickshaw owner/driver union in Jaffna was not a fraternal order of neighborly support and respect (Thiranagama 2018). Though chartered as a form of community representation and empowerment as in many places (e.g., Bedi 2022; Jegathesan 2019), in my research I saw the union more often operate as the first line of policing, the open hand of nonviolent, community-based discipline that, if unsuccessful, could always call in more aggressive responses. Here, I am tempted to agree with French anthropologist Didier Fassin, who boiled down months and months of ethnographic research rather succinctly: "the police are the punishment" (Fassin 2019).

Policing as a Regime of Mobility: Moving Toward a Conclusion

By way of summary, I would like to introduce one more term that encapsulates the overlapping threads of my argument and will help make clear this chapter's investment in mobilities studies. Writing as the "mobility turn" was picking up traction (Sheller and Urry 2006; Urry 2007), anthropologists Nina Glick Schiller and Noel Salazar, perhaps both best known for their work on immigration, ask that we think critically about human (and nonhuman) movements. Rather than emphasizing globalization as the shrinking of the world, the easy movement of global elites, or somehow marking a new age of human civilization, they push us to consider the various regimes that structure both flows and fixity, mobility and immobility in ways that are deeply unequal.

In other words, they ask us to think about globalized human movements as part of larger structures, which themselves are embedded in their own histories and politics that determine what is (and is not) considered appropriate mobility and for whom (Cresswell 2010). Some mobile subjects are welcome as exemplars of a societal ideal (e.g., progress, modernity, freedom), while others are cast as an economic and moral scourge that threatens those very ideals. The refugee is as much a mobile global citizen as a business executive. But the refugee must petition for assistance, must request asylum, must beg and plead and pluck at the heart of immigration systems, while "business class" is literally a designation for flying in comfort, waited on throughout the journey with luxuries both small and large.

As Glick Schiller and Salazar note, regimes of mobility "[call] attention to the role both of individual states and of changing international regulatory and surveillance administrations that affect individual mobility... [and reflect] a notion of governmentality and hegemony in which there are constant struggles" (Glick Schiller and Salazar 2013, 189). In this chapter, I have argued that militarized policing is one such hegemonic structure in postwar Jaffna, though certainly not only there and not without those who challenge it both directly and discreetly. The tragic police shooting at the beginning of this chapter and the more mundane policing experienced by the rickshaw drivers with whom I worked make visible the variable and unpredictable force of this structure. Rather than provide stability and order for all, as the logic of policing suggests, it instead deepens the fault lines of precarity by focusing the brunt of the state's disciplinary forces on those deemed suspicious or susceptible to crime. In Jaffna, these are disproportionately the young men who are already struggling against social marginalization (especially from caste and ethnicity), poverty, and wartime displacement and trauma.

This assemblage of social, political, and economic factors creates a situation that compels young Tamil men to commodify their high degree of motility (Kellerman 2012). Meanwhile, it treats such commodification as inherently suspect, often punishing them for moving (or waiting) "improperly" in a region still overwrought with anxieties. It is this paradox of autonomous movement and ubiquitous policing that I call "driving while Tamil." This chapter has strived to draw attention to the darker potentials of this dynamic given the region's history and present context. In closing, however, I do wish to note that it is not all bad. I have emphasized policing as a regime of mobility because I think it irresponsible to celebrate automobility without noting its costs and consequences (see Adey 2006). Many of the drivers with whom I have worked, however, would insist that I note that it is not without its pleasures and potentials.

Driving while Tamil is the challenge of being in and moving through the tense spaces of Jaffna's streets, a place that even while heavily Tamil is surveilled and patrolled by an equally Sinhala-dominant police force and local allies for whom policing represents order after decades of conflict. Driving while Tamil is also an expression of autonomy and freedom, of joyous and highly valued rights, that allows some of the most socially marginalized in the region to create and maintain meaningful ties to others like themselves and to some within the more privileged classes of society. It is both risk and reward, socially and geographically speaking, presenting one potential route to alter a driver's literal and metaphorical position if they are willing to take the underlying risks involved, most dramatically when navigating the sphere of policing. Viewed this way, it is no wonder there are so many willing to try their luck. But it is still a gamble, and one that could ultimately cost everything, as it did for Nadarasa Gajan and Sundaraj Sulakshan.

References

Adayaalam Center for Policy Research. 2016. *Situation Brief No 1: Student Killings, Aava Gang, and the Securitization of Jaffna.*

Adey, Peter. 2006. "If Mobility Is Everything Then It Is Nothing: Towards a Relational Politics of (Im)mobilities." *Mobilities* 1 (1): 75–94.

Ahmed, Sara. 2014. *Willful Subjects*. Durham: Duke University Press.

Amarasingam, Amarnath. 2015. *Pain, Pride, and Politics: Social Movement Activism and the Sri Lankan Tamil Diaspora in Canada*. Athens: University of Georgia Press.

Amarasingam, Amarnath. 2018. "Post-War Sri Lanka and the 'Big Bad' Diaspora: Sprinkling Some Nuance into the Conversation." In *Sri Lanka: The Struggle for Peace in the Aftermath of War*, edited by Amarnath Amarasingam and Daniel Bass, 201–19. London: Hurst & Company.

Amarasingam, Amarnath, and Daniel Bass, eds. 2016. *Sri Lanka: The Struggle for Peace in the Aftermath of War*. London: Hurst and Company.

Appadurai, Arjun. 2006. *Fear of Small Numbers: An Essay on the Geography of Anger*. Durham: Duke University Press.

Aretxaga, Begona. 2003. "Maddening States." *Annual Review of Anthropology* 32: 393–410.

Bass, Daniel. 2008. "Paper Tigers on the Prowl: Rumors, Violence, and Agency in the Up-Country of Sri Lanka." *Anthropological Quarterly* 81 (1): 269–95.

Bedi, Tarini. 2022. *Mumbai Taximen: Autobiographies and Automobilities in India*. Seattle: University of Washington Press.

Bowling, Ben, and James Sheptycki. 2012. *Global Policing*. London: SAGE Publications.

Brodeur, Jean-Paul. 1983. "High Policing and Low Policing: Remarks About the Policing of Political Activities." *Social Problems* 30 (5): 507–20.

Browne, Simone. 2015. *Dark Matters: On the Surveillance of Blackness*. Durham: Duke University Press.

Camp, Jordan, and Christina Heatherton. 2016. *Policing the Planet: Why the Policing Crisis Led to Black Lives Matter*. London: Verso Books.

Choi, Vivian. 2015. "Anticipatory States: Tsunami, War, and Insecurity in Sri Lanka." *Cultural Anthropology* 30 (2): 286–309.

Chowdury, Romit. 2023. *City of Men: Masculinities and Everyday Morality on Public Transport*. Newark: Rutgers University Press.

Cons, Jason. 2016. *Sensitive Space: Fragmented Territory at the India-Bangladesh Border*. Seattle: University of Washington Press.

Cresswell, Tim. 1996. *In Place/Out of Place: Geography, Ideology, and Transgression*. Minneapolis: University of Minnesota Press.

Cresswell, Tim. 2010. "Towards a Politics of Mobility." *Environment and Planning D: Society and Space* 28 (1): 17–31.

Davis, Angela. 2003. *Are Prisons Obsolete?* Seven Stories Press: New York.

Davis, Angela. 2005. *Abolition Democracy: Beyond Empire, Prions, and Torture*. Seven Stories Press: New York.

De Alwis, Malathi. 2009. "'Disappearance' and 'Displacement' in Sri Lanka." *Journal of Refugee Studies* 22 (3): 378–91.

De Certeau, Michel. 2002. *The Practice of Everyday Life*. Translated by Steven Randall. 2nd ed. Berkeley: University of California Press.

De Mel, Neloufer. 2007. *Militarizing Sri Lanka: Popular Culture, Memory, and Narrative in the Armed Conflict*. New Delhi: Sage.

Devotta, Neil. 2002. "Illiberalism and Ethnic Conflict in Sri Lanka." *Journal of Democracy* 13 (1): 84–98. DOI: 10.1353/jod.2002.0004.

dillon, daniel. 2019. "Stories from a Jaffna Auto Stand." *Roadsides* 27: 9–27. DOI: 10.5070/S527046869.

dillon, daniel 2021. "Pokéwalking in the City: Pokémon Go and the Ludic Geographies of Digital Capitalism." *Streetnotes* 27: 9–27. DOI: 10.5070/S527046869.

Douglas, Mary. [1966] 1984. *Purity and Danger: An Analysis of Concepts of Pollution and Taboo*. New York: Routledge.

Dubber, Marcus. 2005. *The Police Power: Patriarchy and the Foundations of American Government*. New York: Columbia University Press.

Deflem, Mathieu. 2010. *The Policing of Terrorism: Organizational and Global Perspectives*. New York: Routledge.

Ericson, Richard, and Kevin Haggerty. 1997. *Policing the Risk Society*. Toronto: University of Toronto Press.

Ellawala, Themal. 2019. "Legitimating Violences: The 'Gay Rights' NGO and the Disciplining of the Sri Lankan Queer Figure." *Journal of South Asian Development* 14 (1): 83–107.

Fassin, Didier. 2019. "The Police are the Punishment." *Public Culture* 31 (3): 539–61.

Featherstone, Mike. 2004. "Automobilities: An Introduction." *Theory, Culture, and Society* 21 (4/5): 1–24.

Foucault, Michel. 1995. *Discipline & Punish: The Birth of the Prison System*. Translated by Alan Sheridan. 2nd edition. New York: Vintage Books.

Fuglerud, Oivind. 1999. *Life on the Outside: The Tamil Diaspora and Long Distance Nationalism*. London: Pluto Press.

Galtung, Johan. 1969. "Violence, Peace, and Peace Research." *Journal of Peace Research* 6 (3): 261–83.

Gamburd, Michele. 2008. *Breaking the Ashes: The Culture of Illicit Liquor in Sri Lanka*. Ithaca: Cornell University Press.

Gilroy, Paul. 2001. "Driving While Black." In *Car Cultures*, edited by Daniel Miller, 81–104. Oxford: Berg Publishers.

Glick Schiller, Nina, and Noel Salazar. 2013. "Regimes of Mobility Across the Globe." *Journal of Ethnic and Migration Studies* 39 (2): 183–200. DOI: 10.1080/1369183X.2013.723253.

Green, Linda. 1999. *Fear as a Way of Life: Mayan Widows in Rural Guatemala*. New York: Columbia University Press.

Hyndman, Jennifer. 2007. "The Securitization of Fear in Post-Tsunami Sri Lanka." *Annals of the Association of American Geographers* 97 (2): 361–72.

Ismail, Qadri. 2018. "What, to the Minority, is Democracy?" *Groundviews*, November 3. Accessed on February 10, 2019. https://bit.ly/2SJzFK7.

Jauregui, Beatrice. 2013. "Dirty Anthropology: Epistemologies of Violence and Ethical Entanglements in Police Ethnography." In *Policing and Contemporary Governance: The Anthropology of Police in Practice*, edited by William Garriott, 125–53. New York: Palgrave Macmillan.

Jauregui, Beatrice. 2016. *Provisional Authority: Police, Order, and Security in India*. Chicago: University of Chicago Press.

Jeganathan, Pradeep. 2004. "Checkpoint: Anthropology, Identity, and the State." In *Anthropology in the Margins of the State*, edited by Veena Das and Deborah Poole, 67–80. Santa Fe: SAR Press.

Jegathesan, Mythri. 2019. *Tea and Solidarity: Tamil Women and Work in Postwar Sri Lanka*. Seattle: University of Washington Press.

Kaba, Mariame and Andrea Ritchie. 2022. *No More Police: A Case for Abolition*. The New Press: New York.

Kellerman, Aharon. 2012. "Potential Mobilities." *Mobilities* 7 (1): 171–83.

Lacquer, Walter. 1999. *The New Terrorism: Fanaticism and the Arms of Mass Destruction*. Oxford: Oxford University Press.

Lowe, Lisa. 1996. *Immigrant Acts: On Asian American Cultural Politics*. Durham: Duke University Press.

Manalansan, Martin. 2014. "The 'Stuff' of Archives: Mess, Migration, and Queer Lives." *Radical History Review* 120: 94–107.

Martin, Jeffrey. 2013. "Police as Linking Principle: Rethinking Police Culture in Contemporary Taiwan." In *Policing and Contemporary Governance: The Anthropology of Police in Practice*, edited by William Garriott, 157–80. New York: Palgrave Macmillan.

Martin, Jeffrey. 2017. "Affect: The Virtual Force of Policing (Taiwan)." In *Writing the World of Policing: The Difference Ethnography Makes*, edited by Didier Fassin, 91–110. Chicago: University of Chicago Press.

McKittrick, Katherine. 2006. *Demonic Grounds: Black Women and the Cartographics of Struggle*. Minneapolis: University of Minnesota Press.

Miller, Jody. 2011. "Beach Boys or Sexually Exploited Children? Competing Narratives of Sex Tourism and their Impact on Young Men in Sri Lanka's Tourism Economy." *Crime, Law Social Change* 56 (5): 485–508.

Mohan, Rohini. 2014. *Seasons of Trouble: Life amid the Ruins of Sri Lanka's Civil War*. London: Verso Books.

Parmar, Alpa. 2011. "Stop and Search in London: Counter-Terrorist or Counter-Productive?" *Policing and Society*. 21 (4): 369–82.

Perera, Sasanka. 2016. *Warzone Tourism in Sri Lanka: Tales from Darker Places in Paradise*. New Delhi: Sage.

Satkunanathan, Ambika. 2022. "The Tamil Struggle, the Aragalaya and Sri Lankan Identity." *Groundviews: Journalism for Citizens*. Groundviews.Org, May 15, 2022. https://groundviews.org/2022/05/15/the-tamil-struggle-the-aragalaya-and-sri-lankan-identity/.

Schrader, Stuart. 2019. *Badges without Borders: How Global Counterinsurgency Transformed American Policing*. Berkeley: University of California Press.

Sheller, Mimi, and John Urry. "The New Mobilities Paradigm." *Environment and Planning A* 38 (2): 207–26.

Silver, Alan. 1967. "The Demand for Order in Civil Society." In *The Police: Six Sociological Essays*, edited by David Bordua, 1–24. Malden: John Wiley & Sons.

Ralph, Laurence. 2020. *The Torture Letters: Reckoning with Police Violence*. Chicago: University of Chicago Press.
Rudrappa, Sharmila. 2004. *Ethnic Routes to Becoming American: Indian Immigrants and the Cultures of Citizenship*. New Brunswick: Rutgers University Press.
Somosundaram, Daya. 2013. *Scarred Communities: Psychological Impacts of Man-Made and Natural Disasters in Sri Lanka Society*. New Delhi: SAGE Publications.
Subramaniam, Jeevasutah. 2017. *War and Recovery: Psychological Challenges in Northern Sri Lanka*. Colombo: International Center for Ethnic Studies.
Taussig, Michael. 1992. *The Nervous System*. New York: Routledge.
Thiranagama, Sharika. 2013a. "Claiming the State: Postwar Reconciliation in Sri Lanka." *Humanity: An International Journal of Human Rights* 4 (1): 93–116.
Thiranagama, Sharika. 2013b. *In My Mother's House: Civil War in Sri Lanka*. Philadelphia: University of Pennsylvania Press.
Thiranagama, Sharika. 2014. "Making Tigers from Tamils: Long-Distance Nationalism and Sri Lankan Tamils in Toronto." *American Anthropologist* 116 (2): 265–78.
Thiranagama, Sharika. 2018. "The Civility of Strangers? Caste, Ethnicity, and Living Together in Postwar Jaffna, Sri Lanka." *Anthropological Theory* 18 (2–3): 357–81.
Urry, John. 2007. *Mobilities*. Malden, MA: Polity Press.
Venugopal, Rajesh. 2011. "The Politics of Market Reform at a Time of Civil War." *Economic and Political Weekly* 46 (49): 67–75.
Venugopal, Rajesh. 2015. "Demonic Violence and Moral Panic in Postwar Sri Lanka: Explaining the Gsrease Devil Crisis." *Journal of Asian Studies* 74 (3): 615–37.
Visweswaran, Kamala. 1994. *Fictions of Feminist Ethnography*. Minneapolis: University of Minnesota Press.
Wickramasinghe, Nira. 2014. *Sri Lanka in the Modern Age: A History*. Oxford: Oxford University Press.

About the author

daniel dillon (he/they) earned his PhD from the University of Texas at Austin. Their research focuses on Sri Lanka and its Tamil diaspora, especially regarding mobilities, masculinities, the relationship of ethnography and literature, and visual culture. He is working on a manuscript based on research with rickshaw drivers in Jaffna.

5   Adventure Time: Adventure Tourism and the "Annihilation of Space by Time" in Nepal

Mark Liechty

Abstract: If money and technology make possible different traversals of space in time, then the nature of tourist mobilities is going to be closely tied to tourists' relationships with transport technology, time, and money. This chapter traces Nepal's tourism history through three configurations: elderly elite travelers with much time and money (1955–65); young countercultural travelers rich in time but poor in money (1965–75); and, from the 1970s onwards, adventure tourists—people with money but little time. Each phase illustrates how changing transport technology enables changing tourisms. The chapter explores how touristic mobilities in Nepal have always been entangled with (and constituted by) other material and cultural assemblages, from technology and demography to infrastructure and mediated images.

Keywords: Nepal, tourism, adventure, technology, time

If "time is money," and if money and technology make possible different traversals of space in time, then the nature of tourist mobilities is going to be closely tied to tourists' relationships with time and money. This chapter traces the history of tourism in Nepal through three distinct configurations of touristic time, space, technology, and money. In the first phase (ca. 1955–65), elderly Western elites—people rich in both time and money—dominated Nepal's nascent tourism scene. From around 1965 to 1975, Nepal tourism shifted into a second stage with a new prevailing demographic: backpackers, "travelers," and "hippies." Typically arriving overland and on a budget, these young people were rich in time but poor

---

Linder, Benjamin, & Tarini Bedi (eds), *South Asia on the Move: Mobilities, Mobilizations, Maneuvers*. Amsterdam: Amsterdam University Press 2025
doi: 10.5117/9789463726498_CH05

in money. Finally, in a third phase from the early 1970s onward, the Nepali state actively promoted commodified "adventure tourism," aiming to attract a new breed of tourist—vacationing "adventurers," poor in available time but relatively rich financially. This essay traces the social, economic, and technological circumstances of these three modes of touristic mobility while focusing largely on the third—adventure tourism—and the unique forms of transportation and infrastructure that it demands. I argue that touristic mobilities in Nepal have always been entangled with (and constituted by) other material and cultural assemblages, from technology and demography to infrastructure and mediated images.

Nepal's three early touristic phases are closely related to technological developments and infrastructure investments that allowed different kinds of travelers to relate to time and space in new ways. In the first phase, people rich in time and wealth relied on expensive and relatively slow-moving technology (cruise ships and short-haul aircraft) to reach the relatively isolated Himalayan kingdom. By the 1960s, automotive technology, cheap oil, and international road infrastructure across western Asia made South Asia increasingly accessible via overland routes, thereby opening Nepal to a new generation of young travelers with plenty of time but not much money. Then, from the early 1970s onward, new long-haul, high-capacity jet aircraft made mass travel to Asia more and more accessible, while the Nepal government, in turn, invested in rural mountain airstrips and small passenger planes to open up "trekking" and other "adventure" destinations across the country. New technologies helped make possible a new breed of adventure tourists—people with money to spend but limited available time.

As such, this chapter considers what Karl Marx (1857 [1973], 449, 464) referred to in the *Grundrisse* as the "annihilation of space by time," and what David Harvey (1989) later elaborated in his theory of "time-space compression": the ability of new technologies—advances in transport, communications, etc.—to traverse space more rapidly, efficiently, and profitably, thereby transforming the relationships among time, space, and money. At each stage in Nepal's tourism development story, new modes and means of transportation allowed people to use money to overcome the constraints of distance in new ways. But it was only in the early- to mid-1970s that the transport technology and infrastructure were in place to allow large-scale, profitable *mass* tourism to emerge in Nepal. Nepal's newly state-promoted adventure tourism brand actively lured cash-rich but time-poor consumers for commodified, tightly-scheduled holidays in the country's "charismatic" mountain and jungle landscapes. Modern tourism infrastructure allowed privileged, mainly Western consumers to (ad)venture into the imagined timelessness of rural Nepal for allotted periods of self-renewing escape, before being efficiently whisked back to their soul-sapping first-world jobs.

This dynamic of renewal and escape points to a final crucial component of Nepal's experience with tourism and tourists: the shifting cultural, economic, and demographic trends that constituted—and continually *reconstituted*—Nepal as an attractive destination in the minds of mainly first-world would-be tourists. While technology and infrastructure may have facilitated various forms and phases of tourism, these material determinants meshed with other global historical dynamics that continually shaped forms of longing among various classes of first-world consumers, and then allowed those longings to be pursued in Nepal. Elsewhere, I explore at length the story of how the Himalayas emerged in the Western historical imagination as an archetypal land of otherness, and how persistent countercultural disenchantment with modernity, coupled with an intense longing for an "other place," coalesced to make Nepal a land of imaginative escape (Liechty 2017). The otherness that tourists sought changed from one generation to the next, but Nepalis gradually learned to recognize—and then to package and sell—the imagined alterity with which tourists arrived and departed, thinking they had found it in Nepal.[1]

The Golden Age of Tourism: Nepal as Trophy Destination

When Nepal first opened its doors to tourists in the mid-1950s, international travel was a much more awkward, time-consuming, and expensive proposition than it is today. Commercial air service was still mainly *intra*-continental: most people continued to cross the Atlantic and Pacific by ship even if they might travel across Europe and Asia by plane. Because of the time and expense involved, through the 1950s most leisure world travelers to Nepal were wealthy retirees, eighty percent of whom were Americans (Satyal 1999, 75). Additionally, in an era before easy telecommunications, making arrangements for a long trip was so complicated that it *required* a travel agent working in conjunction with tour operators around the world. Steeped in centuries of mystical exotification in the Western imaginary, Nepal was already thoroughly preconstituted as a land of touristic desire

---

1 This chapter draws extensively from Liechty 2017. That book is based on primary and secondary research carried out over an almost three-decade period starting in the mid-1980s. In this chapter any quoted material not accompanied by a formal citation comes from interviews conducted by the author.

(Liechty 2017). But for the country to become an actual tourist *destination* it had to tap into this international travel booking system.

Key to the success of Nepal's first commercially viable international hotel was its ties to the Thomas Cook travel agency. Probably the leading travel and tour operator in the 1950s, Thomas Cook had offices around the world, including in India. It was a Thomas Cook agent in Bombay who gave Russian émigré Boris Lissanevitch the idea of starting Kathmandu's Royal Hotel in 1955. Several luxury cruise lines were bringing tourists to Indian ports from where passengers flew to sightseeing destinations around the subcontinent. The agent reportedly told Lissanevitch, "We'd charter a flight to Kathmandu if there was a hotel."

Thus, ironically for a land-locked Himalayan country, Nepal's first official tourists were passengers on the RMS Caronia, a British Cunard Line cruise ship. In an era when most ocean liners still served the utilitarian function of hauling people across oceans, the Caronia was the first of a new breed that turned cruising into a luxury holiday. Launched in 1947, the Caronia was the first ship with a swimming pool, a bathroom in every cabin, and air-conditioning. In 1951, the Caronia began specializing in round-the-world tours for very wealthy clients and was soon dubbed "the Cunard dollar factory" by *The New York Times* (Rosenthal 1955). In late March 1955, twenty-four wealthy cruisers disembarked from the Caronia at Bombay and flew to Kathmandu. After perfectly playing their epic roles as eager, conspicuously consuming elites, the group flew back to Madras where they rejoined the Caronia.

Newsweek magazine called these first guests at the Royal Hotel "ordinary tourists" (1955, 36), but they certainly weren't ordinary by today's standards. They were among the world's wealthiest people and it's crucial to understand that those who visited Nepal *as tourists* in the decade or so after the Royal Hotel opened in 1955 were, of necessity, rich. Other Westerners came to Nepal as mountaineers, and a few really adventuresome types managed to make it to Kathmandu overland on a shoe-string budget, but the vast majority of those who showed up at the Royal Hotel were big-shots. For people invested in fashion and conspicuous consumption, Kathmandu was a whimsical and chic place to go. Wealthy package tourists traveling in groups, managed and booked by international travel agencies as a side-trip appended to an India visit, were the foundation of the Royal Hotel's business. Notably absent from this mindset was the spiritual, mystical attitude that the next generation of travelers to Nepal brought with them. What lured these elite tourists to Kathmandu in the 1950s and 1960s were the floods of mountaineering and travel images appearing in magazines like *National Geographic* and

Life billing Nepal as a land of heroic, exotic adventure. When it was finally opened to "ordinary tourists" in 1955, Kathmandu became one of the world's most fashionable trophy destinations.

During its almost fifteen years in operation, the Royal Hotel witnessed the dramatic shift in international economics and travel that marked the beginning of the era of modern mass tourism. In 1955, Nepal's first tourists were elderly elites traveling mainly by boat around the world. Ten years later most tourists were traveling by air. What's more, by the mid-1960s tourists who made it to Nepal were more and more likely to be middle-class and young. The 2,000 Westerners who visited Nepal in 1958 were very different people, traveling under very different conditions, than the 45,000 who visited Nepal in the Royal Hotel's last year (1969).

Far Out: Nepal as Countercultural Youth Destination

The year 1965 was the first in which, worldwide, leisure travelers outnumbered business travelers (Rana 1971), as booming Western economies put new forms of consumption within reach of ever more middle-class people. Airlines initiated lower-priced "economy" seating on new, larger planes and added charter flights to encourage greater tourist traffic (Satyal 1999, 5). Declining ticket prices and increased tourist volume sparked a worldwide tourism infrastructure construction boom—including several new luxury hotels that opened in Kathmandu in 1965. The United Nations declared 1967 the "International Tourist Year."

As travel became less expensive, different kinds of people, from different places, began visiting Nepal. In the 1950s, around eighty percent of tourists in Nepal were from the US—declining to about half by 1965, and to a third by 1970, as people of other nationalities joined the tourism trend (Satyal 1999, 8). During those years, Nepal's tourist arrivals rose dramatically with annual growth rates approaching forty percent for most of the 1960s (Satyal 2000, 6–7). But while tourist *numbers* were on the rise between 1960 and 1975, tourists' average *age* dropped significantly. From being overwhelmingly late-middle-aged up to about 1965, by 1972 forty-five percent of Nepal's tourist arrivals were thirty or under, and seventy percent were under forty-five (Satyal 2000, 9, 21). Older tourists continued to come, but their brief, tightly scheduled visits gave them little contact with local people. By contrast, younger travelers wanted not just lower prices but also a more intimate feel for Nepali life. By the early 1970s the average high-end traveler spent three nights in Nepal, whereas budget travelers averaged over two weeks (Burger 1978, 119).

From a trickle of young shoe-string travelers who managed to make it to Kathmandu in the 1950s to a small stream of "beatnik" tourists in the early 1960s, it wasn't until about 1965 that the city emerged as a bona fide youth destination. As the postwar "baby boom" generation came of age, a new wave of anti-modernist discontent revived forms of countercultural longing for the mystical East that had animated generations of "seekers" since at least the mid-nineteenth century (Liechty 2017). By the late 1960s, Kathmandu was one of the principal stops on the famous Hippie Trail that stretched from Europe and North Africa across Western and South Asia to Southeast Asia (Gemie and Ireland 2017). Because Kathmandu was roughly the mid-point of the overland route and, at least for North Americans, as far away from home as one could get—the Hippie Trail was often simply called the Road to Kathmandu, or even just the RTK. Whether hitchhiking or in ramshackle cars and buses, as many as two million young European and American seekers made the roughly eight-week overland journey from Europe to the South Asian subcontinent between the early 1960s and 1979, when the Iranian Revolution and the Soviet invasion of Afghanistan made the trip impossible (Maclean 2006).

According to David Tomory (1996), "two great waves" of young travelers "rolled East" along the RTK. The pioneers staked out territories and lifestyles prior to 1967. Then, from around 1968 to 1972, a much bigger wave of disaffected Western youth surged down the road. "First you get the black sheep, and then you get the flock" (Tomory 1996, 38). Driven by a complex set of developments in Europe and North America—including the suppression of youth political activism, criminalization of recreational "drug" use, and a rise in interest in "Eastern Religion"—the years 1968 and 1969 saw a convergence of factors that generated both a spike in tourist arrivals in Kathmandu and the birth of a new tourist district. By the early 1970s, Kathmandu's "Freak Street" had become a leading destination in Asia for Western budget travelers.

In addition to overland travelers, part of this surge resulted from new airline services to Nepal. In December 1968, Thai Airlines inaugurated passenger jet service between Bangkok and Kathmandu along with a global ad campaign highlighting that "this remote and desirable tourist destination was now open for business" (Dannhorn 1986, 465). Even if it had already been open for tourism for a quarter century, the (late) dawning of the jet era in Nepal meant a dramatic increase in the potential tourist supply. Previously all air transportation to Nepal was via army surplus DC-3 "Dakota" aircraft—crude planes with few windows and passengers strapped to benches along the bulkheads (Morris 1963, 49–50; Bernstein

1970, 58). Whereas DC-3s carried a maximum of twenty-eight passengers, Thai International's Boeing 707s carried 189 passengers (M. B. Shrestha 2000, 32–34). Furthermore, these flights represented Nepal's first direct air link to a non-South Asian hub. Previously, all commercial flights into Nepal had originated in India, making Nepal tourism both susceptible to India's political whims and little more than an appendage of the Indian tourist market. Because Bangkok was on most round-the-world tour itineraries, Kathmandu suddenly had a whole new market to draw from.

Although jets had been in commercial use for over a decade by 1968, what kept them out of Kathmandu was a combination of low demand (too few tourists to justify their use), short runways, and topography: surrounded by high peaks, Kathmandu is a difficult place to land large aircraft. Even after a multi-million-dollar US grant in the mid-1960s doubled the runway's length to two kilometers (Skerry et al. 1991, 170), there was still concern that the landing strip wasn't long enough. In March 1967, a Lufthansa Boeing 707 carrying German diplomats became the first jet aircraft to land in Kathmandu, proving it could be done (McDonald 2005, 104). Even so, early Thai jets carried emergency drag parachutes that could be popped to slow the plane if it was in danger of falling off the cliff at the end of the runway! Returning to Kathmandu after several previous visits, in 1970 Jeremy Bernstein noted "the all but incredible increase in the tourist trade in the last year" (1970, 59). In fact, between 1968 and 1970, annual tourist arrivals almost doubled from 24,209 to 45,970 (Satyal 2000, 10).

The rising numbers and declining ages of tourist were, in part, due to improved air service and lower ticket prices. But large numbers were also arriving overland along the Hippie Trail. Available statistics make it difficult to disaggregate, but from the late-1960s to the mid-1970s, as many as tens of thousands of young Westerners a year arrived in Nepal via the Road to Kathmandu, a veritable mobile countercultural scene (Tomory 1996; Gemie and Ireland 2017; Liechty 2017). Postwar improvements in road infrastructure across West Asia had made overland motor vehicle travel safe and practicable for the first time. Some intrepid souls hitchhiked the whole way, but many others drove their own vehicles from Europe. By the early 1970s the roads around Kathmandu's Freak Street were clogged with battered VW minibuses and other vehicles weary from the two- to three-month overland journey.

Also contributing to the overland flow were various formal and informal bus services that had reached Nepal as early as 1967 (Alderson 1971, 164; Cunningham 1975, 29). Bus transport was especially appealing to women (single or in groups), for whom independent travel through West Asia could prompt unwanted (male) attention. At one extreme were the "freak buses," usually old commercial vehicles or school buses that were rehabbed, filled *ad hoc* with passengers, driven one-way to Kathmandu, and then sold to Nepalis. One Kathmandu expat remembered how in the early 1970s, "there were at least fifteen people running overland trips, three or four times a year, from Europe to Kathmandu. Then they'd sell the vehicles, fly back, and do it again." The no-frills direct route cost around $100 to $150 and took about two months.

At the other extreme were luxury tour bus operators like Penn Overland offering air-conditioned coaches, professional drivers, and experienced guides. In the mid-1970s, its most expensive tour (including meals and the "best available" accommodations) cost £1,250 and attracted mainly rich Americans. (Penn also offered a cut-rate, camping-only youth tour from London to Kathmandu for £288.) One Nepali tourism expert I interviewed estimated that there were ten overland companies operating in the 1970s, each with frequent departures from Europe, spring and fall. Combine these with the dozen or more independent operators, plus the many that came in their own vehicles or even hitchhiked, and it's clear that large numbers of people arrived in Nepal overland (cf. Satyal 2000, 23).

Claiming "Our Commodity": State Branding and the Invention of Adventure Tourism

Prior to the early 1970s, Nepal's official stance toward tourism was basically benign neglect. Like an act of nature, tourism seemed to ebb and flow into Nepal driven by unseen, unknown forces. Nepali entrepreneurs were the main instigators behind tourism development while the state did little more than operate a tour-guide service and print the occasional tourist pamphlet. For Nepalis, what Nepal meant to tourists was still a mystery but, by the mid-1960s, tourism's meaning for Nepal was becoming clearer: money. By then a group of powerful Nepalis, including members of the Rana and royal families, were investing in high-end tourism, including Nepal's first two five-star hotels. Under pressure from Kathmandu business interests, Nepal's official fourth "Five Year Plan" (1971–75) made tourism a national priority (Satyal 1999, 107).

The plan called for a high-level Tourism Development Committee, whose first acts were to 1) hire a German consulting firm to make recommendations for tourism development, and 2) sponsor a "Symposium on Tourism in Nepal." At this meeting, industry leaders laid out a new vision for tourism, noting the industry's phenomenal potential for job creation and foreign currency earning (Rana 1971, 18). But most importantly, committee member Prabhakar Rana signaled a dawning recognition of Nepal's location in a world of competing tourist places: "Nepal is very fortunate. It is a much greater tourism destination than we Nepalese will understand or admit" (1971, 19). The mountains, temples, and culture that Nepalis take for granted and that tourists are eager to spend money to experience—all are there for the taking, he noted. What tourism promoters need to do is harness these resources and turn them into money-makers. Like a general rallying his troops, Rana told his colleagues,

> The destination is already there. It is up to us to improve our commodity by building the infrastructure and not hesitate in selling it vigorously to the outside world... [Nepalis must] take whatever steps might be necessary to improve our product; to constantly improve our product; that is NEPAL [sic]. (Rana 1971, 21–2)

For the first time Nepal had become "our commodity," a "product" to be vigorously sold and constantly improved. Rana's speech marks a radically new objectified understanding of Nepal tourism. It is only when Nepalis began to recognize the tourism "products" that were hiding in plain sight (mountains, temples, culture) that they could begin to intentionally sell them.

But for Nepal to emerge as a destination, it had to extricate itself from under India's tourism shadow. For the wealthy travelers who made up the bulk of Nepal's tourists prior to the late 1960s, Nepal was a secondary destination, typically a side trip added to an organized tour of India (itself often part of round-the-world tour packages). Even Nepali travel agencies were essentially appendages of Indian firms (Rana 1971, 20).

Completed in 1972, the German tourism master plan argued that the only way for Nepal to escape from its place as sideshow to India's circus was to create a stand-alone product centered around adventure tourism broadly and trekking in particular. "The long stay required for a normal trek makes a visit to India or other main attractions in the south of Asia quite subsidiary, so that... direct booking with Nepalese tour operators could be made" (Satyal 1999, 87). The plan also recommended that Nepal promote its other natural and cultural resources. The key, the Germans advised, was to rebrand Nepal as an exciting and exotic *adventure* destination and then to turn those adventures into products sold by *Nepali* businesses.

Almost immediately the German plan launched a flurry of tourism development initiatives in Nepal. In 1973, parliament passed the "National Parks and Wildlife Conservation Act," establishing Chitwan (a former lowland big game hunting reserve) as Nepal's first national park. Shortly thereafter, the state created other parks in the mountainous Langtang, Khumbu, Annapurna, and Dhaulagiri regions (Satyal 2000, 213, 249). Notably, the motive force behind these new parks was less conservation per se, than the need to create protected areas for adventure tourism. The parks were to be habitats for tourists with the conservation of flora and fauna subsidiary to that end.

In Kathmandu the new emphasis on tourism triggered a major surge in activities promoting tourism. Starting in 1972, the new Department of Tourism issued dozens of new brochures (in several European languages) mainly promoting trekking but also festivals and other cultural tourism interests. In 1972, the state launched a national "Hotel Management and Tourism Training Center" that both responded to and further stimulated a surge in hotel construction. Tourism-driven cultural commodification continued through the 1970s in efforts to preserve historically significant monuments in the Kathmandu Valley, culminating in 1978 when the World Heritage Convention recognized seven World Heritage Monument Zones in the Kathmandu Valley.

A crucial element needed to fully exploit Nepal's tourism potential was improved transportation. For Nepal to attract the kind of tourists it now wanted—people *with* money but *without* limitless time (unlike hippies)— these tourists needed an efficient means of getting to and from Nepal. This meant upgrading commercial air service linking Nepal with Europe and major Asian hubs. In 1971, Nepal authorized foreign carriers to bring tourist charter flights into Kathmandu (Satyal 2000, 153), and in 1972 Royal Nepal Airlines Corporation (RNAC), the national carrier, acquired its first jet aircraft and began direct service to Kathmandu from Delhi and, more importantly, several major East and Southeast Asian cities (M. B. Shrestha 2000, 45). Luckily, Nepal's push to improve tourist access coincided with fundamental changes in global aviation. In February 1971, Boeing rolled out its new 747 aircraft. With a seating capacity more than four times that of the 737, and a maximum range of 6,300 nautical miles (more than triple the 737), the 747 transformed global tourist travel (M. B. Shrestha 2000, 34). 747s decreased both ticket prices and travel times by offering more long distance, non-stop flights. The Kathmandu Valley is too constricted to allow 747s to land, but Nepal benefitted nonetheless. Nepal's tourism rates soared by the mid-1970s as 747s brought droves of tourists to major hubs in Europe and Asia, which had direct flights to Nepal.

Nepal's new adventure tourism vision was premised on not just a new kind of tourism, but a new kind of tourist. In place of the increasingly disreputable hippies and other low-budget travelers whose aim had often been to spend as little money, and as much time, as possible in Nepal, Nepal's new tourism brand sought a much more freely spending visitor who could be efficiently shepherded through an intentionally commodified tourism landscape.

Fortunately for Nepal, global cultural and economic trends converged in ways that helped create these new tourists and then deliver them at Nepal's door. The global economic downturn following the 1973 OPEC oil embargo hastened the end of the hippie era. Rising global oil prices had the welcome effect of finally ending the ground war in Vietnam (though bombing continued). Troops returning from Vietnam took some of the political wind out of the counterculture's sails, but more than anything it was global recession that put fear into the hearts of hippie baby boomers. With money tightening and jobs harder to get, the hedonistic and carefree days of the 1960s' Western bull economy were over. Hard times spurred the trend toward social conservatism that characterized the 1970s, a time when young people were less inclined to live for the moment and instead lived for the future by getting serious about education, careers, goals, savings, and responsibility.

A man who drove "freak buses" from Istanbul to Kathmandu from 1970 to 1975 perfectly captured the shifting ethos of those years. When he started, the main question people asked was about cost: "How much?" Five years later the preoccupation had become time: "How long?" (Tomory 1996, 21). With time now the limiting factor, and with airfares dropping, fewer and fewer people were interested in *the journey*—the Kerouac-inspired experience of life *On the Road* (Kerouac 1957). Rather than pursuing travel as an end in itself, people were now focused on *destinations*. This shift away from travel and toward destinations occurred just as Nepalis began actively peddling their country as a stand-alone adventure destination. The global recession briefly hit Nepal's tourist industry, but by the mid-1970s arrival numbers were again climbing fast as adventure tourism took root.

According to Paul Beedie, "adventure tourism" is an activity that combines "travel, sport, and outdoor recreation" (2003, 203). It is a kind of "serious leisure" that introduces a degree of uncertainty and risk into physical activities in unusual places. But if adventure implies peril, the commodified, packaged product offered by adventure service providers guarantees that tourists "have their experiences defined for them" in carefully managed ways that minimize risk (213).

Adventure tourists have a completely different relationship to time and money than Nepal's earlier budget travelers. Hippie travelers were time rich and cash poor. Adventure tourists are the opposite: "rich monetarily but poor in time. They want to squeeze as much experience into as short a time as possible" (Beedie 2003, 211). Lacking time to develop the skills and knowledge needed to pursue exploits on their own, adventure tourists turn to the classic figure of "the guide" (a person or a book) whose presence "supersedes the need for the individual to make choices" (230), and allows them to "rely on the expertise of others to provide the wherewithal to complete their adventure" (221). Trekking in Nepal emerged in the 1970s as the prototypical form of "adventure tourism" as time-poor tourists paid local service providers to make possible experiences they could not efficiently accomplish on their own.

Nepal's transformation into an adventure destination is closely linked to the gradual replacement of overland travelers with those arriving by air (Tomory 1996, xiv). By the mid-1970s the Road to Kathmandu was losing its cachet. Traveling on one's own seemed more and more risky, while joining a tour bus group was not only expensive but vaguely uncool. What's more, thanks to new economies of scale in the airline industry, it had actually become *more expensive* to travel overland with most commercial operators than to fly to Nepal.

The shift produced a subtle change in the character of tourists. Those who had arrived via the Road to Kathmandu were often notably different from those who had arrived by air. "Overland travelers are more tolerant," observed one tourist in 1975. "They can adjust more easily than other travelers." Months spent on the road through Western and South Asia had an "acclimating" effect (Beisler 2006, 128). Making it to Nepal overland was a feat of endurance but also a measure of the traveler's resourcefulness, flexibility, and willingness to adapt to local circumstances. People arriving in Kathmandu by air might have these traits, but without the acclimating and winnowing effect of the RTK, there was a much higher likelihood that they would not.

Many sensed the changing character of tourism that was settling over Kathmandu in the mid-1970s. One returning visitor noted a change in the kind of people she encountered in Kathmandu tourist establishments. On her first visit to Nepal in the early 1970s,

> people tended to be very reflective and thoughtful. I mean they didn't tend to talk in categories. Their responses weren't stereotyped. But the people later, it seemed as though they thought they knew it all and you could predict what they were going to say.

Unlike many budget travelers of the 1960s who left home with few clothes, a bit of money, and a romantic dream of life on the road, these new adventure tourists arrived in Kathmandu equipped with guidebooks that provided them the information and expertise needed to navigate the strange world they had so suddenly descended into. As many Nepalis noted, the new guidebook-guided tourists were more cautious, less open to conversation, more afraid of being cheated, and seemingly less curious.

Whereas the hippies had romantically imagined Nepal's antique timelessness to be the countercultural antithesis of (or antidote to) the West, the new tourists saw Nepal's "backwardness" as part of the risk involved in their temporary "adventures" in Third World living. Now Nepal's imagined non-modernity was reconstituted as an enchanting though vaguely dangerous condition into which brave adventurers could time-travel, experience the thrill of alterity, and then return to the comforting, if monotonous, routines of their modern lives. Over the decade of the 1970s, global tourists and tourism changed, reflecting the swing away from the countercultural radicalism of the previous decade and back toward the more conservative and consumerist end of the economic and cultural spectrum.

But why trekking and adventure tourism in particular? Nepal's rebranding as an eco-adventure land was also a way for the country to strategically hitch its tourism and development wagons to the then-emerging global environmental movement. With environmental consciousness on the rise—and Nepal itself increasingly associated with "ecological crisis"—in the 1970s, Nepal quickly reoriented its development agenda around the new eco-discourses of conservation and sustainability. Notable here is how tourism fit into this new discursive landscape. With international donor agencies eager to fund environmental initiatives, in 1973 Nepal established a new Department of Soil and Water Conservation aimed expressly at reaping a harvest of new environmental aid money. That same year Nepal also established a Department of National Parks and Wildlife Conservation and simultaneously created four new national parks. In so doing, Nepal essentially nationalized its principal tourism assets under the sign of ecological conservation. Nepal attempted to catch and ride the wave of global eco-consciousness to prosperity through "crisis" aid in some areas and ecotourism in others. In modern parlance, one could say that Nepal gave its existing development and tourism interests a good "green washing," transforming them into conservation and eco-adventures.

Trekking had been a well-known tourist and expat activity for decades (Liechty 2017, 49–55), but even as more and more young tourists arrived in the mid to late 1960s, relatively few of them went trekking. This is because the early high-end guide services were prohibitively expensive for budget travelers, and do-it-yourself trekking guidebooks didn't yet exist. That situation changed decisively in the early 1970s with the publication of three new trekking guides aimed squarely at the new breed of adventure tourists. Each book allowed would-be adventurers to transform a vaguely understood possible outing into a thoroughly predictable trek capable of being neatly scheduled into tightly coordinated international and domestic travel plans. In fact, one of the explicitly stated purposes of these books was to allow time-strapped tourists the ability to choose a trek that fit their schedule, from day walks to months-long expeditions. Bezruchka's guide (first published in 1972) actually arranges treks according to the time required to complete them (Bezruchka 1985, 44). All of the guidebook authors were acutely aware of the demands and time constraints under which the new cash-rich/time-poor adventure tourists were operating. Trekking guidebooks were an essential element in the turn toward the tightly scheduled, focused, and agenda-driven ethos of adventure tourism.

To make trekking a realistic option for time-strapped adventure tourists, tourism officials realized that Nepal's trekking areas had to be made accessible by air, even if it meant raising the price of a trek. In a country where huge mountain topography and unstable geology make road building wildly expensive and road travel wildly time consuming, investment in air transportation infrastructure was the only way to get tourists quickly to and from trekking regions. But building airstrips on remote mountainsides also wasn't easy. The solution was for RNAC to phase out its old DC-3s and, beginning in 1970, replace them with a new fleet of small Short Take Off and Landing (STOL) aircraft (Satyal 2000, 148–49). Pilatus PC-6 "Porter" and de Havilland DHC-6 "Twin Otter" aircraft could take off and land on runways less than 200 meters long, even at elevation. The early 1970s saw nineteen tiny new STOL airstrips clinging to mountainsides across Nepal, including Lukla (on the approach route to Everest) and Jumla in western Nepal (M.B. Shrestha 2000, 50). For busy adventure tourists hoping to trek to Everest Base Camp, a flight to and from Lukla was pricey but cut the time required in half—from one month to two weeks. New flights to Meghauli on the Nepal Tarai also made a Chitwan wildlife jungle adventure possible for more tourists. Aircraft were the magic ingredient that transformed remote parts of Nepal into adventure tourism hotspots.

By the mid-1970s all the pieces of a new trekking economy were falling into place: an emerging adventure ethos among a new breed of tourists, detailed guidebooks to help schedule a trek, government promotion of trekking and investment in air transportation, and a burgeoning service economy featuring trekking agencies, restaurants, and gear shops. Nepalis actively responded to and created demand for their "product" and watched as tourist numbers climbed by almost twenty-five percent per year for most years between 1970 and 1980 (Satyal 2000, 17). Trekking played a large part in this rise. For example, between 1970 and 1973, the number of trekkers in the Everest region rose from 300 to 3,000 and continued to rise apace thereafter (Rogers 2007, 44). In 1970, 1.2% of tourists went trekking; by 1974, 13% were trekkers (H.P. Shrestha 2000, 14; Satyal 2000, 18). By 1980, those rates had risen to 17% and, by 1990, about 25% of tourists went trekking (Satyal 2000, 193). These percentages may seem on the small side, but when calculated *without* South Asian tourists (mainly Indians arriving in summer to escape the heat), then well over half of international arrivals in Nepal went trekking (Satyal 2000, 144). What's more, while sightseeing tourists averaged three days in Nepal, trekkers averaged around three weeks (Satyal 2000, 102–4). With ever more trekkers pouring into the country, in 1976 tourism moved into first place as Nepal's leading foreign-exchange earner (Satyal 1999, 114).

Conclusion: Nepal as "Incredibly Spiritual and Marvelous"

Now, fifty years after Nepal began to actively promote trekking and other adventure opportunities, tourism remains one of the country's leading employers and foreign-currency earners (though remittances from millions of Nepalis working abroad now dwarf all other sources of currency inputs). But in those fifty years, surprisingly little has changed in the tourism sector, aside from scale. Nepal now receives more Chinese visitors than ever before (Linder 2019). Religious or dharma tourism is on the rise, with the government promoting Lumbini (the birthplace of the Buddha) as a destination and even attempting to build a new international airport nearby. A new international airport in Pokhara in west-central Nepal aims to bring more tourists directly to this popular trek staging area. Other forms of tourism are important, but the bulk of Nepal's tourist trade is still centered around trekking and other adventure tourism activities.

This chapter has traced Nepal's tourism development through successive permutations of global class dynamics, advances in transportation technologies and tourism infrastructure, and the cultural trends that constituted Nepal as an attractive destination in the minds of would-be tourists. That relatively little has changed since the country's self-branding as an adventure tourism mecca suggests that Nepalis have hit upon a reliable long-term formula for success. Nepal's unique geographic and cultural "products" continue to attract new generations of adventure seekers serviced by international and national air carriers that make it possible to, for example, squeeze an Everest base camp trek into a meticulously scheduled two-week vacation.

Yet, for all the tangible assets, technologies, and infrastructures that make Nepal tourism what it is, there are also crucial intangible forces that continue to be fundamental to Nepal's global appeal. Tied to the Himalayan region's long history of exoticization in the Western imagination, these forces have been crucial factors in luring generations of tourists to Nepal in search of alterity, enchantment, and an imagined antidote to Western modernity (Liechty 2017).

But how long can these delicate fantasies persist? By some accounts it appears that Nepal's romantic allure is as strong as ever. For example, the 2016 Hollywood fantasy/science fiction film *Dr. Strange* uses contemporary Kathmandu (including the bustling Thamel tourist district) as the seemingly natural setting for the hero's (played by Benedict Cumberbatch) mystical enlightenment. In an interview, Cumberbatch (who had previously visited Nepal as a tourist) proclaimed Kathmandu to be "exotic" and "incredibly spiritual and marvelous." The film's director added, "I've been all over the world, but there's no place on the planet like Kathmandu. It is a city with almost no Western influence in it. It is a large city that is so deeply mystical and religious in all operations, and in a most peaceful, beautiful, colorful way" (Radio Times Staff 2016).[2] Echoing remarks made by enraptured European and American visitors to Nepal for much of the past 200 years, in these voices Nepal's mystical attractions seem alive and well.

Romantic images of Nepal have been in global circulation for centuries but only in the past roughly fifty years have geopolitical shifts, changing class formations, and major transformations in transportation technology and infrastructure meant that Nepal could increasingly be touristically "consumed" in situ and in person. If in the early twentieth century, almost no one could visit Nepal outside of flights of the imagination (quite literally in the case of James Hilton's "Lost Horizon" [1933], which begins with a plane crash in Shangri-La in the high Himalayas), today virtually anyone with some disposable income and time can follow their dreams to their imagined source. Yet, fantasies aside, how anyone could visit Kathmandu and not find a crowded, traffic-jammed, noisy, air-polluted, bustling, *thoroughly modern metropolis,* is an enigma. The "incredibly spiritual and marvelous" city "with almost no Western influence" exists, but only in the minds of tourists who bring these fantasies with them to Nepal and then—through what would

---

[2] Thanks to Ben Linder for bringing this interview to my attention.

seem to be increasingly difficult imaginative labor—manage to leave Nepal, fantasies still intact. However enigmatic this mystical experience may be, it is precisely upon this enigma that much of Nepal tourism's future seems to depend. For generations, Nepalis have skillfully managed and profited from the dreams that tourists bring with them to Nepal, but it remains to be seen just how sustainable those fantasies may be in the face of the very technological advances in human mobilities that have made it possible for tourists to visit this place of their dreams.

References

Alderson, Frederick. 1971. *The New 'Grand Tour': Travelling Today Through Europe, Asia Minor, India and Nepal.* Newton Abbot: David & Charles.

Beedie, Paul. 2003. "Adventure Tourism." In *Sport and Adventure Tourism*, edited by Simon Hudson, 203–39. New York: The Haworth Hospitality Press.

Beisler, Jerry. 2006. *The Bandit of Kabul.* Oakland: Regent Press.

Bernstein, Jeremy. 1970. *The Wildest Dreams of Kew: A Profile of Nepal.* New York: Simon & Schuster.

Bezruchka, Stephen. 1985. *A Guide to Trekking in Nepal.* 5th ed. Seattle: Mountaineers.

Burger, Veit. 1978. "The Economic Impact of Tourism in Nepal: An Input-Output Analysis." PhD diss., Cornell University.

Cunningham, John S. 1975. *Kingdom in the Sky.* London: Souvenir Press.

Dannhorn, Robin. 1986. "Nepal: The All-Seeing Presence." In *Fodor's India, Nepal and Sri Lanka, 1986*, 463–85. London: Hodder and Stoughton.

Gemie, Sharif, and Brian Ireland. 2017. *The Hippie Trail: A History.* Manchester: Manchester University Press.

Harvey, David. 1989. "Time-Space Compression and the Postmodern Condition." In *The Condition of Postmodernity*, 284–307. Oxford: Basil Blackwell.

Hilton, James. [1933] 1998. *Lost Horizon.* Delhi: Book Faith India.

Kerouac, Jack. [1957] 1972. *On the Road.* London: Penguin.

Liechty, Mark. 2017. *Far Out: Countercultural Seekers and the Tourism Encounter in Nepal.* Chicago: University of Chicago Press.

Linder, Benjamin. 2019. "'This Looks Like Chinatown!': Contested Geographies and the Transformation of Social Space in Jyatha, Kathmandu." *City & Society* 31 (2): 164–87.

MacLean, Rory. 2006. All You Need is Luggage. *Sunday Times,* June 18 (online). Available at https://www.thetimes.co.uk/article/all-you-need-is-luggage-73vrwx0pl9s

Marx, Karl. [1857] 1973. *The Grundrisse.* https://www.marxists.org/archive/marx/works/1857/grundrisse/index.htm

McDonald, Bernadette. 2005. *I'll See You in Kathmandu: The Elizabeth Hawley Story*. Seattle: Mountaineers.
Morris, John. 1963. *A Winter in Nepal*. London: Rupert Hart-Davis.
Newsweek. 1955. "Nepal: Into a 'Forbidden Land.'" Newsweek, March 28, 1955: 34–37.
Radio Times Staff. "Doctor Strange: When Benedict Cumberbatch Went to Kathmandu." *RadioTimes* (website). Accessed on November 4, 2016. http://www.radiotimes.com/news/2016-10-25/doctor-strange-when-benedict-cumberbatch-went-to-kathmandu.
Rana, Prabhakar S. 1971. "Untitled speech." In *Symposium on Tourism in Nepal*, 12–23. Kathmandu: Panchayat Coaching Institute.
Rogers, Clint. 2007. *The Lure of Everest: Getting to the Bottom of Tourism on Top of the World*. Kathmandu: Mandala.
Rosenthal, A. M. 1955. "Nepal's Open Door: First Tourists Admitted to Himalayan Kingdom Call It High Spot of Trip." *New York Times*, May 1, 1955: X19.
Satyal, Yajna Raj. 1999. *Tourism in Nepal: A Profile*. Delhi: Adroit Publishers.
Satyal, Yajna Raj. 2000. *Tourism Monograph of Nepal*. Delhi: Adroit Publishers.
Shrestha, Hari Prasad. 2000. *Tourism in Nepal: Marketing Challenges*. Delhi: Nirala.
Shrestha, Maheswor Bhakta. 2000. *Nepalese Aviation and Tourism*. Kathmandu: ATM Consult.
Skerry, Christa, Kerry Moran, and Kay M. Calavan. 1991. *Four Decades of Development: The History of U.S. Assistance in Nepal, 1951–1991*. Kathmandu: USAID.
Tomory, David. 1996. *A Season in Heaven: True Tales from the Road to Kathmandu*. London: Harper Collins.

About the author

Mark Liechty is a professor of Anthropology and History at the University of Illinois at Chicago, USA. Liechty has been a student of Nepali history and culture for over three decades. He is author or editor of six books on modern Nepal, middle-class culture, tourism, and development.

6   After *Eat, Pray, Love*: Tourism, Orientalism, and Cartographies of Salvation

Rumya S. Putcha

Abstract: This chapter examines certain kinds of travel and tourism as extensions of colonialism and examples of neocolonial forms of Orientalist engagement between the Global North and Global South. Focusing on areas that border the Indian Ocean, and the South Asian context in particular, I interrogate the gendered, racial, and geopolitical attachments that have historically drawn and continue to draw travelers to the region for tourism. I refer to these attachments as cartographies of salvation. In connecting the history and representations of travel to the area to the forms of leisure and spiritual tourism popularized by the 2006 memoir *Eat, Pray, Love*, I argue that the Indian Ocean region remains for many a paternalistic endeavor or an exotic playground, where one can project a sense of purpose or indulge in an escapist fantasy. This chapter combines critical tourism studies, feminist ethnography and theory, and critical race studies.

Keywords: tourism, Orientalism, representation, yoga

In November of 2018, a young man and adventure tourist from the United States, John Chau, traveled to a remote island off the east coast of India, where he was subsequently killed by a member of an indigenous tribe, the Sentinelese. The island, North Sentinel, is among a small group of isolated union territories, the Andaman and Nicobar Islands, an archipelago which was occupied by Europeans beginning in 1755 and was ceded by the British Empire to the Indian government after independence in 1947. Since Indian independence, these islands have remained relatively cut-off from the mainland, primarily because at least one of the indigenous tribes who

---

Linder, Benjamin, & Tarini Bedi (eds), *South Asia on the Move: Mobilities, Mobilizations, Maneuvers*. Amsterdam: Amsterdam University Press 2025
doi: 10.5117/9789463726498_CH06

reside in the area, the Sentinelese, has consistently expressed hostility to visitors. The Indian government has protected the Sentinelese and their right to privacy, so travel to the area is strictly controlled and, in most cases, prohibited. Considering this history, Chau's visit surprised many. How did he travel to the island, which is only accessible by boat? Why did he want to visit the island when he had to have known that his presence would be unwelcome?

In the months since his death, news reporting has uncovered that Chau was in fact an Instagram influencer as well as a Christian missionary, trained by the evangelical organization All Nations. Chau relied on his expertise in adventure tourism to reach places and people who were otherwise unreachable. News outlets highlighted his social media posts, particularly on the platform Instagram, which is popular among travelers, food photographers, and nature enthusiasts, to piece together a story of a young man who traveled to remote areas of the world—areas known as the "10/40 window," a term coined by a Christian missionary strategist named Luis Bush to describe regions of Africa and Asia that lie between ten and forty degrees north of the equator and are home to the majority of the world's Muslims, Hindus, and Buddhists. In his travel diaries, Chau described his commitment—what he described as his "burden"—to save the Sentinelese. In entries only days before his death, he wrote, "You guys might think I'm crazy in all this… but I think it's worth it to declare Jesus to these people." Is this "Satan's last stronghold," he asked God—a place "where none have heard or even had a chance to hear your name?"

In this chapter, I engage closely with how South Asia as a place and South Asian representations of mysticism and orientalism are mobile and mobilized imaginatively. As Linder's introduction to this volume argues, a South Asian mobilities perspective need not restrict itself to only focus on the physical mobility of people or objects; rather, the mobilities of imagination and representation are equally important. This perspective from South Asia illustrates how mobility is created in representational domains through a mystification and Orientalizing of South Asian practices and lifeworlds such as yoga. I also illustrate how these imaginative and representational mobilities reshape these practices and lifeworlds both in their places of origin and in the places to which they travel.

The following discussion connects standardized representations of South Asia as an undiscovered, uncivilized space (see Bandyopadhyay 2009; Bandyopadhyay and Morais 2005), echoed in John Chau's story, to the gendered forms of wellness tourism popularized by the 2006 memoir *Eat, Pray, Love,* written by US-based author Elizabeth Gilbert, which was subsequently adapted into a film starring Julia Roberts in 2010 (see Aggarwal et al. 2008; Bowers and Cheer 2017; Williams 2014). Bringing these disparate, but intertwined, forms of contemporary travel and tourism to South Asia into one frame, I argue that such forms of engagement, established during the colonial era and in the name of the "White Man's Burden," have today become popular and legible through what is known as "Instagram tourism," a form of neocolonial performative travel. I refer to such forms of travel as cartographies of salvation, a version of what Cherie Ndaliko (2016) has theorized in her work with international non-governmental organizations (NGOs) in the East Congo as a form of "charitable imperialism... which is often more charitable for the intervener than for the intervened upon, but also illuminates how this dynamic works in an age when people believe they know better" (11).

Applying this critique to forms of wellness tourism and voluntourism, I also rely on the methods of critical transnational feminists like M. Jacqui Alexander and Chandra Talpade Mohanty (2010, 38) who have argued that cartographies, which are often called into existence in order to locate difference and produce otherness, enact "different border crossing(s) of geography and nation state, of time and the continued, albeit dis-continuous, traffic between the colonial, the neocolonial, and the imperial; among and between different colonized spaces." In this chapter, a transnational lens not only allows me to examine how South Asia and its inhabitants remain a racialized other in the US context; it also reveals how the Indian nation-state has capitalized on such rhetoric to increasingly violent and ethnonationalist ends, especially since the election of Prime Minister Narendra Modi and his right-wing Hindu nationalist party, the Bharatiya Janata Party (BJP), in 2014.

Both Chau and Gilbert's travels to South Asia are predicated on entrenched Orientalist notions of those in the Global South as eternally destitute (see also Hallaq 2018). This attitude positions formerly colonized areas as places to which one can travel to find a true purpose and saviorhood, which can and will teach you how "to engage, surrender, and transform your body, mind, and spirit" (Brown 2015). Following this recognition of how leisure tourism and contemporary missionary work align, in the first part of this chapter, I apply a critical transnational feminist lens to focus on how leisure and wellness forms of travel also reproduce colonial-capitalist relations through ideologies of mobility. I examine a wide range of sensory, consumptive, and thus mobile Orientalist practices associated with yoga tourists, voluntourists, and missionary workers (see also Jain 2015). Drawing on over a decade of ethnographic participant-observation in yoga studios in the United States, and extending from feminist and cultural studies work on US imperialism and Global South tourism (see Conran 2011; Skwiot 2012; Vivanco and Gordon 2006), I argue that cartographies of salvation are inspired by a somatic (rather than simply literary) Orientalism. Somatic Orientalism draws tourists to study yoga or engage in missionary or volunteer work in South Asia, Indonesia, and more recently Central America—locales which are easily affordable for those traveling on the US dollar or other Global North currencies that have benefited from the colonial logics of "as good as gold." In the second half of the chapter, I examine the legacy of missionary work in India and connect it to both voluntouristic work as well as to the Orientalist and "re-Orientalist" aesthetics common in commercial yoga industries, even those emerging from India (see Bandyopadhyay and Patil 2017; Lau and Mendes 2014). Ultimately, I consider the uneasy marriage of contemporary forms of travel and mobility with cultural consumption and the touristic relationship between the Global North and Global South.

White Saviors, Moving Images, and Yoga Tourism

> The camera has often been a dire instrument. In Africa, as in most parts of the dispossessed, the camera arrives as part of the colonial paraphernalia, together with the gun and the bible, diarizing events, the exotic and the profound, cataloguing the converted and hanged. (Vera 1999)

My first day at the studio was a snowy Monday evening in small-town Indiana. I arrived with my colleague, a white woman in her forties and a dedicated yoga practitioner. Entering an otherwise unremarkable red brick building in the historic part of town, we walked up a steep flight of stairs, which led us to the second floor, above a French bakery and luxury women's clothing boutique. As soon as I entered the reception area, I was greeted by the overwhelming scent of incense, a collection of bronze statues, and a wall of bright and colorful photos featuring Indian women and children. Scanning the photos for details that might help me locate where they were taken, I guessed somewhere in North India, probably Rajasthan—a popular tourist area—judging by the terrain and the clothes the women and children were wearing. The photos were voyeuristic, intrusive almost, and part of a larger affective economy popularized by *National Geographic* over the past century—most notably for framing previously colonized areas as destitute and underdeveloped. One photo in particular caught my eye. Centered on the wall was a photo of a young woman staring into the camera with a red shawl framing her face. The photo bore an unmistakable reference to the now infamous photograph "Afghan Girl." Photographed in 1985 by Steve McCurry, this photo has since come to signify the aestheticized and poverty-pornographic connection many in the Global North maintain with previously colonized areas.

The owner of the studio, Elise, a white woman in her forties as well, did not introduce herself, nor did she ask me my name. She did earnestly inquire, as I removed my shoes, if I was "Indian." Without waiting for an answer, she proudly pointed to the wall of photos, sharing with me that she had taken all of them herself during a recent trip to study yoga in India. She was animated and enthusiastic as she told me about how transformative the trip had been for her—how India had really helped her "find herself" and "heal." Drawing my attention back to the photos, she said she had capitalized on the time in India to learn how to use her Nikon and to hone her amateur photography skills. We stood in silence in front of the photos for a few moments. I asked if she remembered their names, but she said she had not asked, she did not know how to—she did not speak their language. They were "just souvenirs," she explained, "a way to bring India back home with her."

It is by now a truism that photographs and other forms of visual, mobile art which position South Asia as an Orientalist fantasy reproduce what many have theorized as the white racial frame (see, for example, Dyer 1997; Feagin 2009; Seshadri-Crooks 2000). In her work on the circulation of images in Global North news media, Zeynep Gursel (2016) refers to images like those found in magazines like *National Geographic* as "indexed bodies," which are meant to represent an entire country's population. After all, for years after Sharbat Gula was photographed by McCurry, *against her wishes*, the photo did not identify her, but rather signposted the war-torn region metonymically *through* her, as it often appears in the US racial and geographic imagination—"an aggregate of what is portrayed as Afghanistan's timeless, almost naturalized plight of despair and poverty" (Gursel 2016, 20).

Photography, as a documentary, affective, and cartographic tool, cannot be understood as separate from the colonial encounter in which it first emerged as a method of anthropological inquiry. In their respective work, Zahid Chaudhary (2012) and Teju Cole (2019) both describe the extent to which photography was adopted and utilized as "a weapon of imperialism." In British India, in particular, photography became a disciplining or "census" tool and a means by which colonial authorities and missionaries alike studied local populations in the service of administration, surveillance, and rule. The weaponization of census data relied most obviously on the influence of Enlightenment thought and its rationalist projects, including inquiries of "racial science" (see Dhawan 2014). Ideologies of representation became essential to installing ideas of white racial superiority and identifiers like "Caucasian" through the specious logics of craniometry and anthropometry (see Painter 2010). Indeed, by the mid-nineteenth century and at the height of imperial and settler-colonial projects, biologists like Johann Fredrich Blumenbach were postulating racial hierarchies using tools of measurement, ethnology, and other forms of visual representation. In other words, travel photographs like "Afghan Girl" belong to a longer history of white racial framing, despite or perhaps precisely because of their coercive origins. Thus, emotionally charged, moving images like "Afghan Girl" and those inspired by its aesthetic must be understood as genealogical in contemporary imaginations of the white man's burden. Today, such photographs, as highly mobile artifacts, underscore *both* epistemologies *and* affective economies of race and place that call tourists like Elise to document their travels through photographic souvenirs and on social media platforms like Instagram and Facebook.

Today, social media's discursive formations have produced a powerful aesthetics of mobility and tourism, particularly in the context of missionary work. In the aftermath of John Chau's death, for example, the Instagram missionary community, known through hashtags like #missionary, #jesus, and #volunteer, has received new and perhaps unprecedented coverage in news media. This is an active and young community, represented through its massive digital footprint, like the numerous websites that offer advice on how to take the best photos for Instagram to help inspire others to engage in missionary work. One blog entry by the prolific missionary group, Youth with a Mission, is simply titled "24 Instagram Pictures That Will Inspire You to Become a Missionary." The photo captions from this post offer a glimpse into how Gursel's (2016) argument might be applied to new forms of stock images and Orientalist affective economies. For example, the captions for the photos include phrases like "sleep in a luxurious hut" and "hold a baby in every country."

In this regard, Instagram accounts that fetishize missionary work are arguably contemporary examples of the travel diary or the tourist postcard, offering an opportunity for the traveler to bring, send back, or own a souvenir of the experience. Recent work on the colonial era postcard in British India offers some compelling parallels with contemporary social media trends. A recent conference and exhibition through the University of London's School of Oriental and African Studies curated a selection of picture postcards from the Indian cities of Chennai and Bengaluru (previously known as Madras and Bangalore) from the early twentieth century. This new research explores "how postcard practices imagined, figured and performed a colonial encounter by depicting... monuments... people and places" (Hughes and Stevenson 2018). The colonial postcard, alongside other forms of cheap print and advertising media, forged a new kind of Orientalism, a commercial and materialist variety, which arguably collapsed discursive formations of "burden" with "escape" (see also Tchen 2001, xx–xxiii). Under these early twentieth-century logics, the Orient emerged as an underdeveloped space, in need of saving, but also as an untouched, magical world, a place where time and space somehow stood still.

It is within the context of missionary work and its deep connections to travel photography that Chau's story begins to come into focus as part of a longer and messier narrative about how inhabitants of certain parts of the world understand themselves as saviors while others can only exist in need of saving. This long-standing binary, mapped onto cartographies of the Occident and the Orient—what Sara Ahmed (2004, 113) identifies as the etymology of the "orient in orientation"—captures why inequitable relations between the Global North and Global South have endured, not only through touristic engagements, but also through the discursive formations that first encouraged white Europeans to travel to places where brown and Black people come from.

Somatic Orientalism

In the fifteen years I have been conducting ethnographic fieldwork in Euro-American yoga studios, images of India as an inherently spiritual space have appeared as a consistent tool in cultivating an affective tether and a somatic experience for practitioners and consumers, who are overwhelmingly upper-middle-class white women (see Birdee et al. 2008; Park et al. 2015). In the studio in Indiana, the owner, Elise, a lawyer by profession and a photography enthusiast, had traveled to India in the aftermath of an acrimonious divorce. She was part of a new era of yoga enthusiasts inspired by *Eat, Pray, Love* (*EPL*). This book, part memoir, part travel diary, part self-help guide, reinvigorated a somewhat dormant, but long-standing escapist relationship between white women and India. Joining a larger body of work set in the Global South in the post-9/11 era, the memoir particularly valorized yoga but also alternative forms of spirituality and medicine as a way for well-to-do white women, and those who might seek to identify with them, to "find themselves" as well as claim their sexuality outside of the confines of marriage. Feminist scholars like Shefali Chandra (2014) have noted the Orientalist logics at the heart of such engagements.

> Skillfully navigating between twentieth-century imperial history, the rise of the War on Terror, and a barely-contained obsession with Hindu female sexuality, each of these texts is driven by the conviction that India, and Indian women, will heal the mind and body of the white woman. India enables the American woman to cure herself. (Chandra 2014, 488)

To be sure, *EPL* and other cultural texts like it (see, for example, the movie *Wild*) valorize travel and escapism from accountability and difficult emotions through the rhetoric of "feminism" or "spirituality."

A recent tourism advertisement by Incredible !ndia, the international campaign maintained by the Government of India since 2002, animates such logics. Opening with a shot of a white woman juxtaposed with a Hindu goddess, the imagery of the ad is underscored by a guitar, piano, and a drone. Importantly, the instruments featured in this arrangement, particularly the drone, are not idiomatically Indian, but rather an ambiguous collection, most likely provided by a synthesizer. The white woman, we learn as the advertisement progresses, has come to study yoga in India. Dressed in plain, white cotton, reminiscent of the style popularized by Indian nationalists like Mohandas Karamchand Gandhi in the early twentieth century, she becomes more skilled at yoga through instruction from an Indian woman, her *guru*. In a series of shots, as the music builds, we see the white woman gaining confidence and exploring uninhabited areas, marveling at the wildlife and untouched vistas. In a final shot, as the music climbs to a crescendo, she is balancing on a boulder, overlooking a beautiful scene by a river, performing a yoga pose, demonstrating the completion of her training and transformation. As the advertisement ends, we hear a woman's voice in an Indian accent say, "Come to the land of yoga, rejuvenate your soul, experience India." As the scene fades out, the Incredible !ndia logo fades in, and we hear the jingle for the advertising campaign, a pentatonic sequence that unequivocally, if redundantly, signals the Orient.

I first saw this ad while I was in India, perhaps paradoxically enough, while I was running on a treadmill in New Delhi. Indeed, the advertisement is rarely broadcast on channels outside of India, raising interesting questions about who is meant to identify with this ad. The inspiration for the instrumentation is easily identifiable—the sonic landscape would be familiar to anyone who participates in commercial yoga industries in the United States. I have come to understand the affect this kind of music is meant to evoke for its listeners as a kind of somatic Orientalism, an emotional experience that invokes India, and specifically a Hindu India, if only as a simulacrum.

The genre label for such music in the US context is New Age. New Age music, associated with the broader countercultural trends that popularized yoga and meditation in the 1960s and 1970s, particularly in California, did not attract much industry attention until the 1990s (see Hall 1994). Since the 1990s, however, New Age artists have capitalized on the growth of the yoga industry by adopting the themes of spirituality and healing. One New Age artist whose work is popular across the US yoga industry goes by the stage-name Deva Premal (Deva translates to God). Premal, who was born in Germany and whose legal name is Jolantha Fries, spent time studying yoga in India and now credits herself with introducing "the West" to the power of the Sanskrit *mantra* or chant. Through her music career, Premal is deeply intertwined in the yoga industry in the US context and its Orientalist fascination with Sanskrit. Her commercial success can arguably be attributed to one track in particular, her interpretation of the "Gayatri Matra," which first appeared on her 1998 album, *The Essence*. The track follows the conventions of New Age spiritual music and, like the Incredible !ndia advertisement, features a synthesizer and drone-like texture.

Premal and other New Age musicians like her produce music specifically for the yoga consumer market in the United States by maintaining that such music is not geolinguistically grounded in any way. This argument reveals a new, neoliberal twist to the logics of imperialism. Since 1998, the yoga industry has exploded world-wide under the premise that yoga is spiritual, not religious. Indeed, there is an ever-present demand for music like Premal's, which boasts a "5000-year old tradition that predates religion" and claims magical, healing powers for its listeners (Louise 2016). A recent review of Premal's new, self-titled album builds on this trend, describing the sounds as "sensual... mantra medicine" (Wood 2018). It seems of no consequence to fans of Premal or of her fellow New Age stars, like Snatam Kaur, who performed at the 2019 Grammy Awards ceremony during the pre-televised programming, if their music uses language in any way that might allow it to be intelligible. Much like Premal, Kaur's performance style relies on racialized signposting and a combination of costuming and spectacle. In other words, the communicative potential of the sound is arguably secondary to its somatic power and the means by which consumers can experience an altered state.

Sara Ahmed (2006) has noted that affective tools, like images, and also scent, taste, and sound, work in tandem to produce a cultural politics of emotion—the very kind mobilized in the Incredible !ndia advertisement described above—to solidify the notion that India offers white women a chance to "rejuvenate" themselves. Inherent in this claim is the idea that those who visit India to study yoga will be able to return to an original state of good health, one the world they live in otherwise depletes. Incredible !ndia advertisements as well as New Age artists like Premal's or Kaur's mobilize this idea to depict India as a fountain of youth, relying on Orientalist branding.

This logic can be found in food cultures as well, most notably in recent dietary trends of "returning to nature." For example, the heightened sensitivity around unprocessed, organic, and non-GMO foods, along with the recent spike in farm-to-table restaurant ventures is an extension of a larger movement to encourage those from the Global North to live, eat, and exist more sustainably, supposedly like those in the Global South. Indeed, this attitude toward primitive "raw" food (see also the paleo diet) makes an appearance in John Chau's biography, too. His influence on Instagram among adventure tourists garnered the attention of California-based, outdoor apparel company Huckberry, as well as Colorado-based Perky Jerky, for whom Chau served as an official brand ambassador. In fact, it was reportedly through his partnership with Perky Jerky, and for which he posted photos of their products in picturesque, wilderness settings, that Chau was sent to India in 2017. In other words, capitalist enterprises dovetail with the kinds of somatic Orientalism and affective logics that combine eco- and adventure tourism with missionary practices today.

These logics, relying as they do on the weaponization of otherness through representations of the mystical or natural, produce what Ahmed (2010) terms affective communities as well as affective economies, both of which functionally cultivate a sense of "we," "us," or "here" in contradistinction to "them" and "there." Understanding John Chau's story as part of a larger affective economy allows for a more robust understanding of how and why Orientalist leisure industries, like yoga, have achieved a foothold in US consumer markets, relying as they do on stereotypes of India as a spiritual and exotic, but dirty and impoverished, locale that can provide not only culture and escape but also the sanctimonious feeling of "helping the local economy" for white travelers.

Colonialism and Cartographies of Salvation

The arguments for "charitable" travel to India belong within a long history, of course, dating back to the early colonial era and are well documented in the diaries of Catholic missionaries of Portugal and Italy from at least the sixteenth century. However, the missionary call to save those living in the

Orient by, as John Chau phrased it, "declaring Jesus," is most often credited to the Baptist preacher William Carey, also known as the "father of modern missions," and his work *An Enquiry into the Obligations of Christians to Use Means for the Conversion of the Heathens* (Carey 1934 [1792]). Carey's work in India was massively influential and must be contextualized within the broader colonial-capitalist project as the East India Company was absorbed into the Crown. Carey and other men like him were not initially welcome by the colonial authorities, especially the East India Company. As historians have noted, "early British involvement... specifically prohibited the evangelizing of the Indian public until the early 1800s, in line with the company's policy of cultural non-interference to facilitate commerce" (Johnston 2003, 18). British administrative officials well into the nineteenth century were explicit about the need to avoid any semblance of collusion with missionary work, arguing,

> once they [Indians] suspect that it is the intention of the British Government to abandon this hitherto inviolate principle of allowing the most complete toleration in matters of religion... there will arise in the minds of all so deep a distrust of our ulterior designs that they will no longer be tractable to any arrangement intended for their improvement. (Bentick 1829)

The preceding quote is particularly telling in regards to how drastically the attitudes toward missionary work shifted in the late nineteenth century and how it became possible, in the twentieth century and later, to collapse and equate "improvement" with "conversion," among other things. Bentick's sentiment, for example, appears within his "Minute on Sati," in which he debated the merits of intervening in the indigenous practice of *sati*, or widow immolation. In his consideration of the matter, Bentick was circumspect, revealing his concern that were the British to force their beliefs on the local population, they would be seen as no better than their predecessors, "the Mahomedan conquerors" (Bentick 1829). Like many other British administrative interventions, the *sati* issue was cast as a civilizational problem and applied colonial logics to local understandings of gender and religion.

If one follows the broader nineteenth-century discourse about gender, especially the mounting conversations about marriage, race, and what women's studies scholars have described as the "cult of domesticity," it is possible to understand how and why British administrative authorities became less resistant to missionary work in India and why, in turn, certain forms of travel like volunteer-tourism (today also known as "mission trips") to India, by white women, especially from the United States, became more common (see, for example, Singh 2013). In other words, somatic Orientalism, particularly its capitalist modalities, must be understood as an extension of European imperial projects, including missionary work. The gendered imperatives of somatic Orientalism are therefore fundamental to the forms of travel and tourism which today draw upper-middle-class white women to India to "find themselves" and simultaneously "uplift and save" impoverished Indian women and children (Bandyopadhyay and Patil 2017, 651).

What becomes clear, especially if one listens carefully to the rhetorical slippage between the sights and sounds of India constructed by these missionaries and travelers, is that it is not India, but a version of India—what Pavithra Prasad (2015, 203) has described in her work as racially motivated "nostalgia"—which these musicians, consumers, and missionaries sought and continue to seek (see also Rosaldo 1989). Others have noted this trend, highlighting the fact that many travelers in the early modern era wrote accounts of India that challenged the belief that European civilization was superior. In her work, for example, Sonia Sikka argues that the dominant view of European and therefore Christian cultural superiority—the brand we see in Chau's biography—

> with its concomitant image of non-European cultures as childlike and backwards, was constructed. It was entirely possible for Europeans to think differently. Some did and they related enough information, with enough thoughtfulness, about the inclination towards partiality, for others to do so as well. If these latter perspectives did not win out historically… it is due to a deliberate refusal to hear, on the part of the Europeans, with an interest in maintaining a hierarchical view of their relations with others. This can only be explained, I believe, as a function of what Nietzsche calls "will to power"; that is, the desire to enhance one's own being through a demonstration of mastery over others. (Sikka in Beaman and Sikka 2018, 13)

One could reasonably argue that in the case of yoga industries, this form of mastery and power over others fuses with gender politics in the US context, which have historically marginalized women and otherwise ignored their health and wellness needs. That said, the commercial yoga industry, despite its claims to the contrary, is not an inclusive or even nominally diverse landscape. Women of color are remarkably absent in the US context, as either producers or consumers. In other words, despite its claims to humanitarianism, this is an industry run for and by white women, with the most recent industry data reporting that yoga consumers in the United States are ninety percent white, and seventy-five percent identify as women (see especially Park et al. 2015). In this light, it makes sense that some women might flock to a place where they can feel superior by virtue of their nationality and race, but also where they can seek access to alternative forms of wellness, since it is now well-documented that their own medical communities often cannot and will not listen to their pain (see, for example, Adler and Rehkopf 2008; Chetty et al. 2016). As I discuss in the final section, however, such forms of travel not only rely on inequitable global flows of capital and access but also reveal the lasting residue of British colonialism, which makes it possible for someone like John Chau to gain access to an otherwise restricted island.

Tourism and "The Land of Yoga"

Discourses of diaspora and cosmopolitanism can often gloss over the enduring role of colonial-derived valuations in the story of the Indian nation-state, particularly in the aftermath of the 1991 International Monetary Fund (IMF) mandate, which forced the Indian government to abandon its carefully laid plans for self-rule and liberalize its economy instead (see Sengupta 2009; Spero and Hart 2010). Facing a financial crisis in August 1991, the government of India turned to the World Bank (WB) and IMF. India had landed in an acute balance of payments crisis. The WB and IMF were willing to offer aid, but on the condition that the centrally-planned economy convert into a market-driven one, which whittled down the role of the government, cut trade barriers, and allowed foreign investment into the economy. In the end, the IMF mandate, as it has come to be known, recommended and pushed through economic reforms that liberalized the Indian economy. By requiring India to open its markets in order to access aid, these two US-based financial watchdogs effectively coerced the Indian government, ending four decades of central planning, significantly shifting resource allocation decisions from the public sector to the private sector and markets, and ultimately integrating the country into the world economy.

The liberalization of the Indian economy, occurring as it did while the Hindu nationalist party, the BJP, emerged as a political force in the 1990s, also ushered in new possibilities for what was now branded as "heritage tourism" and travel to India (see Bandyopadhyay et al. 2008). Increasing revenue through tourism that exclusively highlighted India's Hindu identifications featured prominently in economic planning beginning in the post-IMF era. The Incredible !ndia Campaign (IIC), a prime example of this trend, was launched in 2004, and was, according to its principal architect, Amitabh Kant, aimed at "(1) extending international business and leisure travelers' length of stay and yield in India; and (2) promoting domestic tourism—all the while positioning India away from a low-cost destination to one of luxury" (Kant 2009, as cited in Kerrigan, Shivanandan, and Hede 2012, 319). The strategic objectives emphasize the importance of class identification within the key demographics: "Target the age group of 40–65 belonging to affluent, well-educated, married, white-collar segments for a value-based strategy" (321). In other words, officials who run the IIC and related projects are well aware of the perception that traveling to India has not historically been understood as a leisure activity either among domestic or international travelers.

To address this perception and, arguably, to provide an incentive to encourage leisure and conspicuous forms of travel, in 2016 the Indian government introduced a new visa category exclusively for those who wish to travel to India to study yoga. A subset of the tourist visa, this category allows the government to track tourism sectors while also creating an opportunity for revenue since the "yoga visa" is now available to around 150 countries through what is known as the e-visa or visa on arrival program. In the US, however, this visa program is priced, for those who can afford the convenience, at twice the cost of a traditional visa. It is worth noting that this was the kind of visa that John Chau used and arguably abused, to travel to India and conduct missionary work.

Conclusion

Ultimately, John Chau's story indexes a longer and unsettling history of travel and cartography. Such narratives remind us that contemporary forms of tourism are deeply intertwined with racism, and therefore neither can nor should be understood as ahistorical forms of culture. As the Indian government continues to brand the nation-state as a homeland for dominant-caste Hindus (see Kaur 2020), this chapter has demonstrated that cartographies of salvation, established through the legacies of colonialism and its forms of governmentality, continue to locate and dislocate humanity when presented with the opportunity. Indeed, how else can one explain the affection—the somatic forms of Orientalism—that draw travelers from the Global North to the Global South to experience spiritual, adventure, and other forms of tourism and feel benevolent in the process? If we expand our lens to view these sedimented economic and cultural formations together, it is hard to dispute that what is positioned as "affordable" tourism unequivocally demonstrates the lasting impact of imperialism.

More recently, scholars of commercial wellness and tourism industries have noted the uninterrogated attachment to mobility that draws missionaries like John Chau, as well as self-help yoga consumers like Elizabeth Gilbert, to India and other areas positioned as tropical (see, e.g., Barendregt 2011; Kassabian 2004). Such critiques acknowledge a complex and uneven relationship between the Global North and South. In the case of South Asia in particular, this relationship belongs to a genealogy Vijay Prashad (2007, 68) describes as a "textual orientalism," which relies not only on the imagined exoticism of South Asian goods and bodies, but also on fictions cultivated by transcendentalist writers like Henry David Thoreau and Ralph Waldo Emerson. These critics suggest that to continue to participate in and reenact colonial and imperial dynamics by utilizing objects from historically oppressed or colonized peoples for libidinal enjoyment or monetary gain stands in direct opposition to any semblance of reparative justice. To be sure, the sights, sounds, and economies I have charted above rely on discursive coordinates which were set long ago, and which continue to ferry some at a cost paid by others. In a sense, yoga tourism and its affective imperatives offer the direct inverse of John Chau's supposedly altruistic mission while relying on synonymous logics. In either case, the Global South remains a spiritual oasis or a cautionary tale; a timeless, imagined place where one can either save or be saved.

Acknowledgments

Portions of this chapter appeared in *Tourist Studies* in 2020. I have received permission from the publisher to reprint.

References

Adler, Nancy E., and David H. Rehkopf. 2008. "U.S. Disparities in Health: Descriptions, Causes, and Mechanisms." *Annual Review of Public Health* 29: 235–52. DOI: 10.1146/annurev.publhealth.29.020907.090852.

Aggarwal, Ardarsh Kumar, Meenal Guglani, and Raj Kumar Goel. 2008. "Spiritual and Yoga Tourism: A Case Study on Experience of Foreign Tourists Visiting Rishikesh, India." Presented at Conference on Tourism in India-Challenges Ahead, IIMK, Kozhikode, India, 15–17 May: 459–64.

Ahmed, Sara. 2004. *The Cultural Politics of Emotion*. Durham: Duke University Press.

Ahmed, Sara. 2010. *The Promise of Happiness*. Durham: Duke University Press.

Alexander, M. Jacqui, and Chandra Talpade Mohanty. 2010. "Cartographies of Knowledge and Power: Transnational Feminism as Radical Praxis." In *Critical Transnational Feminist Praxis*, edited by R. Nagar and A. L. Swarr, 23–45. Albany, NY: SUNY Press.

Bandyopadhyay, Ranjan. 2009. "The Perennial Western Tourism Representations of India That Refuse to Die," *Tourism* 57 (1): 23–35.

Bandyopadhyay, Ranjan, and Vrushali Patil. 2017. "'The White Woman's Burden': The Racialized, Gendered Politics of Volunteer Tourism." *Tourism Geographies* 19 (4): 644–57.

Bandyopadhyay, Ranjan, and Duarte Morais. 2005. "Representative Dissonance." *Annals of Tourism Research* 32 (4): 1006–21.

Bandyopadhyay, Ranjan, Duarte Morais, and Garry Chick. 2008. "Religion and Identity in India's Heritage Tourism." *Annals of Tourism Research* 35 (3): 790–808.

Barendregt, Bart A. 2011. "Tropical Spa Cultures, Eco-Chic, and the Complexities of New Asianism." In *Cleanliness and Culture: Indonesian Histories*, edited by Kees van Dijk and Jean Gelman Taylor, 159–92. Leiden: KITLV Press.

Beaman, Lori G., and Sonia Sikka. 2018. *Constructions of Self and Other in Yoga, Travel, and Tourism: A Journey to Elsewhere*. New York: Palgrave Macmillan.

Bentick, William Cavendish. 1829. "A Minute on Sati." November 8, Calcutta. Available at: http://chnm.gmu.edu/wwh/p/103.html.

Birdee, Gurjeet S., Anna T. Legedza, Robert B. Saper, Suzanne M. Bertisch, David M. Eisenberg, Russell S. Phillips. 2008. "Characteristics of Yoga Users: Results of a National Survey." *Journal of General Internal Medicine* 23 (10): 1653–58.

Bowers, Hana and Joseph M. Cheer. 2017. "Yoga Tourism: Commodification and Western Embracement of Eastern Spiritual Practice." *Tourism Management Perspectives* 24: 208–16.

Brown, Coral. 2015. "Why Make a Yoga Pilgrimage to India?" *Yoga Journal*, March 31. Available at: https://www.yogajournal.com/lifestyle/make-yoga-pilgrimage-india.

Carey, William. 1934 [1792]. *An Enquiry into the Obligations of Christians to Use Means for the Conversion of the Heathens*. London: Baptist Missionary Society.

Chandra, Shefali. 2014 "'India Will Change You Forever': Hinduism, Islam, and Whiteness in the American Empire." *Signs* 40 (2): 487–512.

Chaudhary, Zahid R. 2012. *Afterimage of Empire: Photography in Nineteenth-Century India*. Minneapolis: University of Minnesota Press.

Chetty, Raj, Michael Stepner, Sarah Abraham, Shelby Lin, Benjamin Scuderi, Nicholas Turner, Augustin Bergeron, and David Cutler. 2016. "The Association between Income and Life Expectancy in the United States, 2001–14." *Journal of the American Medical Association* 315 (16): 1750–66.

Cole, Teju. 2019. "When the Camera Was a Weapon of Imperialism (and When It Still Is)." *New York Times*, February 6. Available at: https://www.nytimes.com/2019/02/06/magazine/ when-the-camera-was-a-weapon-of-imperialism-and-when-it-still-is.html.

Conran, Mary. 2011. "They Really Love Me! Intimacy in Volunteer Tourism." *Annals of Tourism Research* 38 (4): 1454–73.

Dhawan, Nikita. 2014. *Decolonizing Enlightenment Transnational Justice, Human Rights and Democracy in a Postcolonial World.* Opladen: Budrich Barbara.

Dyer, Richard. 1997. *White.* New York: Routledge.

Feagin, Joe R. 2009. *The White Racial Frame: Centuries of Racial Framing and Counter-Framing.* New York: Routledge.

Foxen, Anya P. 2017. *Biography of a Yogi: Paramahansa Yogananda and the Origins of Modern Yoga.* New York: Oxford University Press.

Gursel, Zeynap Devrim. 2016. *Image Brokers: Visualizing World News in the Age of Digital Circulation.* Oakland: University of California Press.

Hall, Dennis. 1994. "New Age Music: A Voice of Liminality in Postmodern Popular Culture." *Popular Music and Society* 18 (2): 13–21.

Hallaq, Wael B. 2018. *Restating Orientalism: A Critique of Modern Knowledge.* New York: Columbia University Press.

Hughes, Steven Putnam, and Emily Stevenson. 2018. "Postcard Journeys: Image, Text, Media." Presented at Conference Organized by the School of Oriental and African Studies, London, September 14.

Jain, Andrea R. 2015. *Selling Yoga: From Counterculture to Pop Culture.* New York: Oxford University Press.

Johnston, Anna. 2003. *Missionary Writing and Empire, 1800–1860.* New York: Cambridge University Press.

Kassabian, Anahid. 2004. "Would You Like Some World Music with Your Latte? Starbucks, Putumayo, and Distributed Tourism." *Twentieth-Century Music.* 1 (2): 209–23.

Kaur, Ravinder. 2020. *Brand New Nation: Capitalist Dreams and Nationalist Designs in Twenty-First-Century India.* Palo Alto: Stanford University Press.

Kerrigan, Finola, Jyotsna Shivanandan, and Anne-Marie Hede. 2012. "Nation Branding: A Critical Appraisal of Incredible India." *Journal of Macromarketing* 32 (3): 319–27.

Lau, Lisa, and Ana Cristina Mendes. 2014. *Re-Orientalism and South Asian Identity Politics: The Oriental Other Within.* New York: Routledge.

Louise, Sri. 2016. "The Globalization of the Gayatri Mantra." Lecture Presented at the Third Annual Race and Yoga Conference, Berkeley, April 26.

Ndaliko, Chérie River. 2016. *Necessary Noise: Music, Film, and Charitable Imperialism in the East of Congo.* New York: Oxford University Press.

Painter, Nell Irvin. 2010. *The History of White People.* New York: W.W. Norton.

Park, Crystal L., Tosca Braun, and Tamar Siegel. 2015. "Who Practices Yoga? A Systematic Review of Demographic, Health-Related, and Psychosocial Factors Associated with Yoga Practice." *Journal of Behavioral Medicine* 38 (3): 460–71.

Prasad, Pavithra. 2015. "Paradiso Lost: Writing Memory and Nostalgia in the Post-Ethnographic Present." *Text and Performance Quarterly* 35 (2–3): 202–20.

Prashad, Vijay. 2007. *The Karma of Brown Folk*. Minneapolis: University of Minnesota Press.
Puar, Jasbir K. 2017. *The Right to Maim: Debility, Capacity, Disability*. Durham: Duke University Press.
Rosaldo, Renato. 1989. "Imperialist Nostalgia." *Memory and Counter-Memory: Representations* 26: 107–22.
Sengupta, Mitu. 2009. "Making the State Change Its Mind: The IMF, the World Bank and the Politics of India's Market Reforms." *New Political Economy* 14 (2): 181–210.
Seshadri-Crooks, Kalpana. 2000. *Desiring Whiteness: A Lacanian Analysis of Race*. Abingdon: Taylor & Francis.
Singh, Maina Chawla. 2013. *Gender, Religion, and "Heathen Lands": American Missionary Women in South Asia (1860s–1940s)*. New York: Routledge.
Singleton, Mark. 2010. *Yoga Body: The Origins of Modern Posture Practice*. New York: Oxford University Press.
Skwiot, Christine. 2012. *The Purposes of Paradise: U.S. Tourism and Empire in Cuba and Hawai'i*. Philadelphia: University of Pennsylvania Press.
Spero, Joan Edelman, and Jeffrey A. Hart. 2010. *The Politics of International Economic Relations*. Boston: Wadsworth Cengage Learning.
Tchen, John Kuo Wei. 2001. *New York before Chinatown: Orientalism and the Shaping of American Culture, 1776–1882*. Baltimore: Johns Hopkins University Press.
Vera, Yvonne. 1999. *Thatha Camera: The Pursuit for Reality*. Bulawayo, Zimbabwe: National Gallery of Zimbabwe. Published in conjunction with an exhibition of the same title, organized by and presented at the National Gallery of Zimbabwe.
Vivanco, Luis A., and Robert J. Gordon. 2006. *Tarzan Was an Eco-tourist... and Other Tales in the Anthropology of Adventure*. New York: Berghahn Books.
Williams, Ruth. 2014. "Eat, Pray, Love: Producing the Female Neoliberal Spiritual Subject Eat, Pray, Love." *Journal of Popular Culture* 47 (3): 613–33.
Wood, Leanne. 2018. "Deva by Deva Premal," *LA Yoga*, October 4, 2018. Available at: https://layoga.com/ entertainment/music/deva-by-deva-premal/.

About the author

Rumya S. Putcha is Associate Professor of Music and Women's Studies at the University of Georgia. Her first book, *The Dancer's Voice: Performance and Womanhood in Transnational India* (Duke University Press, 2023), develops a transnational feminist approach to Indian performance cultures.

7   The Mobility of Regional Labor Hierarchies: Nepali Employment and Entrepreneurialism in the "South Asian" Gas Stations of North Texas

Andrew Nelson

Abstract: Through an ethnographic portrait of music videos, wage labor, and entrepreneurialism related to the Nepali migrant experience working in North Texas gas stations, this chapter examines how multiple dimensions of mobility (physical, social, infrastructural) shape a pan-ethnic economy of South Asian-owned gas stations. Rather than understanding the gas stations as an "occupational niche" based on ethnicity, I apply a mobility paradigm for the more holistic framework it provides. A mobility approach highlights the regimes of migration that funnel temporary visa holders into the stigmatized and precarious service labor of gas stations often organized according to a South Asian diasporic hierarchy. At the same rate, a mobility trajectory approach emphasizes the creative agency of migrants to craft and enact narratives of cross-immigrant mutual help and solidarity, and gas station innovation.

Keywords: regimes of mobility, mobility trajectories, South Asian diaspora, gas stations, immigrant service labor

Introduction: The Nepali Gas Station Dream According to PSPN and Swami D

Near the end of the 2016 Nepali hip-hop (Nep-hop) song "Malai Baal Ho,"[1] the rappers PSPN and Swami D pay homage to "all of my gas station people,

---

[1]   I would like to thank Premila van Ommen for notifying me of this video.

Linder, Benjamin, & Tarini Bedi (eds), *South Asia on the Move: Mobilities, Mobilizations, Maneuvers.*
Amsterdam: Amsterdam University Press 2025
doi: 10.5117/9789463726498_CH07

gameroom people, my mall people, F1, H1, TPS people."[2] For this group of Nepali migrants in the US working on temporary visas, the song's lyrics and video charts an aspirational social mobility rooted in gas station labor. The video begins with PSPN carrying his pistol from his car into the gas station, implying the threat of gas station violence. While greeting a group of a multiethnic group of men standing outside, he gives "shout-out" references to Dallas, Fort Worth, and Irving, the main cities of the Dallas Fort Worth (DFW) metroplex. Although introducing himself as *saahu* (owner), the video shows him working alongside workers mopping the floor and stocking the beer collection of the gas station. The video portrays not just the grind of gas station labor, but also its jovial side of gambling machines and employee-customer flirtations. These images link the gas station with the video's more glamorous second location, a mid-sized yacht, where PSPN is joined by Swami D and a multicultural group of bikini-wearing women for more rapping, gambling, and dancing.

By associating the gas station with the yacht, the video represents the former as a stepping-stone to upward social mobility but also provides a certain working-class credibility to the migrant worker short on opportunities. The video's narrative counters the prevailing devaluation of gas station labor in the US. Despite selling a product, gasoline, that is central to the US "cultural imagination of nationhood" (Huber 2009, 476), gas station labor has increasingly become stigmatized and exploited due to cost-cutting measures that depend on migrant workers, particularly those on temporary visas. As I discuss, the devaluation of gas station work has coincided with an increase of working-class Asian immigration to the US. The video seeks to reverse the gas station's negative image by glamorizing its immigrant milieu often at the intersection of South Asian and Latino DFW. The rappers pepper "Malai Baal Ho" with Spanish phrases (*que paso*, Dallas *gracias*) and brag about their sex appeal to multiple races of women. In their subsequent 2017 video, "Whoz Yo Daddy?," they repeat the English title in Spanish, Hindi, and Nepali, and allude to their global fanbase in Nepali cities (Kathmandu and Pokhara), Indian metropolises (Mumbai and Delhi), and Spanish-speaking cities (El Paso and Cancun).

For PSPN and Swami D's version of the migrant dream, the gas station marks a stepping-stone to a materially successful life. While the reality

---

2   These references combine the precarious labor in gas stations and malls with the non-immigrant visa categories of H1, F1, and TPS. As discussed later in the chapter, H1 visas are granted to workers in "specialty occupations," F1 visas are granted to students, and TPS refers to Temporary Protected Status, a humanitarian visa granted to migrants from countries deemed unsafe to return to.

of gas station-based social mobility is, of course, far more complex than the video suggests, the general arc resonates with many entrepreneurial Nepali immigrants who similarly aspire to become entrepreneurs. As one community leader explained to me, something has switched in the new generation of Nepali immigrants since 2010. He claimed, "We have gone from the mentality of go and work for someone else to go and work for myself, start a business." In "Whoz Yo Daddy?," they project a further transformation of the gas station owner into a real estate mogul. The yacht of the first video is replaced by a massive suburban house that represents the next step up the ladder of entrepreneurship from the gas station into real estate. As another Nepali entrepreneur explained, "We are just replacing the Indians. As they move more into motels/hotels and real estate, we are buying their gas stations."

The South Asian ethnic "niche" of North Texas gas stations is, however, not a simple story of entrepreneurial transfer from one nationality to the next. It is engulfed in the wider social politics of class, gender, and visa status. Feeling forced into gas station jobs reflects, I argue, the intersection of multiple structural forces, what I interpret as mobility regimes, or the structural forces that condition the uneven politics of mobility (Glick Schiller and Salazar 2013). For example, a Kathmandu migration industry that sells the "developed country" destinations without preparation for specific jobs or success; US immigration policy that funnels temporary visa holders into undesirable jobs; a colonial legacy of South Asian labor hierarchies reconstituted in diasporic locations; and, finally, the ethnicization and exploitation of service labor. However, it also reflects the creative adaptations of immigrant workers and entrepreneurs to convert the multi-ethnic milieu of the gas station into social support and business opportunities.

A Short History of South Asian Gas Stations

With the exception of scant media attention to the concentration of Punjabi Sikh owners in New York gas stations (Dhingra 2012; Foreman 1997; Lorch 1992), there is little reliable data regarding South Asian ownership and employment in gas stations and convenience stores. My two years of ethnographic research indicates, however, a pervasive trend of Indian, Pakistani, Nepali, and Bangladeshi nationals involved in the gas stations of DFW. Further, the South Asian prevalence has reflected an alignment between shifts both in immigration policy and trends, and the prevailing market and practices of gas station labor.

From contacts at the US-India DFW Chamber of Commerce, I learned that the "pioneers" of gas stations were an unrelated group of Pakistani and north Indian entrepreneurs who arrived on professional or family reunification visas in the late 1970s and 1980s, often residing and working in the town of Irving (located in the mid-cities stretch between Dallas and Fort Worth). This period aligns with the so-called "third wave" of Asian immigration to the US. While the 1965 Immigration and Nationality Act lifted national quotas and eased entry for "professional" immigrants (called the "second wave"), the bill's provision for family reunification provided a labor supply to meet the neoliberal restructuring of the US economy in the 1980s that increased the low-wage and de-skilled labor of the service economy (Das Gupta 2006, 101).

The third wave also happened to coincide with the conversion of many gas stations into convenience stores. In the wake of the 1970s oil embargo, gas stations needed new ways to maintain their status as a "secular temple" devoted to the country's addiction to cheap gasoline (Huber 2009; Tweedy 2014, 75). The transformation into convenience stores provided one solution by offsetting reductions in gas profits with markups for other products such as beer, bread, and milk (Jakle and Sculle 1994, 80). The shift also feminized and ethnicized gas station labor, and coincided with the economic marginalization of, particularly smaller-scale, shops (Tweedy 2014). For instance, gas stations gained a gendered association with being "man caves" selling cheap food, beer, and possessing dirty bathrooms, while increasingly reliant on female and migrant labor (Tweedy 2014, 119). Further, as Min (1990, 15) notes of Korean-owned gas stations in Los Angeles, the increase of migrant labor was a direct product of companies seeking immigrant owners, who were assumed to have access to cheaper labor sources.

The first Nepali owners invested in their gas stations in the late 1990s just when Nepali immigration to the US started to grow through the diversity visa (or DV) and student visas. Interestingly, of all the owners with whom I spoke, all recalled a similar starting point as workers in stores owned by Pakistanis or Indians. It was not until the later 2000s that Nepalis began investing in gas stations in larger numbers. This moment has coincided with further structural challenges for the gas station market. According to the National Association of Convenience Stores, from 1994 to 2013, the number of US gas stations decreased from 202,800 to 152,995, and early data from the pandemic suggests the situation has since worsened. This decline is often attributed to the drop in gas consumption among rising energy alternatives for personal vehicles as well as a downswing in cigarette sales. As I will discuss, Nepali gas station entrepreneurs have met this challenge with innovating food sales and forming alliances with Latino workers and communities.

From Ethnicity to Mobility: The Regimes and Trajectories of Labor Migration

The concentration of South Asian gas stations in DFW might qualify as an "occupational niche," defined as an over-representation of an ethnic group in one job sector (Brettell and Alstatt 2007; Portes 1995).[3] In the sociology of occupational niches, ethnicity represents a symbol of social capital and networks organized according to trust, solidarity, and reciprocity (Portes and Bach 1985; Portes 1995), which may also be exploited for economic gain (Mahler 1995; Menjívar 2000). Scholarly debates tend to focus on whether ethnic economies exist because of "exceptional" cultural resources (Basu 1998; Werbner 1984), structural discrimination (Bonacich 1993; Min and Bozorgmehr 2000; Portes and Rumbaut 2014; Waldinger and Lichter 2003), or a combination of reasons (Kloosterman and Rath 2001). However, while these debates add insights into the relationship between entrepreneurialism, social networks, and xenophobia, they tend to treat ethnicity unproblematically, often conflating it with nationality.

The conflation of ethnicity and nationality not only perpetuates methodological nationalism (Wimmer and Glick Schiller 2002) but also fails to account for regional cultural similarities that extend beyond national identity. A few ethnographic studies have shown glimpses of how pan-ethnic identities function in various contexts. Low's (2017, 182–94) ethnography of a pan-ethnic Latino market in Brooklyn documents how the nationality of entrepreneurs is spatially marked between Puerto Ricans in the center and Mexicans and Nicaraguans at the periphery. In the case of voluntary associations in DFW, Brettell (2005, 876) has demonstrated examples of social solidarity across Hindu, Indian, South Asian, and Asian organizations. However, while looking beyond nationality, the invocation of a pan-ethnic or regional identity runs the risk of reproducing the "ethnic lens" of methodological nationalism, in which migrants remain understood as fundamentally separate from and outside of national society (Çağlar and Glick Schiller 2018). In this case, although we might understand the category of South Asian immigrant as cut into numerous national, religious, class, and ethnic

---

3 I use occupational niche to distinguish it from ethnic niche, which refers to businesses that predominantly serve co-ethnic or co-immigrant communities (Brettell and Alstatt 2007, 384).

categories, we might still overlook the "common conditions of precarity and displacement that mark the lives of many urban residents" (2018, 12).

Pieke and Xiang (2009) argue that the forces of a post-Fordist global economy based on a deregulated and commercialized international labor market reduce the importance of ethnic economies. According to their study of Chinese migrant laborers in the UK, ethnic ties have become "purely transactional and ephemeral" (2009, 39). Similarly, Jones and Ram (2007) highlight the shared challenges of business that have been overshadowed by ethnic concerns in the literature of immigrant entrepreneurialism. They state, "As a general rule we would argue that immigrant origin entrepreneurs are heavily over-concentrated in a small range of inherently poorly remunerated, labour-intensive activities, some of which are sunset industries on their last legs, *which would be problematic for any entrepreneur of whatever origin*" (2007, 451; emphasis added).

To recognize the politics of ethnicity, as well as social networks, economics, and migration status, I propose we understand the Nepali experience in a South Asian gas stations through a mobility framework, particularly through the concepts of regimes of mobility (Glick Schiller and Salazar 2013) and mobility trajectory (Schapendonk et al. 2020). Such a move is not to remove categories of nationality, or regional ethnicity, from our analysis, but to rather undo the fixed binaries of mobility and stasis, migration and settlement, that tend to privilege a state-centric focus on integration. Further, a mobility framework is not to celebrate movement as emancipatory, but rather to emphasize the uneven power relations and politics of movement (Cresswell 2010; Glick Schiller and Salazar 2013). The concept of regime draws attention to state and international regulation of movement, as well as to how individuals embody subjectivities attached to dislocation. While regimes smoothen the travel of some, often elite travelers, they create barriers, containment, and exploitation for others. The politics of mobility do not simply dictate who can and cannot move, but also how they move, or what Linder (introduction) calls a "second axis" of mobility that "plots the qualities and institutional contexts of such movements."

Schapendonk et al. (2020) have contributed further nuance to the regimes approach by proposing the concept of mobility "trajectory" to emphasize the agency of migrants, particularly from the global south. Instead of studying migrants *in places*, trajectory refers to migrants *through places* to highlight how migrants respond to changing dynamics and challenges imposed by mobility regimes. They refer to a process of "re-routing" to describe the constant adaptations of migrants to the turbulence and uneven conditions of working-class migration. Here, I borrow trajectory to consider migrant narratives of labor as practices of improvisatory agency within the restrictions of US immigration policy and neoliberal conditions of gas station economics. The following ethnographic accounts illustrate the alienation and struggles of gas station labor, while also highlighting the creative adaptations and aspirations of those occupying such ethnicized and forgotten places.

"We Had No One": The Labor Isolation of Diversity & Student Visa Holders

Recognizing the lack of European immigrants after the 1965 reforms, the US Congress included the Diversity Visa (DV) program in the 1990 Immigration Act with the goal of increasing arrivals from Europe, specifically Ireland and Italy (Goodman 2023; Law 2002). The DV grants visas on a lottery system to countries with less than 50,000 annual immigrants to the US. In what Piot (2019, 10) calls "a history in which postcolonial theorists would find delight," the DV has contributed to the post-1965 upward trends of non-European immigration, especially from Asia and Africa (Goodman 2023; Imoagene 2017). Notably, since the US stopped issuing DVs to Bangladesh in 2013 and Nigeria in 2014, Nepal has become the top recipient, averaging 3,400 visas per year since 2015 (US Department of State 2019). Concurrently, the number of Nepali student visas has also consistently risen in the twenty-first century, from the 2,411 in 1999–2000 to 11,581 in 2008–2009, and more recently, 13,270 in 2017–2018, making Nepal the eleventh highest nationality (IIE 2018).

Unlike professional visas, the DV and student visa programs have created a consistent supply of laborers without prearranged jobs or extensive social networks. As Imoagene (2017) documented in her study of Nigerian DV-holders, the program does not provide support for immigrants once they reach the US, often leaving them compelled to take difficult and exploitative jobs. For Nepalis, the lack of choice is also the consequence of a Kathmandu sending industry that recruits through a developmentalist discourse highlighting the destination country while underemphasizing the actual job details (Shrestha 2018). For example, student visa applicants often rely on educational consultancies to gain admission letters and obtain visas, even inflating their family's income to prove self-sufficiency (Adhikari 2010; Thieme 2017). Unsurprisingly, consultancies do not prepare students for life in the US, leaving many unable to cover tuition and living expenses. As a result, they are forced into taking low-paying service-sector jobs and often into discontinuing their education (Hangen 2018, 235; Sijapati 2011).

Where they find those jobs is often dependent on South Asian business networks within low-paying service economy occupations.

Arjun arrived in the US in 2014 on a DV. Inspired by the possible earnings of the US and the educational opportunities for their daughter, he and his wife, Smriti, decided to use the visa to relocate and leave their rented Kathmandu apartment and her civil service job. While most of Arjun's friends had migrated to *khadi desh* (Arab Peninsula), he felt much luckier to be able to go to the US. However, this optimism quickly faded when confronted with a lack of support upon arrival in the US. When Arjun and Smriti received news of the DV, everyone they knew in the US called them over the phone, saying *aijao, aijao* (come, come). But, after arriving, they found that their contacts did not have time to help them. They added, "They talk one way, but their behavior is a different way." Smriti attributed the change to the *pāch minet hisāb* of American life. Literally translated as "five-minute math," this phrase reflects the calculated and regulated nature of work in the US. Arjun continued, "In Nepal, if you are supposed to show up at ten, people arrive at eleven. We have a culture of sitting around and chatting, but not in the US." Although the DV application required a "letter of sponsorship" from his *bahini* ("cousin sister") in Denver, when they arrived, they found that she did not have time to help, and they found Colorado unaffordable.

Smriti and Arjun then moved to the Jackson Heights neighborhood of Queens, New York, an area historically associated with Indian immigrants but more recently inhabited by Bangladeshis, Nepalis, and Tibetans (Hangen 2018). Arjun recalled, "A friend called me saying it was easy here, lots of jobs, and that we wouldn't need a car in New York." But they found it was too difficult to find work and reliable housing in the big city. Arjun explained, "I would cry at night" out of fear that they would not be able to pay off loans. To obtain the visa and airline tickets, they sought the services and debt of a Kathmandu consulting agency, leaving them with just enough savings for one to two months of living without an income in the States.

While in New York, Arjun conducted a frantic Facebook search for social contacts in the US. He connected with a friend from his village in the southwestern district of Kapilvastu. After becoming reacquainted virtually, they started talking over the phone. The friend then invited Arjun to North Texas and promised, like his other contacts had, to find him housing and work. Arjun recalled, "I said no, imagining it would be the same as before. Why go through the pain again?" But, then his friend did something the others had not. He bought Arjun a ticket to come to Dallas.

As soon as Arjun arrived, he started working at a gas station. He was trained by an Indian coworker, someone he described as "despite being

Indian, he was just like us, from a village." He referred to his boss, Mr. Manzoor, with a similar phrase: "Even though he is a Pakistani, he has honor." This "honor" was earned by keeping a promise to hire Smriti to work alongside Arjun within one year of starting. They referred to Mr. Manzoor as eating the same food and speaking the same language ("Hindustani"). But, their similarities end there, Arjun insisted, refusing any identification with the term "South Asian." Arjun pointed to the gas station's taqueria to explain: "The women behind the counter are Nicaraguan, not Mexican, even though we see the two as the same, Spanish. Like that, Nepalis and Pakistanis."

The social isolation of new immigrants is common to hear, especially among DV holders. While Arjun ultimately found work and a permanent location due to a village contact, others often seek work through labor agencies. In interviews, immigrants referred to such agencies as "consultancies," which are often run by South Asians and considered exploitative for taking commissions. According to a consultancy manager I interviewed, jobs in gas stations are always available but least desired. He repeated the cultural perception of Nepalis as "loyal" and "hardworking," as well as their understanding of Hindi, as reasons for South Asian owners to hire them, an observation that multiple owners confirmed. Perhaps accounting for Arjun's "even though" reluctance, he noted that Nepali workers tended to think of Indians and Pakistanis as likely to cheat them.

Nepalis Working for Indians: The Subtle Adaptations within a Pan-ethnic Labor Hierarchy

Arjun's reluctant entrance into Indian and Pakistani work partnerships reflects a long history of Nepalis tending to occupy subordinate positions within South Asian labor configurations. Whether as labor migrants for the expansionist or military projects of British imperialism (des Chene 1993; Hutt 2003; Nath 2003) or as guards and domestic workers in postcolonial Indian cities (Thieme 2006), the open border and long history of binational labor migration between Nepal and India has often positioned Nepalis as neither foreigner nor native (Sharma 2018). Their liminal situation accounts for their perception in India as "brave, hardworking, trustworthy, honest and cheap labor" (Bruslé 2008, 244).[4] The more recent global expansion of

---

4 Of the three major waves of Nepali migration history, the first two are connected to India (Gellner 2018). The first wave emerged out of the labor created through colonial needs to build

Nepal's migration industry since the 1990s has further contributed to the economic marginalization of migrants in South Asian frameworks.

In some cases, Nepalis must travel via informal outlets in India to avoid the governmental regulation of migrant labor destinations (Ahmad 2017; Coburn 2016). More commonly, it is recruitment, or "manpower," agencies in Kathmandu that send working-class migrants directly to employers who provide contract-based visas in the Arabian Peninsula, or Gulf, and in Southeast Asia, often in the construction or service industry (Kern and Müller-Böker 2015). There, as well, the image of Nepali workers as "brave, hardworking, obedient, and easy to satisfy" (Bruslé 2018, 213) reinforces their subordinate position at the bottom of migrant hierarchies (Gardner et al. 2013).

Although Nepali immigrants to the US tend to be more educated than their conationals working in India and the Gulf, many experience a similar downward mobility stuck in "South Asian enclaves." Bohra-Mishra (2011) attributes the precarious condition of Nepalis in the US to timing, in that they have immigrated to the US after other South Asian groups. She claims, "Given the relatively new nature of Nepalese migration and the abundance of pre-existing and incoming South Asians, these Nepalis often become part of the South Asian enclave" (1533). Especially for migrants without college degrees or sufficient English ability, they turn to migrant-focused employment agencies who can find work rapidly, but with little to no possibility for advancement (Hangen and Ranjit 2010, 20). For example, the ability to understand Hindi "opens up some employment opportunities" with Indian employers, but mostly for low-paying jobs (20).[5]

In Hamal Gurung's (2015) ethnography of Nepali domestic laborers working for Indian employers in New York City, "South Asian" refers to an identity imposed by non-South Asians.[6] She claims, "Although in the United States

---

roads, clear forests, and work in mines and plantations in the northeast areas of Sikkim, Assam, Burma, and Bhutan, as well as the Gurkha regiments serving in the British and Indian militaries. The second wave emerged in the postcolonial moment of urbanization which attracted laborers for domestic work, security, and factories to Indian cities.

5   Hangen and Ranjit (2010, 21) note that exploitation is not limited to Indian employers but includes "other South Asian employers… including the Nepali employers." Similarly, Nepalis are not the only South Asians occupying subordinate positions, as Kibria (2007) notes, "Bangladeshis and Nepalis are far more likely to be working for Indian or Pakistani business owners than the other way around."

6   While commonly used among social scientists, it is debatable to what extent "South Asian" qualifies as a category with which immigrants identify in the North American diaspora. In Canada, for instance, Ghosh (2013, 44) argues that South Asian is configured according to the racial logics of white settler society, which is, in turn, internalized as only referring to

Indians and Nepalis are lumped into a single pan-ethnic category as South Asian, outside of this context Indians and Nepalis do not see themselves as part of the same group" (2015, 69). While the employers seek out Nepali domestics for their comprehension of Hindi, familiarity with vegetarian food, and Hinduism, such cultural proximity allows for a "colonial mentality" of exploitation to pervade these relationships (2015, 69–71). To the more established Indian employer, Nepali nationality symbolizes poverty and desperation regardless of the migrant's actual socioeconomic background (2015, 68). Amid the exploitation of Nepalis working for foreign employers, studies also show the occasional and subtle responses to unequal conditions. In the fuzzy relations of domestic laborers in between family member and foreigner, Ahmad (2017) highlights conversions to Islam as a gradual process of adaptation, while Hamal Gurung (2015) stresses how workers leverage the subtle codependency of South Asian employers. I observed similar tactics of Nepali migrants in Chile and Ecuador to exploit immigration policy loopholes and pan-diasporic labor relations to further migration possibilities (Nelson 2023).

The worker-to-owner story of Gyanu provides a similar narrative of subtle adaptation within the South Asian diaspora of Texas gas stations. She arrived in the US in 1996 on a business visa to Los Angeles but soon thereafter had to move to Texas to care for an ill nephew.[7] In the northern Dallas suburbs, she found work in a Pakistani-owned gas station. After four months, the boss promoted her to manager, which required her to be responsible for the store's banking and ordering. This promotion allowed her to bring her children to the US three years later, as well as to start considering buying her own gas station.

As most of her contacts in the Nepali community were students, she knew few people who could invest in her business. Importantly, she felt alienated from the "professional Nepalis" in DFW at the time whom she recalled "keeping their distance from us gas stations workers." She explained, "They were not helpful, didn't want to deal with us, especially the ones who were settled." She used the term "settled" to refer to those with established businesses. She went on to describe the Nepali bias against gas station work:

university-educated, young, and middle-class migrants. Additionally, it remains unclear to many whether the category extends beyond areas colonized by the British to also include Nepal, Afghanistan, or Bhutan (Ghosh 2013, 36). For our purposes, it is worth asking how South Asian or the more colloquial reference of *desi* create relations of solidarity across national identities or are undermined by unequal relations based on social differences.

7   A business, or B-1 visa, to the US is a non-immigrant temporary visa given to individuals for the purpose of consultation, conference attendance, or contract negotiation.

"They think of us as lower, as working long hours, always on our feet working in very dangerous settings." She also experienced gender discrimination in the doubts she heard about a woman owning a gas station. She remembered, "They would say they were worried about a female in the dangerous space of the gas station, so I had to be tough."[8]

A distinction between professional and service labor speaks to a class differentiation within the Nepali diaspora in the US that is often based on visa status. Gyanu and her station's workers pointed out to me an internal hierarchy separating permanent from temporary visa-holders. Permanent resident (or green card) card-holders are further divided between the professional (employment-based or "EB" visas) and the seemingly more working-class DV or refugee visa-holders. Similarly, temporary, or non-immigrant, visas split the more prestigious H-1B-holders (employer-sponsored for jobs that require specialty knowledge) from the F1-holders (students), followed by undocumented migrants, and those covered under the post-2015 Temporary Protected Status (TPS) program.[9]

Without access to investor networks based on shared Nepali nationality, Gyanu sought support through personal contacts. When her boss learned of her entrepreneurial interest, he offered to help. But, she responded, "I told him, 'I don't want to work with you, I wouldn't be comfortable. I know how you are.' He was an okay boss, but only good for himself, he was picky, not bad, just okay." Instead, she turned to a friend, another gas station owner who also happened to be Pakistani, for business advice. Importantly, though, she insisted on limiting his role in the venture, as she "didn't want to work for someone else." Instead of partnering with him, she saw him as a mentor who guided her to a contact at a financing bank. He helped her apply for her licenses, a sales tax permit, and tobacco permit because, as she clarified, "I didn't want to hire an agent and waste $1,500 for advice I could learn on my own." She explained that she now had her children to rely on: "Eventually, my son taught me the computer. He knows how to run the station, our family business." She has since purchased and sold additional gas stations and a laundromat with several Nepali partners, but significantly looks back at

---

8   The threat of violence represents the largest fear of workers with whom I spoke. They each had a story of being robbed or of a coworker who has been robbed. According to my informal observations of news stories, I counted seven Nepalis having been murdered in US gas stations over the past decade, four of whom were in Texas.

9   Temporary Protected Status grants temporary visa and work status to citizens of countries that are deemed unsafe. The program was granted to Nepalis by the Obama administration after the 2015 earthquake but rescinded by the Trump administration in 2018. As of writing, the Biden administration has renewed the program through 2025.

her original business with pride—as a leader for both Nepalis and women in gas station ownership.

Gyanu's success reflects her selective alliances with other South Asian gas station owners, but also with the connections to the Latino community surrounding her business. Referring to Latinos in the area, she explained, "They have been here for 200 years, so they are as old as any other community." She counts many Spanish-speakers as "loyal customers, people who I have known for twenty to thirty years. They've even invited me to their children's weddings." She knows a bit of Spanish, and her son is fluent. Further, she has embraced the adoption of her store as the day laborer pick-up spot in town, a space associated with undocumented migrant workers. She identified the benefit of the workers in saying, "Them standing there much of the day makes the store much safer. It creates business and keeps away anyone planning a robbery." In addition to providing safety, she saw the surrounding community's loyalty as economic protection against the growth of mega-gas stations, which can afford to offer lower gas prices because of their substantial convenience store earnings.

Working in the "Other America"

As seen in the multicultural references of Swami D and PSPN, gas stations owned by South Asians in DFW tend to be located in diverse, working-class neighborhoods.[10] For one Nepali worker, who goes by Kancho Bhai (meaning "youngest brother"), the nationality of his boss was irrelevant (he happened to be Nepali); rather, it is his customers from what he called the "other America" that informed his work experience. As a resettled refugee from Bhutan,[11] he joked about the misleading cultural orientations he received before leaving the camps in southeast Nepal, which focused primarily on financial matters of survival in the US with very little social education. He recalled, while laughing, being told to "never make eye contact with Black Americans." Being initially resettled in the poorer Seminary Boulevard area of Fort Worth, he quickly became acquainted with the multiracial prevalence of US poverty. He characterized his customer base at a nearby gas station

---

10   One gas station owner, who had stores in both "rich and poor neighborhoods," lamented that wealthy neighborhood stations are not profitable because the rich looked down upon gas station food.

11   Although refugees technically receive temporary visas, they automatically become eligible to apply for permanent residency after one year, and citizenship after five years in the US.

as "white, black, brown, and all poor." From my observations at the store, I have heard Kancho be called "Indian," but most often people assume him to be a Spanish-speaking Latino. Kancho played with this perception as seen in the following dialogue that occurred when a customer requested a money order in Spanish:

> Kancho: *Cuantos*? (How much?)
> Customer: *Cien* (A hundred)

Kancho winked at me and explained in Nepali that he can count to a thousand in Spanish.

> Customer: *Conoces* Cleburne? (Do you know Cleburne? [a nearby town])
> Kancho: *No soy Espanol, soy Nepali, solo apriendo Espanol* (I am not Spanish, I am Nepali, I'm only learning Spanish.)

As Hamal Gurung (2015, 69) observes about Nepalis (and other South Asians) in the States, they are often mistaken for East Asian, Middle Eastern, Black, or Latino. This phenotypic confusion is by no means unique but rather common for how immigrant groups in the US are racialized into an ambiguous middle space between the dominant poles of white and Black (Ong 2000). The ambiguous racialization of South Asian gas station attendants can be exploited as witnessed in the brown-face caricature of Apu on *The Simpsons* (Melamedoff 2017), or even made violent as in the post-9/11 hate crimes at DFW gas stations that killed Waqar Hasan and Vasudev Patel, and injured Rais Bhuiyan (Brettell 2006, 108). However, for Kancho, racial ambiguity creates space to explore solidarities that he might not otherwise experience. Based on his experience as a refugee in Nepal, he related to the marginalization of the "other America."

The Momo Gas Station

While the narrative of Nepali gas station worker-to-entrepreneur has followed a South Asian example, the emergence of gas station "momo stands" follows a Latin American immigrant tradition of gas station taquerias. Although gas stations often serve food, the specific restaurant-within-store idea in North Texas started with convenience store taquerias opening in the 1980s. While the restaurant entrepreneur benefits from the cheaper rent of the gas station, the station ownership benefits from more customers entering to buy not only gas, cigarettes, and other items but also food. Due to the decrease of gas and cigarette sales, industry experts see food and restaurants as the future of the industry (Mastroberte 2017).[12] The menu of the Nepali gas station counter is based on the popular snack food of the *momo*, a Nepali-style dumpling.

Prajwal owns one such *momo* stand counter in a gas station. He arrived on a student visa in 2006, and immediately took a job in a Pakistani-owned gas station. He left this work as soon as he graduated and became a corporate accountant. However, with his brother, who was working as a banker in Dallas, they aspired to own their own business. They noticed that none of the area South Asian restaurants offered delivery services, but they did not want to commit to opening their own restaurant. Instead, they rented an industrial kitchen and started delivering *momos*. Responding to demand, but still uncertain about the liability of a full restaurant, they negotiated a deal with a Nepali friend who owned a gas station to convert the station's small back area into a momo counter. The success inspired them to open a second momo counter in another Nepali-owned station that already had a taqueria connected to it and a larger eating area.

In hopes of expanding his market, Prajwal defined his mission to "educate" non-Nepalis about the momo. At the opening of his business, he estimated that ninety percent of customers were Nepalis, the other ten percent South Asian. But, due to outreach at food festivals, non-South Asian consumers are increasing, arguably part of a growing trend of "foodie" interest in the momo (Kugel 2019). He has since gone on to start an annual Momo Fest where area restaurants serve the dish during a party in the central public park of the DFW mid-city, Arlington.

According to Prajwal, the problem facing his and other momo stands is the stigma associated with the gas station. Whereas the taqueria is an established gas station option in Texas, other food traditions have not taken root. The gas station stigma applies to Prajwal's struggles to hire and keep staff. He reluctantly admitted that the momo counter has not changed the perception of gas station labor. He imagined that "If I were selling momos inside a restaurant with waiters and white table-cloths, staff would come because that is prestigious. No one wants to work in a gas station, and especially not in a kitchen in a gas station." Nonetheless, he has noticed

---

12   Although receiving little academic attention, gas station restaurants, often serving "ethnic food," have gained media attention in Washington D.C. (Rosenwald 2013), Los Angeles (Wang 2017), and across the urban spectrum (McLaughlin 2011) for their attractive "low start-up costs, guaranteed foot traffic and a little bit of kitsch" (Rosenwald 2013).

other professionals, like himself, more willing to invest in gas stations. Unlike the early days of Gyanu's entry in the 1990s, when the professional class shunned gas station enterprises, the emergence of a larger Nepali community, even a Nepali Chamber of Commerce, has elevated the industry's perception. Gas stations, as one key community member explained to me, "are a stepping stone to bigger money-making opportunities in real estate and consultancies."

Conclusion

By all accounts, the mobilities of global migrants often reproduce diasporic social relations that extend beyond nationality to include regional connections based on shared cultural practices, language, and political histories. Similar to the experiences of Nepalis working in India and the Gulf, South Asian hierarchical labor structures in the US tend to reproduce a paternalist treatment of Nepalis as pliable workers who share certain cultural attributes. The experiences of Nepalis working in North Texas gas stations offers one such case in point. However, if we understand this case from a mobility framework, the case reveals much more than a pan-ethnic labor diaspora.

The common trend of Nepalis working in Pakistani- or Indian-owned gas stations is a product of a US mobility regime funneling temporary visa holders into undesirable service labor. Of the four highlighted participants in this study, all but one (the DV is technically an immigrant visa) entered the US on a temporary visa with few job options other than the South Asian gas station. All expressed mixed experiences with South Asian bosses, often finding a select boss or coworker in whom to place trust and seek support, regardless of their nationality. Further, their workplace locations tend to inhabit neglected and disinvested urban areas more associated with poverty than any one ethnicity. As Prajwal and Gyanu indicated, a class stigma remains attached to working in the gas station despite the prevalence of the job for recent immigrants from Nepal.

And yet, although none of the four envisioned the gas station work as a professional goal, their migrant labor trajectories remain rooted in the gas station, two as workers and two as owners. Regardless of their current status, however, they tended to share two points with PSPN and Swami D's portrayal. One, the social relations of their gas station experience reflect a cross-ethnic and cross-immigrant social milieu that occasionally blossoms into innovation, mutual help, and solidarity. Second, and finally, the gas station remains at the foundation of their aspirations.

References

Adhikari, Radhika. 2010. "'The Dream-Trap': Brokering 'Study Abroad' and Nurse Migration from Nepal to the UK." *European Bulletin for Himalayan Research* 35–36: 122–32.

Ahmad, Attiya. 2017. *Everyday Conversions: Islam, Domestic Work, and South Asian Migrant Women in Kuwait*. Durham: Duke University Press.

Basu, Anuradha. 1998. "An Exploration of Entrepreneurial Activity among Asian Small Businesses in Britain." *Small Business Economics* 10: 313–26.

Bohra-Mishra, Pratikshya. 2011. "Nepalese Migrants in the United States of America: Perspectives on Their Exodus, Assimilation Pattern and Commitment to Nepal." *Journal of Ethnic and Migration Studies* 37 (9): 1527–37.

Bonacich, Edna. 1993. "The Other Side of Ethnic Entrepreneurship: A Dialogue with Waldinger, Aldrich, Ward and Associates." *International Migration Review* 27 (3): 685–92.

Brettell, Caroline B. 2005. "Voluntary Organizations, Social Capital, and the Social Incorporation of Asian Indian Immigrants in the Dallas-Fort Worth Metroplex." *Anthropological Quarterly* 78 (4): 853–83.

Brettell, Caroline B. 2006. "Wrestling with 9/11: Immigrant Perceptions and Perceptions of Immigrants." *Migration Letters* 3 (2): 107–24.

Brettell, Caroline B., and Kristoffer E. Alstatt. 2007. "The Agency of Immigrant Entrepreneurs: Biographies of the Self-Employed in Ethnic and Occupational Niches of the Urban Labor Market." *Journal of Anthropological Research* 63 (3): 383–97.

Bruslé, Tristan. 2008. "Choosing a Destination and Work: Migration Strategies of Nepalese Workers in Uttarakhand, Northern India." *Mountain Research and Development, International Mountain Society* 28 (3–4): 240–47.

Bruslé, Tristan. 2010. "Who's in a Labour Camp? A Socio-economic Analysis of Labour Migrants in Qatar." *European Bulletin of Himalayan Research* 35–36: 154–70.

Bruslé, Tristan. 2012. "What Kind of Place is this? Daily Life, Privacy and the Inmate Metaphor in a Nepalese Workers' Labour Camp (Qatar)." *Samaj* 6. doi.org/10.4000/samaj.3446.

Bruslé, Tristan. 2018. "'No One Wants to Go Abroad; It's All about Obligation': What Migration Means to Nepali Workers in Qatar." In *Global Nepalis: Religion, Culture, and Community in a New and Old Diaspora*, edited by David Gellner and Sondra Hausner, 210–28. New Delhi: Oxford University Press.

Çağlar, Ayşe, and Nina Glick Schiller. 2018. *Migrants & City-Making: Dispossession, Displacement, and Urban Regeneration*. Durham: Duke University Press.

Coburn, Noah. 2016. *Labouring under Fire: Nepali Security Contractors in Afghanistan*. Kathmandu: Centre for the Study of Labour and Mobility (CESLAM). Research Paper VIII.

Cresswell, Tim. 2010. "Towards a Politics of Mobility." *Environment and Planning D: Society and Space* 28 (1): 17–31.

Das Gupta, Monisha. 2006. *Unruly Immigrants: Rights, Activism, and Transnational South Asian Politics in the United States.* Durham: Duke University Press.

Des Chene, Mary. 1993. "Soldiers, Sovereignty and Silences: Gorkhas as Diplomatic Currency." *Comparative Studies of South Asia, Africa and the Middle East* 13 (1/2): 67–80.

Dhingra, Pawan. 2012. *Life Behind the Lobby: Indian American Motel Owners and the American Dream.* Stanford: Stanford University Press.

Foreman, Jonathan. 1997. "Bombay on the Hudson." *City Journal* (Summer). Accessed on June 1, 2022. https://www.city-journal.org/html/bombay-hudson-11881.html

Gardner, Andrew, Silvia Pessoa, Abdoulaye Diop, Kaltham Al-Ghanim, Kien Le Trung, and Laura Harkness. 2013. "A Portrait of Low-Income Migrants in Contemporary Qatar." *Journal of Arabian Studies* 3 (1): 1–17.

Gellner, David. 2018. "Introduction: The Nepali/Gorkhali Diaspora since the Nineteenth Century." In *Global Nepalis: Religion, Culture, and Community in a New and Old Diaspora*, edited by David Gellner and Sondra Hausner, 1–26. New Delhi: Oxford University Press.

Ghosh, Sutama. 2013. "'Am I a South Asian, Really?' Constructing 'South Asians' in Canada and Being South Asian in Toronto." *South Asian Diaspora* 5 (1): 35–55.

Glick Schiller, Nina, and Noel B. Salazar. 2013. "Regimes of Mobility Across the Globe." *Journal of Ethnic and Migration Studies* 39 (2): 183–200.

Goodman, Carly. 2023. *Dreamland: America's Immigration Lottery in an Age of Restriction.* Chapel Hill: University of North Carolina Press.

Hamal Gurung, Shobha. 2015. *Nepali Migrant Women: Resistance & Survival in America.* Syracuse: Syracuse University Press.

Hangen, Susan. 2018. "Transnational Politics in Nepali Organizations in New York." In *Global Nepalis: Religion, Culture, and Community in a New and Old Diaspora*, edited by David Gellner and Sondra Hausner, 229–46. New Delhi: Oxford University Press.

Hangen, Susan, and Luna Ranjit. 2010. *Snapshots of the Nepali-Speaking Community in New York City: Demographics and Challenges.* New York: Adhikaar for Human Rights and Social Justice.

Huber, Matthew. 2009. "The Use of Gasoline: Value, Oil, and the 'American Way of Life.'" *Antipode* 41 (3): 465–86.

Hutt, Michael. 2003. *Unbecoming Citizens: Culture, Nationhood, and the Flight of Refugees from Bhutan.* New Delhi: Oxford University Press.

Imoagene, Onoso. 2017. "Affecting Lives: How Winning the US Diversity Visa Lottery Impacts DV Migrants Pre- and Post-Migration." *International Migration* 55 (6): 170–83.

Institute of International Education (IIE). 2018. *Report on International Education Exchange*. New York: IIE Research.

Jakle, John A. and Keith A. Sculle. 1994. *The Gas Station in America*. Baltimore: Johns Hopkins University.

Jones, Trevor, and Monder Ram. 2007. "Re-Embedding the Ethnic Business Agenda." *Work, Employment and Society* 21 (3): 439–57.

Kern, Alice, and Ulrike Müller-Böker. 2015. "The Middle Space of Migration: A Case Study of Brokerage and Recruitment Agencies in Nepal." *Geoforum* 65: 158–69.

Kibria, Nazli. 2007. "South Asia." In *New Americans: A Guide to Immigration Since 1965*, edited by Mary C. Waters, Reed Ueda, and Helen B. Marrow. Cambridge: Harvard University Press.

Kloosterman, Robert C., and Jan Rath. 2001. "Immigrant Entrepreneurs in Advanced Economies: Mixed Embeddedness Further Explored." *Journal of Ethnic and Migration Studies* 27 (2): 189–201.

Kugel, Seth. 2019. "A Whirlwind, Round-the-World Food Tour of Queens." *New York Times*, July 1, 2019. Accessed on June 1, 2022. https://www.nytimes.com/2019/07/01/travel/queens-new-york-city-international-food-scene.html.

Law, Anna O. 2002. "The Diversity Visa Lottery: A Cycle of Unintended Consequences in United States Immigration Policy." *Journal of American Ethnic History* 21 (4): 3–29.

Lorch, Donatella. 1992. "An Ethnic Road to Riches: The Immigrant Job Specialty." *New York Times*, January 12, 1992.

Low, Setha. 2017. *Spatializing Culture: The Ethnography of Space and Place*. Abingdon: Routledge.

Mahler, Sarah. 1995. *American Dreaming*. Princeton: Princeton University Press.

Mastroberte, Tammy. 2017. "Reflections and Learnings from Outgoing NACS Chairman Rahim Budhwani." *Convenience Store News*, October 10, 2017. Accessed on June 1, 2022. https://csnews.com/reflections-learnings-outgoing-nacs-chairman-rahim-budhwani.

McLaughlin, Katy. 2011. "Introducing Texaco-Mex." *Wall Street Journal*, February 26, 2011. Accessed on June 1, 2022. https://www.wsj.com/articles/SB10001424052748704900004576152603082214370.

Melamedoff, Michael, dir. 2017. *The Problem with Apu*. TruTV.

Min, Pyong Gap. 1990. "Korean Immigrants in Los Angeles." ISSR Working Papers in the Social Sciences, Institute for Social Science Research, University of California at Los Angeles.

Min, Pyong Gap, and Mehdi Bozorgmehr. 2000. "Immigrant Entrepeneurship and Business Patterns: A Comparison of Koreans and Iranians in Los Angeles." *International Migration Review* 34 (3): 707–38.

Nath, Lopita. 2003. *The Nepalis in Assam: Ethnicity and Cross Border Movements in the North-East*. Calcutta: Minerva Associates.

Nelson, Andrew. 2023. "Going to 'Let-in America': Transit, Geographic Imagination, and Labor in Nepali Migration to and through South America." *Studies in Nepali History and Society* 28 (1): 3–34.

Pieke, Frank N., and Biao Xiang. 2009. "Legality and Labour: Chinese Migration, Neoliberalism and the State in the UK and China." *Geopolitics, History, and International Relations* 1 (1): 11–45.

Piot, Charles. 2019. *The Fixer: Visa Lottery Chronicles*. Durham: Duke University Press.

Portes, Alejandro. 1995. "Economic Sociology and the Sociology of Immigration: A Conceptual Overview." In *The Economic Sociology of Immigration*, edited by Alejandro Portes, 1–41. New York: Russell Sage Foundation.

Portes, Alejandro, and Robert L. Bach. 1985. *Latin Journey: Cuban and Mexican Immigrants in the United States*. Berkeley: University of California Press.

Portes, Alejandro, and Rubén G. Rumbaut. 2014. *Immigrant America: A Portrait*. Berkeley: University of California Press.

Ong, Aihwa. 2000. "Cultural Citizenship as Subject Making: Immigrants Negotiate Racial and Cultural Boundaries in the United States." In *Race, Identity and Citizenship: A Reader*, edited by Rodolfo Torres, Luis Mirón, and Jonathan Xavier Inda, 262–94. Malden: Blackwell Publishers.

Rosenwald, Michael. 2013. "Gas Station Restaurants are Becoming the Next Big Thing in Cuisine." *Washington Post*, September 28, 2013.

Schapendonk, Joris, Ilse van Liempt, Inga Schwarz, and Griet Steel. 2020. "Re-routing Migration Geographies: Migrants, Trajectories and Mobility Regimes." *Geoforum* 116: 211–16.

Sharma, Jeevan Raj. 2018. *Crossing the Border to India: Youth, Migration, and Masculinities in Nepal*. Philadelphia: Temple University Press.

Shrestha, Tina. 2018. "Aspirational Infrastructure: Everyday Brokerage and the Foreign-Employment Recruitment Agencies in Nepal." *Pacific Affairs* 91 (4): 673–93.

Sijapati, Bandita. 2011. *Learning Democracy: Political Socialization, Transnationalism and the Nepali Diaspora*. PhD diss., Syracuse University.

Thieme, Susan. 2006. *Social Networks and Migration: Far West Nepalese Labour Migrants in Delhi*. Münster: LIT Verlag.

Thieme, Susan. 2017. "Educational Consultants in Nepal: Professionalization of Services for Students Who Want to Study Abroad." *Mobilities* 12 (2): 243–58.

Tweedy, Amy Jo. 2014. "Laboring Lesbians at Gas Stations: Pumping the 'Good Life'." PhD diss., Syracuse University.

US Department of State. 2019. "Diversity Visa Program Statistics." Accessed June 19, 2022. https://travel.state.gov/content/travel/en/us-visas/immigrate/diversity-visa-program-entry/dv-2018-selected-entrants.html.

Waldinger, Roger, and Michael Lichter. 2003. *How the Other Half Works: Immigration and the Social Organization of Labor.* Berkeley: University of California Press.

Wang, Andy. 2017. "Some of the Best Indian Food in L.A. Is Served Inside a Gas Station." *Food & Wine*, October 3, 2017.

Werbner, Pnina. 1984. "Business on Trust: Pakistani Entrepreneurs in the Manchester Garment Trade." In *Ethnic Communities in Business*, edited by Robin Ward and Richard Jenkins, 166–88. Cambridge: Cambridge University Press.

Wimmer, Andreas, and Nina Glick Schiller. 2002. "Methodological Nationalism and the Study of Migration." *European Journal of Sociology* 43 (2): 217–40.

About the author

Andrew Nelson is an applied cultural anthropologist at the University of North Texas. His scholarship has focused on Nepali urbanism, refugee resettlement, and transit migration. With Rob Curran, he is the author of *Journey without End: Migration from the Global South through the Americas* (Vanderbilt University Press, 2022).

8 Sometimes She Stands Like a Statue: Immobility in the Archives of Colonial Psychiatry

Sarah Pinto

Abstract: This chapter considers the way the body, especially the still and silent body, has elicited theorizations on the nature of the social and its relationship to selves and bodies. Asking how diagnosing was the site of tacit theorization in early twentieth-century India, it considers connections between psychiatry, colonial rule, documentary knowledge, and politics of knowing. In late colonial India, psychiatrists, often working in carceral institutions, used interlinked concepts such as hysteria, melancholic stupor, and psychocoma to ask how bodies respond to the world. Their diagnostic efforts reinscribed, and in some instances resisted, racialized and gendered moral categories.

Keywords: stillness, immobility, psychiatry, colonial medicine, racialization, India

The concept of "mobility," as descriptor, analytic, and critical intervention, arguably has diverse genealogies. Influential concepts, texts, and orientations in philosophy, literary studies, dance studies, and the social sciences all bring their political, cultural, and infrastructural contexts to bear on the concept. As more recent interventions in mobility studies have shown, the valorization of movement, as defined against stasis and immobility, is no longer tenable, as the introduction to this volume and Friedner and Staples (Chapter 9, this volume) note. Rather, it becomes important to consider genealogies not just of movement but also of *theorizations* of movement, and of movement and stillness together, to ask what political architectures may orient the analytics of "mobility," past and present. The interdependence

---

Linder, Benjamin, & Tarini Bedi (eds), *South Asia on the Move: Mobilities, Mobilizations, Maneuvers*. Amsterdam: Amsterdam University Press 2025
doi: 10.5117/9789463726498_CH08

and entanglement of movement and stasis in theorizations bring to light, often, the parameters of what might be considered a "disability," and, to paraphrase Friedner and Staples (this volume), mobility in and of conditions of "disorder." Movement and stasis as disorder provide conditions that can be historicized, with possibilities for understanding the ways concepts of "mobility" are deployed in our own era.

One such genealogy for "mobility" is medicine and, especially, medicine as it was practiced and theorized in colonial times and places, and on and by colonized peoples. In such contexts, it becomes clear that the parameters of disorder and abnormality become raced as they become "cultured" at the points of contact of movement and stasis, of broken and disordered movement and pathological stillness. In other words, stillness as pathology is part of an archive of theorizations of mobility that link the latter, indelibly, to histories of forced movement and of forced stillness.

Another point of entry for this history is to ask, how does a symptom such as stillness become paradigmatic of cultural difference? What are the stakes of such a process? And what other, contrapuntal work might come of the way movement/stillness come to stand for difference in racial and cultural terms?

In the later years of British rule in India, as the Indian medical system was increasingly "indigenizing" and new, large psychiatric institutions were emblems less of colonial power and neglect than of the potential of modern science for an emerging nation, the political stakes of understanding mental affliction condensed around a hoary diagnosis—hysteria—and a set of symptoms deemed, in some quarters, characteristically "Indian." Catatonia, temporary paralysis, trance-like states, syncopes, waxy rigidity, and other instances of stilled movement were, by the early twentieth century, grounded in divergent kinds of thought work. In those decades, doctors often stumbled onto, and over, "peculiar" crises of movement, frozen postures deemed "queer" and "fantastical," their "silent and motionless" patients defying and frustrating by failing to divulge their histories (Ewens 1908, 71; Noronha 1926). But in offering inscrutable subjects, immobile bodies and inaccessible subjects also fascinated, stirring doctors to draft and send copious cases to medical journals.

Crises of movement invited not one but several repertoires of attention. For many, the still body was a mystery for which the answer was *locality*—culture, custom, psychological traits tied to race or ethnicity or gender in many instances, more diffuse senses of environment in others. That *immobility* was read toward locality in contexts of violent *displacement* suggests as much about colonial medical logics and their relationship to political orders as it does about bodies, minds, and violent conditions.[1] Thus, in the early decades of the twentieth century, as individuals and groups were relocated through colonial rule, physicians—Indian and European—discussed the prevalence of symptoms of immobility in India, whether and how they were characteristically "Indian," asking what that difference might consist of. In their attentions, acts of clinical difference-making, often in the form of differential diagnosing, met civilizational difference-making, in the form of race and nascent concepts of culture, in some instances on a continuum with environments, politics, social worlds, and their violences, in others severed from them. Importantly, Indian doctors were very much part of this scene. They were a diverse cadre of practitioners working in difference scenes of colonial rule and writing to diverse audiences. Many of their engagements with immobility were counterpoint to the work colonial medicine did with immobile bodies. So, too, they challenge our own sense that colonial knowledge practices were singular or seamless in their use of mental affliction to enforce racialized difference.

Frozen movement had long prompted colonial medical observers to wax theoretical. In the nineteenth century, immobility, a problem that raised basic questions about the human condition, troubling notions of will, agency, and consciousness, met colonial expediencies and racial theorizing, prompting nineteenth-century discussions of the effects of climate, custom, and moral capacity, establishing translation as a method for aligning the familiar with the (supposedly) unfamiliar—hysteria with spirit possession, religious trances, and the strange postures adopted by religious adepts and "fakirs." English language Indian medical journals frequently ran cases of "curious," "mysterious," and "fascinating" paralyses, catatonias, and odd movements, while doctors touted the effects of their treatments and trickery, posing the efficacy of ritual cures as a way of understanding the psychological, often "hysterical," nature of such illnesses (Pinto 2016). Catatonia and catalepsy were particularly confounding symptoms, at once potentially a matter of psychology, heredity, and disease, and illuminating the complexity of an Indian landscape where multiple afflictions, lacks, and racial shortcomings might plague a body. Without theorizing "culture" as such, colonial medicine lay the groundwork for social theorizing that spanned a global colonial infrastructure. Across diverse scenes of medical practice—large government asylums, missionary hospitals, and private homes and surgeries—such mysteries allowed for paradoxical work with violence and causation, in many cases at once pointing to and effacing trauma.

1   I am grateful to Benjamin Linder for pointing out this connection.

In conditions of Empire, persons seemingly stuck in time were frequently described as ciphers; yet, as ciphers they offered openings for diverse clinical imaginings. Though their place in the archive might be considered similar—stalled movement challenges readers of its record with opacity—what does become clear is another kind of flourishing: the inscrutability of frozen movement allowed for expansive imagination. The motionless were available to be made over *into* something: an idea, a theory, a case, an article. In colonial India, they were fodder for the projects of others, seeds for other intellectual harvests, for the making of careers. Many anonymous patients disappear from the archive upon release from the institutions that held, and sometimes cured, them. While they may seem knowable to us only through the parallax of brief clinical scrutinies, most doctors are only slightly more knowable, visible in short and performative bursts of assertion through their published work. Thus, the supposedly discursively unavailable catatonic patient may not necessarily be much less accessible *to us* than their physicians, whom we know through self-productive publications and fragmentary clinical scrawlings, costumes, and patches. Moreover, it is not the case that silent patients are necessarily ciphers in the *wider* record in the same way they were ciphers to their physician observers and to the readers of medical journals. (Indeed, it is not clear that doctors' statements about catatonic patients' unknowability are in good faith.) In some cases, as we shall see, patients were, in fact, widely present in other archives as loudly vocal, rangely mobile historical actors.

And yet, the fact that stillness *was* scrutinized for its mysteries offers the archival gift of fascination. Frozen bodies were useful for diverse kinds of understanding. They produced counterpoints of affect and action—the "misery" of immobility and the revelation of sudden "awakening"—that were bound to violence and pointed toward questions of containment and freedom that ground so much writing in this period.

"In a Curiously Fixed Position"

In the final years of the nineteenth century, a man in Punjab, identified in the medical record only by the ethnic signifier "Pathan," shot and killed his wife with a pistol. Imprisoned awaiting trial, he grew "morose" and dull, with a certain heaviness. Over time, he ceased speaking and resigned to a motionless state. Brought to the Punjab Lunatic Asylum in Lahore, he was put under the observation of G.F.W. Ewens, author of influential medicolegal guidelines for India. The court found the woman's death to be accidental but sentenced her husband to six years in prison for owning an unlicensed revolver (Ewens 1902). In the ward, Ewens described the man's condition as one of "absolute misery": "He stands or sits or lies perfectly motionless and silent in any position in which he is placed," with his "head bent the eyes fixed on the ground... the forehead deeply wrinkled transversely and the features presenting a picture of absolute misery" (Ewens 1902, 382). Though he "moved aside" to pass excreta, the patient required force feeding. After thirteen months, he was returned to his family "a silent, motionless, huddled-up heap" (Ewens 1902, 382).

A wave of similar cases passed through Ewens's ward: a man "found wandering" in the Northwest Provinces who leaned against the wall with a "folded up" posture and an "expression of deep misery," a stuporous man who had "murdered his own mother," a man convicted of murdering a "little girl" out of revenge on her mother, whose movements cycled between action and rigidity, and mood between agitation and "ordinary, simple melancholia" (Ewans, 1902, 382–83). In his 1902 article in the *Indian Medical Gazette*, and six years later in his influential medicolegal text *Insanity in India*, Ewens (1908, 70) named their condition "melancholic stupor," a form of insanity "not at all infrequent in Indian asylums of a very remarkable and distinctive character."

> A man will be for many months, even one or two years, practically in one position, motionless, silent, passing his excreta under him, making no reaction to any form of sensory stimulation. You may pinch him, strike him, shout to him, use any form of cutaneous irritation, he will not move or speak, or indeed show any signs of perceiving the same. (Ewens 1908, 70)

Ewens (1908, 71) distinguished "melancholic stupor" from the effects of dementia, mania, and proper "katatonia," a distinction that, he declared, championing his own skill, was challenged by Indian conditions in which "no previous history is obtainable and you only see the patient when he is brought to you silent and motionless."

Though "no two cases are exactly alike" (Ewens 1908, 80), there were continuities. Such patients seldom demanded food; most required feeding by nasal tube, and no organic signs could be discerned from post-mortem examinations. In most cases, when they did not "die of tuberculosis, disease of the lungs, and chronic diarrhoea," most patients recovered (Ewens 1908, 71). Ewens (1902, 385; 1908, 81) observed a similarity to nonmedical states: "There is little doubt that many of the cases of trance, &c., so often found in literature would, if examined, be found to usually consist of people suffering from this disease which, from its striking peculiarities, lends itself well to description and the sufferers from which must always have excited great interest."

Many of Ewens's patients claimed to have been conscious throughout their ordeal, saying that they felt "compelled to act as they did in consequence of some great dread or great depression or sense of misery or some powerful 'feeling' which they could not help but obey" (1908, 78). Ewens thus connected melancholic stupor to a breakdown of will, "intense volitional exertion" that "overpowers the normal impulses," "inhibits all the usual movements," and "culminates in the state of absolute silent immobility and non-reactions" (Ewens 1908, 77–78). In prose stuttering with negatives, Ewens noted there was "little doubt as to the condition not being involuntary" (Ewens 1908, 77). Melancholic stupors occupied a grey area between malingering and illness, mendacity as much a crisis of unregulated action and lapsed will as murder.

Evidence for dysregulation came not from psychological exploration, but from the courts and prisons, official reports of violence and rage. Ewens little discussed patients' backstories or the violent acts that recurred in the cases. His sense of emotion landed less on guilt than on "misery," and his etiology relied on stereotypes validated by ethnology of the time, shared understandings, scholarly and everday, of tendencies toward homicidal madness among men in Punjab and the Northwest Frontier (Condos 2016). The "peculiarity," "mystery," and "queerness" already associated with stuporous states in the East materialized in the silent, mournful, rageful male prisoner, the crumpled heap who refused intimate knowledge. Voids in medical and court records spoke volumes. Ewens did not need to describe the tense and violent political conditions of the Punjab—his readers would know the colonial map, and their ideas about race and culture could be cued with passing mention of ethnic identities like "Pathan."

By the early twentieth century, once-blurry diagnostic categories were increasingly clarified. In the *Indian Medical Gazette* alone, the scope of "unusual" paralyses and catatonias was narrowing, "mysteries" winnowed by expanding categorizations, as articles about illnesses with unclear etiologies were increasingly associated with specific diagnosis (Garden 1867; Shah 1891). Indian colonial medicine had contributed to clearer understandings of Landry's paralysis (Russell 1909; Thompson 1902; Bannerjea and De 1941; Dutta 1948; Vishvanathan 1929; Lal 1931), "infantile paralysis" (latterly poliomyelitis) (Mazumdar 1921), malarial effects (Murray 1878), paralysis caused by poisoning (Hume 1876), paralysis related to alcohol abuse, paralysis caused by accidents (Morris), chorea related to rheumatic fever (late stage streptococcus infection), paralysis related to pregnancy (Shah 1891), hereditary paralysis (Khan 1935), and, especially, "general paralysis of the insane," an outcome that, with the arrival of the Wasserman test, could be definitively tied to syphilis (Wide 1869; Pearce 2012; Ghani et al. 2018).

The remainders of this list, paralyses and afflictions of movement, speech, and volition that could not be explained by new disease concepts, were informed by writings on hysteria which, though often concerned with female patients, established translational connections between culture—in the form of afflictions, behaviors, "customs," and tendencies—and medical disorder properly defined.

"Of a Remarkable and Distinct Character"

In 1926, a twenty-seven-year old Moplah man was found wandering in the forest in the Andaman Islands. "Absent from his station for three days" was the only back story provided by the physician, A. Bayley de Castro (1928, 132), who recorded his case, but the man's ethnic identification tells us he was among those deported from Madras in the wake of the 1921 Moplah uprising, likely sentenced to Andaman labor camps to clear the forest for resettlement. Found with a "vacant expression" and "no interest in his surroundings," he was shifted to a hospital in Port Blair, where he defied efforts to take a medical history (Bayley de Castro 1928, 132). A course of antimalarial treatment was given "with the hope that all the trouble was due to this," which improved his physical state but not his mental condition (Bayley de Castro 1928, 132). The "Moplah man" stayed "in his cell in queer postures (sits at times bent over to the right side, or while in squatting posture throws his head either forwards or backwards or else lies on his left side curled up)" (132). Preferring to lie on his left side, "with his legs fixed (thighs flexed on the abdomen, lower leg from the knee down flexed on the back of thigh)," he resisted efforts to open his eyes and, though at first "coaxed to eat," soon refused food, requiring a nasal tube (Bayley de Castro 1928, 132). There were brief periods of consciousness. After two weeks, he "opened his eyes and spoke," asked for water, then "laid down, coiled himself up, shut his eyes and lapsed into his former state" (Bayley de Castro 1928, 132). After five months, "a very sudden and wonderful change occurred. The patient now suddenly woke up." From that point, until the "date of his transfer to India," a few months hence (ten months from his arrival in the hospital), "there [was] nothing special to record;" he regained "intelligence" and even "had become fat" (Bayley de Castro 1928, 132).

Bayley de Castro, a junior medical officer in Port Blair, positioned the "Moplah man's" case in support of Ewens's claims that melancholic stupor was a legitimate diagnosis distinct in and to India. To strengthen his argument, de Castro cited a brief case published by an Indian Medical Service (IMS) officer at the Berhampore Lunatic Asylum, St. John Moses, who described an anonymous patient suffering melancholia that advanced to "psychocoma," leaving him with "utter loss of volitional power," unresponsive to "words addressed to or shouted at him," and "totally unaffected" by a visit from his mother, even as she "sat beside him" issuing "most affectionate addresses" (Moses 1920, 281). Moses rejected the notion of malingering because of the "extraordinarily consistent manner in which he kept up appearances" under even the observation of "a most watchful and intelligent staff" (Moses 1920, 281). Like de Castro's patient, after three years Moses's catatonic patient suddenly woke "as if from a long dream," and asked, "in a feeble whisper," for a pen and paper so that he might write "in a perfectly legible though somewhat shaky handwriting… a few lines which had a perfectly rational meaning" (Moses 1920, 281). Moses did not say what the lines contained.

Emphasizing wonder and mystery ("His recovery has been as remarkable in its suddenness as his entire illness has been in its mysterious nature" [Moses 1920, 281]), Moses used his patient's example to validate Ewens's diagnostic concept, and de Castro affixed it to his own to argue with Ewens's detractors, who suggested that such cases were better "diagnosed as dementia praecox straight away, instead of calling them by the fanciful names of melancholic stupor, atonia, or psychocoma" (Stoddard, cited in Bayley de Castro 1928, 132). But beneath the exercise of sketching a picture of diagnostic similarity, the writing strategies of these interconnected texts—anonymity, spare narrative history, use of ethnic terms and signifiers—at once evacuated political context and the identity of "cases" and made visible institutional connections. The use of ethnic glosses (e.g., Pathan, Moplah, etc.) highlighted as much as it hid, highlighting the similarity of contexts—imprisonment and forced relocation—and the place of psychiatry in colonial efforts to quell rebellion, move populations, and exploit resources, including human ones. These writing strategies established a larger sense of locality—the geographic and cultural formulation "India," a place at once racially marked and home to diverse races.

Doctors who bemoaned the "absence of a patient history" in cases of melancholic stupor nonetheless erased from the clinical record the histories that were available to them; at the same time, their accounts depend on the widely shared understanding of political conditions among the articles' readers, not least the fact that all of their patients were prisoners. Much could be communicated in phrases such as "a young well-developed Moplah" "absent from his station" (Bayley de Castro 1928, 132). Is there irony in de Castro's note that, in melancholic stupor, "obstinate resistance with retention of memory and consciousness are marked and indeed essential features" (Bayley de Castro 1928, 132)? Certainly, this description resounded with debates about the moral status of Moplahs, brought to the Andamans as "rebel" deportees—that is, criminals—yet vital to the violent civilizing labors of settling the Andamans (Sen 2000). To see the political nature of the "Moplah man's" condition requires barely a scratch into the surface of differential diagnosing, bringing to light conditions of violence, suppression, forced migration, and forced labor, and the colonial irony of deploying "convict" populations to "civilize" the Andaman Islands (Sen 2000; Panikkar 1989). The forced movement of communities and the degradation of environments are legible in the conditions that signal "absence" of patient history.

It is not too strong to say that "melancholic stupor" was built from the wrecked lives of incarcerated men. But while it is a step too far to argue that Bayley de Castro's patient, or any other beset with "stuporous" stillness, was, "in fact," immobilized by trauma, just as it is inadequate to insist that the murderous men of Punjab and the Northwest Frontier were victims of unbearable grief, or that they re-enacted political violence in domestic scenes, such psychologized readings are at once suggested and swatted away by colonial clinicians writing with the same coy willfulness they attributed to their patients. A better reading may be to dwell less on misunderstood self-processes than to note that doctors' unwitting invocations of violence interrupted their own public efforts to think and write in other terms, a doubling that echoes the doubleness of deforestation/development, criminal/civilizer, and rebel/settler.

What is clear is that doctors wrote not in ignorance of political facts but knowingly against a chorus of voices, including a Bengali public for whom Moses's patient was anything but anonymous.

"A Rigid Self-Hypnotized State"?

In January 1917, Jyotish Chandra Ghosh, a schoolteacher and revolutionary with a small following of young men in Hooghly, Bengal, was arrested under the Defense of India Act and committed to the Hooghly Jail. Six years earlier, he had been accused but acquitted of playing a role in in the bomb plot that sent revolutionary sage Aurobindo Ghosh to prison. Now, having acquired a cadre of his own, Ghosh was arrested for masterminding a bombing in Calcutta. The local magistrate, a friend "morally convinced of his innocence" went with Ghosh's male relatives to visit him in jail and offered encouragement that he would be released ("The Case of…" 1918). Instead, Ghosh was moved from prison to prison, held in solitary confinement, abused, and stricken with tuberculosis. His communications with the outside world ceased. Ultimately, Ghosh's mother learned that her son lay in an uncommunicative stupor, his legs paralyzed, and that he had been moved to the Berhampore Lunatic Asylum. Ghosh's mother began writing letters to the authorities, begging for information, to be permitted to visit her son, imploring that he be released so she could secure better care in Calcutta Medical College. She took the case to the Bengal Legislative Council, who took it up in earnest, writing letters, petitioning officials, seeking information, and agitating for Ghosh's release.

Ghosh's mother's letters were eloquent and fraught with grief, describing the way solitary confinement, ill treatment, disease, and prison conditions could "turn a prisoner mad" and imploring for the better care she could provide at Calcutta Medical College. In addition, worried about her own survival, she requested an increase in the government's meager compensation payment for her son's imprisonment, saying they did not cover her living costs as, not just a widow but head of a household of widowed daughters and daughters-in-law. Reprinted in progressive newspapers, in English and vernacular languages, across India, her letters and reports of Ghosh's condition fueled public outrage. Articles about Ghosh's condition ran in series, blaming his "wretched" and "moribund" condition of "utter physical and mental wreck" on prison conditions and the "reign of suspicion" induced by the Defense of India Act ("The Case of Detenu…" 1918; "A Sheaf of Internment Cases" 1918).

In Berhampore, Ghosh improved slightly, an uptick that raised suspicions of malingering and questions about whether his legs were not legitimately paralyzed but organically immobilized by Ghosh's "rigid self-hypnotized state" (Government of India Home Department 1918, 7). Ghosh remained unresponsive and continued to be fed by nasal tube. However, after a year in this condition, one of Ghosh's primary doctors, St. John Moses, informed officials that Ghosh's jaw had become stiff and could only be opened by force. Both the authorities and Ghosh's mother feared he was dying. At the recommendation of his mother, Ghosh was examined by Medical Board physician Mrigendralal Mitra, who declared Ghosh insane, writing that "an attempt should be made" to change the "environment of detention," as freedom would create an "awaken[ing] in consciousness" (Government of India Home Department 1918, 4). Colonial officials expressed concern about the effect of the case on political sentiments in Calcutta and the possibility that his transfer to Calcutta Medical College might incite "public interest."

In April 1920, after three years, Ghosh suddenly "awoke." At first, unable to speak, he communicated only by writing. His first written words were to ask if he was to be tried. By this time, the government was offering amnesty to political prisoners, and decided that Ghosh would not be tried but could be released only when his condition improved. A government memo noted, "The case is a most interesting one from a medical point of view, and will no doubt receive considerable attention in medical publications" (Government of India Home Department 1920, 9). Not long afterwards, Moses published Ghosh's case—as that of an anonymous patient—in the *Indian Medical Gazette*.

"Waggles Her Head About as if She Could Not Hold It Up"

Catatonia connected to culture in diverse ways. Indeed, the link between political conditions and concepts of cultural difference would be hard to trace were lines drawn only via diagnostic categories (like melancholic stupor) and not traced symptomatically, body to body. It is possible to imagine gender as a deciding element, such that what was termed melancholic stupor in male prisoners may have been diagnosed as hysteria in young women. The former was treated with various physical techniques (that receive little attention in cases), the latter with psychological manipulations that characterize accounts of medical heroics.

In the early 1920s, two sisters were brought to the Baptist Missionary Society Hospital in Bhiwani, some distance from Delhi, to be seen by the locally famous "lady doctor."[2] Both girls were deemed to be "suffering from hysteria" and for this reason were brought before Dr. Ellen Farrer, who was known for her effective treatments of hysterical girls. Farrer herself bemoaned this status, and worried that her reputation as a healer of hysterical paralyses, fits, and pains would induce villagers with all manners of insanity—which she would be unable to cure—to flood her clinic. The girls themselves were creating a ruckus in the private ward. Crowds of kin clustered around them, the watchful audience of gazes creating, in Farrer's estimation, ideal conditions for hysterical symptoms to flourish. The younger girl, Dulari, was thirteen and unmarried. Her legs were withered

---

2   Baptist Missionary Society Archives, IN/148, 1891–1933, Oxford University, Angus Library at Regent's Park College, retrieved by Lauren Minsky.

"from disuse." She had been bedridden for two years and "profess[ed] an inability to sit up." Most often, she lay under her quilt, "peeping... furtively with one eye" when the hospital staff approached her. When asked to sit up, she "waggles her head about, as if she could not hold it up," though there was nothing "really wrong with her neck." Her family was anxious for her to improve, as "it would soon have been considered a disgrace to her family if she was not married; but who would want a girl who lay in bed with a stone on her chest, and needed constant waiting on all the time, being unable apparently even to sit up?" The other girl, eighteen, was recently widowed. She suffered stomach pains at night. "Suspecting the nature of her trouble," Dr. Farrer instructed a nurse to administer a "hypodermic of plain water," gleefully noting "that she had gone to sleep within half an hour and was still sleeping as a result of it!!! Which amply confirmed my diagnosis." Dulari was "a different matter." Dr. Farrer doubted that she wanted to get better. This, she said, was "half the battle."

Farrer, a Baptist mission doctor from England, had joined the Bhiwani hospital in 1897 and by the 1920s was widely admired for treating hysteria. Where others singled out cases of dysfunctional movement as "mysterious," "interesting," and "peculiar," Farrer portrayed such symptoms as common and predictable, though interesting enough to merit detailed mention in letters to her sisters. These symptoms included unusual movements, paralysis, pain, running away, and "hysterical fits," a term that seemed to require no explanation.

Six weeks after her sister's cure, with Dulari still in hospital, her "men-folk" told Farrer they would pay any fee for as long as it took to make Dulari "marriageable" and gave Farrer "remarkably free hand." Farrer developed an antagonistic relationship to Dulari, involving "one or two mighty battles of will." She did not elaborate on these battles, but they were likely to have looked like others she experienced, such as "a great trouble" with a fourteen-year-old girl, "who had got her hips and knees bent up so that she was always in a sitting posture." Farrer administered chloroform and then straightened the girl's legs with straps and weights. The next day, "in spite of a Morphia injection," the patient was noisy and disruptive, ultimately tearing off the apparatus. Farrer was upset to discover the next day that, "My beautiful extension arrangement was quite spoiled and useless, damaged beyond repair." Farrer gave up trying to treat the girl and sent word to her village that she should be taken home.

Whatever the battles, Dulari, however, improved, eventually walking by herself, chatting sociably, and greeting hospital staff with "smiles and *salaams* [Urdu greeting]." Farrer was hopeful for her progress, but nervous about its implications—"an influx of all the queer hysterical cases of the district and even some that are quite mad, in the expectation that we can cure them too!" Farrer's cures resemble those of nineteenth-century accounts in which doctors deployed trickery to rationalize a patient's grip on her symptoms or induced a cure with performative techniques and threats of unpleasant methods. As famed physician and medicolegal writer Norman Chevers (1886, 733–34) wrote in the 1880s, recalling an "East Indian lady" he had frequently treated for convulsions, unconsciousness, retained urine, and "delirious singing," the threat of catheterization by her own husband was enough to end the problem of urine retention, for the reason that a "native woman might be unwilling to be touched by her husband or a 'native' man"; psychological trickery mirrored the illness's cause—a female mind prone to self-deceit.

If trickery allowed insight into the psychological nature of distresses, the strategy required enough "cultural" understanding to manipulate therapeutically. For Farrer, though her cures were effective in psychological terms, culture was evident, too, in her sense of the cause of so many illnesses—girls' apprehension about marriage and fear of a future as a widow, evident in the fact that so many of her cases were newly married, soon-to-be-married, and recently widowed women. She wrote, "It is surely not wonderful considering the unnatural conditions of pardah etc under which they live, that hysteria in multitudinous manifestations should be quite prevalent among Indian women, and we saw much more of it than of organic nervous disease." At once a sign of cultural and moral disorder, hysterical paralysis allowed Farrer to at once acknowledge entrenched gender inequities and approach her patients with disdain and antagonism. Where melancholic stupors in men were linked to poorly regulated will and racialized formulations of masculinity, for female patients, Farrer reckoned, the body bore struggles of life and pathologies of kinship by having the effect of creating at once too much and too little will, an arrangement that remains in contemporary practice (Marrow 2013). The punitive and moralizing nature of such paralysis manifested in deeply gendered postures of resistance—willfulness, "naughtiness." Signs of violence were systemic, at once the cultural ground of distress and integral to a therapeutic repertoire.

"Guided by the Passions of the Mind"

Paralyses and catatonias were not just obsessions of Europeans or the colonial medical establishment. Long-established as key symptoms of afflictions that, across non-European medical systems, came to be connected, historically and translationally, to "hysteria" (see Pinto 2020), immobility figured in Bengali medical writing in the late nineteenth and early twentieth centuries as characteristic of hysteria, "fits" often occurring in proximity to outbursts of laughter and crying, urine retention, and "globus hystericus," the sense of an obstructing object rising from belly to throat and relieved, hydraulically, by crying or urinating ("*Histiriya*," Anon. 1901). These afflictions attached less to racialized notions of difference than to gendered visions of a morally compromised mind and will, ill-effects of British education and modern enjoyments such as novels, theater, and urban life. For Calcutta homeopath Chandrasekhar Kali (1895b, 244), "attention-seeking" and the inability to "contain... mental passions" characterized hysterical women, producing a range of often horrifying behaviors: "It is impossible to fathom what hysteric patients can do when guided by the passions of the mind" (Kali 1895b, 245).

As in English-language medical writing, in Bengali accounts it often fell to the doctor to distinguish the hysterical "fit" of unconsciousness from other disorders. Writing in the journal *Chikitsak o Samalochak* (Doctor and Critic) in 1895, Kali (1895a, 224) noted that the body often overcame conscious will: "Often paralysis or fits from this disease prevent the patient from moving her paralysed organ in spite of her will to do so." Many of the cases Kali described involved frozen postures and prolonged unconsciousness, with bodies bearing the ability to show no signs of morbidity even after prolonged periods without food. One woman, a mother of four, who would fall unconscious for up to eleven days, "lying down as though sleeping," was, nonetheless, not visibly thin (Kali 1896, 84). Patients' odd postures were signs of trickery, conscious or not, and Kali described his efforts as reading the body for signs of hysterical postures such as the telltale "bow" or "hysterical arch," misread as abdominal bloating (Kali 1896, 85). Unlike his European peers, however, upon disarticulating the body's own trickery through its various iterations of immobility, Kali typically prescribed homeopathic medication rather than resorting to his own deceptions.

Bodily trickery might be circumvented by clever attendants, "cheerful conversation," removal to a happier, quieter, more peaceful place, and keeping busy. Encouragement was preferable to angering the patient, as was connecting the curative potential of distraction to the nature of paralysis: "If shrewd conversation can divert the minds of the patient, you will see that the paralyzed organ works just fine." But it was not just trickery or distraction that healed; doctors also prescribed a range of pharmaceutical and material therapeutics including splashes of water and electric shock (conception, too, was considered instigator and cure for hysteria). Kali

(1896) provided readers with a compendium of medicines, homeopathic and conventional, including anacardium, arsenic, asafoetida, colophylum, ignatia, and others. There was no single drug for hysteria, but a medicine chest of options, depending on symptoms and their variations.

While Bengali physicians discussed cultural habits, they did so to parse and reconsider diagnoses, often leaning *away* from hysteria and toward other illnesses, poisoning, and the dangerous side effects of medicines. Describing the limitations of sulphonal, a widely touted sedative, an anonymous physician related a dangerous misdiagnosis ("Calcutta Medical Society" 1891). A young woman given sulphonal for a tendency to "fall into a hysterical fit," fell promptly. By morning, she was catatonic, staring unmoving and apparently unconscious at her sister and unresponsive to her friends' forceful shaking and tickling with a feather. When the doctor lifted her hand, it stayed in that position, a waxy rigidity that struck her legs as well. He asked the girl's friends to raise her veil so he might "assess her level of consciousness" and was struck that she "did not show any shyness and shame," an aberration that led him to understand that patient as cataleptic, not hysterical. He prescribed a different medicine, and, on his return in the afternoon, found her happily conversing with her friends. "This catalepsy," he said, "was certainly caused by sulphonal" ("Calcutta Medical Society" 1891).

While paralytic conditions could be understood through cultural manipulation and understanding in such cases, such conditions were not categorized as "Indian" or "Bengali" or reckoned comparatively in racial or cultural terms. But such discussions were not without the sense of moral failure, a sense that was applied in terms of gender. In place of the racialized sense of difference in European doctors' case-writing, Bengali accounts of hysterical paralysis emphasized the moral deficiencies of women. As deft at ignoring the possibility for trauma as his English colleagues, Kali (1896, 85) observed the case of an eleven-year-old girl who told her mother-in-law she had been bitten by a snake (a figure of fright that recurs in diverse cases): "I was called in and saw that there was no puncture on her foot. I waited by the patient for a few moments, after which she began to have a hysterical fit, I then came to understand that she was pregnant and with that was displaying hysteria. But many hysterias are also cured as soon as a person conceives."

"Not Quite Alright"

In later colonial Indian medicine, a sense of traumatic causation for paralytic and catatonic states was not altogether absent, found less in British colonial medicine than in "indigenizing" psychiatry in South India, and visible less in published cases than in hospital files. In 1938, a young mother, from an educated, middle-class family, was brought by her husband to the Mysore Mental Hospital in Bangalore. Three months earlier, a cold had developed into a fever that left her "not quite alright."[3] Gradually, the woman stopped talking and moving, mutely standing or sitting for hours at a time. When admitted to the hospital, she "refused" to speak, so the job of supplying a history was left to her husband and condensed by the duty doctor: married at thirteen to a man thirteen years her senior; first child, born when she was fifteen, died in its sixth month, her second after seven days; the third, born nine months earlier, was alive and healthy. Her husband described her as an ideal wife, "very obedient, modest and loving." She was diagnosed with a "depressive reaction," admitted to the ward, and given the usual barrage of treatments—a magnesium sulphide enema, iron supplements for anemia, Benzedrin, an amphetamine to be taken in the mornings, and paraldehyde, a sedative for evenings. Chart records during her three weeks in the ward were scant, noting only small adjustments to her medical regimen and concluding with the corrected note: "Discharged against advice improved at request."

Intriguingly, by comparison with other settings, the terms "hysteria," "hysteric," "hysterical reaction," and so on are relatively scant among the diagnostic assignments in the Mysore Mental Hospital's case files. When hysteria began appearing as a formal diagnosis (beginning in 1930), it was often appended with a question mark, occasionally crossed out and replaced with other labels, more a question than answer, never the florid diagnostic entity it was for Ellen Farrer or Chandrasekhar Kali. In the 1930s, its phenomenology narrowed to "strange," "fantastical," "queer," and "theatrical" postures, while catatonia, stupors, fits, and paralysis moved freely across the diagnostic landscape, attached to diverse diagnoses, including dementia praecox/schizophrenia, hysteria, depressive states, and confusional reactions, a catch-all compendium of loosely affiliated symptoms (weakness, agitation, incoherence, emotional volatility, disinterest in food, sleeplessness, delusions, hallucinations, stupors, and fainting) often appended with a cause—an infectious or chronic disease, puerperal, pyrexial, etc. Catatonia also appeared as a separate diagnosis—"catatonic stupor," "catatonia after childbirth," "post-pyrexial catatonia," and "catatonic."

While hysteria's minimal presence speaks to its source—records of a hospital in-patient unit, whereas most hysteria cases would likely have been

---

3   Case notes from the Mysore Mental Hospital are held in the archives of the National Institute of Mental Health and Neurosciences.

seen in non-hospital setting—it also has to do with the clinical philosophies of Mysore Mental Hospital's leadership, an orientation toward organic understandings of mental illness, which continues to be characteristic of South Indian psychiatry. This orientation produced pointed critiques of reading paralyses and catatonias as neurotic symptoms. Frank Noronha (1926), Mysore Mental Hospital's director in the early decades of the twentieth century, was concerned about the limits of standard diagnostic taxonomies and the practice of organizing diagnoses by etiology. He preferred the formulations of Emile Kraepelin, who organized disorders by symptoms. In contexts such as India, where multiple etiologies might shape a disorder, Noronha (1926, 540) felt that etiological taxonomies "often give rise to fallacies." "Until we have an undisputed aetiology or pathology of mental diseases, we have to rely on symptoms" (Noronha 1926, 540).

Noronha (1925, 416) noted, "it may not be inappropriate to allude to a tendency prevalent among the public—and shared by some medical practitioners—of dubbing any case of disordered conduct as hysterics, especially if it happens to be in a female, even when definitely insane symptoms are manifested. It is needless to point out the danger of glossing over a serious disease by calling it simply hysterics and treating it as such." Noronha described cases with complex presentations (two of which contained an excessive fondness for climbing trees), including disorders of movement and consciousness, expressing suspicion of pronouncements of "cure," especially in situations in which a patient's "environment" contributed to their illness (Noronha 1926, 542). Of particular concern was that dementia praecox (schizophrenia), which often bore symptoms of catatonia, was too readily diagnosed as hysterical (Noronha 1925, 416).

This does not mean that difference was not at stake in clinical practice. M.V. Govindaswamy (1939, 506), Noronha's successor as hospital superintendent observed of "Indian patients" that a "far greater proportion... suffer from organic states—post-pyrexial, toxic, or exhaustive," with "states of excitement... commoner than states of depression," noting the influence of "both climate and diet," especially the fact that "most patients are undernourished and weak." Later, he observed that among the factors influencing mental health were "diseases of the brain tissues, head injuries, bacteria, poor heredity and also a quarrelsome mother, a tyrannical father, acute poverty, pangs of conscience, social disgrace, jealousy, religious difficulties, political troubles and businessmen's worries" (Govindaswamy 1970, 72), a list that orients difference toward conduits between organic bodies and minds and environments in which political and economic conditions shaped material realities and possibilities for living. The orientation toward material conditions and organically understood diseases, bodies, and minds that characterizes the school of psychiatry associated with the influential Mysore Mental Hospital, later National Institute of Mental Health and Neuro-Sciences, emerged at a juncture of clinical orientations toward the most mysterious and perplexing symptoms—crises of movement, stillness, and consciousness. Here, points of difference in understanding bodies and minds were read less by working through grand etiological mysteries of mind and culture than by reckoning with diverse and entangled symptoms, conditions, and cures, aligning political critique and social concern with perhaps paradoxical approaches to care.

"A Good Fit"

Around the time that the young mother was admitted to the female ward of Mysore Mental Hospital, a seventeen-year-old boy was brought to the male ward for "frequent attacks of stuporous conditions." His father, who delivered him to the hospital, described him glowingly—a dutiful son, active and sporting, sociable, never idle, and liked by others. His medical troubles had started a year earlier, when feelings of strangulation in the throat, pain, and inability to speak sent him to a local physician, then to the district hospital, where he received "electric treatment" to his tongue. Though he improved, after ten days a new set of symptoms—increased psychomotor activity in his limbs—sent him back to the hospital for three weeks. Again, he improved and relapsed, a pattern that would continue over several months, until, when his fits sent him into a "stupor," he was taken to Bangalore. In the ward, as well as receiving the usual medicines and supplements, he began receiving treatment with a cutting-edge therapy—chemical "shock" treatment with cardiazol.

Before the dawn of modern psychopharmaceuticals, the Mysore Mental Hospital, through the influence of Govindaswamy, was an early adopter of intense somatic treatments that, though little understood, were aimed at shocking the body and brain into recalibration. Such therapies were mostly chemical, seizures and comas induced by insulin, cardiazol, and ammonium chloride (as well as the use of electricity on paralyzed limbs and body parts). Such therapeutics were used to treat a range of afflictions, especially those involving catatonias and tenacious depression (Govindaswamy 1939, 507). Cardiazol, which induced seizures, was favored at Mysore Mental Hospital, where it was introduced in 1937 to replace coma-inducing insulin therapy, which Govindaswamy considered more dangerous for weak and malnourished patients. Cardiazol was used to treat schizophrenia and "allied states," notably catatonia, catatonic stupor, depressive state, and hysteria. Resounding with a familiar term, in Govindaswamy's case files of cardiazol patients, the immediate effects of this form of chemical shock therapy were often described as "a good fit," and daily ward notes from the cardiazol era are full of the short sentence, "had a good fit."

The effects of cardiazol were touted as radical and immediate, including the dramatic "awakening" of catatonic patients. In a 1939 article, Govindaswamy described 34 patients who had received cardiazol, fourteen men and twenty women, most diagnosed with schizophrenia with catatonic or "dull and seclusive" presentations, others included "depressives," "hysterics," "confusional reaction types," and simply "catatonic" (Govindaswamy 1939, 506). Most were reported "improved." Govindaswamy highlighted two cases, a man and a woman. In one there was an "awakenings" like response: a twenty-eight-year-old woman who went into a "stupor" two weeks after the birth of fourth child and was admitted to the hospital, "immovable" and "in a cataleptic trance" (Govindaswamy 1939, 508). After four months with no response to medications, she was given cardiazol and immediately, "came out of her trance-like condition, became friendly and cooperative, and her conversation was sustained, sequential, and relevant" (Govindaswamy 1939, 508). However, after three more treatments, the woman returned to a state of stupor. Another injection revived her, but only for a few hours. The dosage required to cause a convulsion had quintupled and "the lucid intervals depend entirely on cardiazol. She has had nearly fifty injections and is living a cardiazol life analogous to the insulin life of a diabetic" (Govindaswamy 1939, 508). The other case closely resembled that of the young man cited above, a college student in a "catatonic stupor" who, "with one convulsion with cardiazol (5 mg)… came out of his stupor and became friendly and cooperative" (Govindaswamy 1939, 506).

One of the noted effects of cardiazol was a feeling of intense dread in the moments before the "fit." Knowledge of this effect must have spread beyond the circle of experts because in 1941, K.N.H. Rizvi, Deputy Medical Superintendent at Agra Mental Hospital, noted "extreme apprehension and fear of treatment… in almost every case" (Rizvi 1941, 575), so much that some patients refused treatment. Rizvi noted other "complications," including "the dislocation of the jaw, shoulder or hips, fractures of the arms or leg, sometimes the thigh, fracture of the spine, and decalcification" as well as, in rare cases, cerebral hemorrhage and lung abscesses (Rizvi 1941, 575). Rizvi preferred to induce seizures with intravenous ammonium chloride, which was cheaper than cardiazol, produced less violent seizures, and only "slight apprehension," though its results were less miraculous, with only a thirty-five percent cure rate, and forty percent unimproved (Rizvi 1941, 576).

The sense of the humane that pervades Indian psychiatry's discourse on violent chemical therapies may seem ironic to those accustomed to associating the severity and danger of such techniques with the idea that biological understandings rob mental conditions of social context. Yet, in Bangalore, the violence of induced seizures coincided with a therapeutic ethos of comfort and care as well as with a sense that even bodies denied basic needs might be recalibrated by just the right jolt to the system. In light of the prevalence of catatonias—and discussion of how to make sense of them in racialized terms—in the context of colonial medicine, cardiazol and other chemical shock therapies, with their potential for "awakening," were part of a wider clinical philosophy that emphasized a psyche understood as at once organic and social, a psyche whose social, political, and environmental contexts were present in, not erased from, understandings of it. Such treatments were attuned to the needs of the impoverished and malnourished, allowing an organically oriented psychiatry to indicate not depoliticized medicine but the expanse of political imaginations possible of medical practice. It is not a paradox that Govindaswamy (1970, 73), practitioner and advocate of chemical shock therapies (and later leucotomies, or lobotomies), wrote about the appeal of a life of peace, free from tumult, a cultivated inward turn that is decidedly different from psychoanalysis: "Freudian psycho-therapy and psycho-analysis has not met with the same success as once was anticipated. We have to think of simpler modes of living, simpler ideas. 'The Gods approve of the depth, but not the tumult of the soul.' This quotation of Wordsworth is the teaching of the Geetha, the Upanishad and the Mahabharata. We have to go back to them for peace—shanti." It makes a certain kind of sense that, in a clinical archive in which excitability, frozen rigors, and "clouded consciousness" were recurring symptoms, a tumultuous soul would find refuge in the false peace of stupor and be cured through the clarity of a "good fit." That the catatonic patient of the Mysore medical archive is an unsettled, unquiet self, and her treatment an "awakening" signaled what doctors may have understood to be at stake in postures of misery and resignation.

Archives of Broken Movement

Friedner and Staples (this volume) note the critical potential for thinking with what they term "failed mobilities," a possibility that enacts a scholarly/

critical reversal on histories of medicine in which "failed mobilities" fell under a vast pathologizing gaze. We might also ask, what do "failed mobilities" do for compounded knowledge practices, those of the original actors, and those—ours—that come long after the fact? In other words, what does immobility—the frozen body, the stilled voice—do, not just for medicine, or politics, but in and for an archive? Different colonial conditions generated different kinds and stakes of psychiatry, not only different approaches to catatonia but different senses of what an unresponsive person might mean, do, and offer for medical understanding under colonial rule. In Bengal, where anti-colonial movements often rejected Gandhian nonviolence and passive resistance, revolutionary Jyotish Chandra Ghosh's "stuporous" condition seized medical knowledge, grabbing and freezing the gazes that turned to it, at the same time allowing for a flourishing public debate over the violences of colonial policing. The clinical records of the Andaman Islands, Punjab, and Bengal, places where medicine was intrinsically tied to policing, surveillance, and incarceration, scenes, too, of violent displacement, read catatonias as wondrous accounts of inscrutable illness and sudden awakening, theorizing at the blurred juncture of cultural and racial difference. Beyond these settings, but drawing on the medical science that happened in them, concepts of "culture" were taking shape, informed by colonial psychiatry's comparative work, in which, though race was slowly replaced with concepts of culture and acculturation, it remained implicit in broad reference to heredity, custom, and environmental differences (Vaughan 2007; Lucas and Barrett 1995; Redfield, Linton, and Herskovits 1935; Guarnaccia and Hausman Stabile 2016; Pinto 2020a). While the concept of "culture-bound" disorder was not coined until the 1950s (also, notably, based on Asian source material, Yap 1951, 1952), its genealogy includes such scenes, including the way physicians in India mapped the environmental, cultural, and racial contours of "odd" afflictions, few meriting as much scrutiny as paralysis and stupor. The "queer" remainders of differential diagnosing of crises of immobility filled in the sense of "culture" and difference. Intrinsic to this conceptual history, diagnoses of catatonias, fits, and stupors were never far from scenes of violence, judgment, and incarceration, and it takes a modest but reparative trick of reading (replacing race/culture with colonial infrastructures) and the insertion of a psychological mechanism (trauma) to restore politics to discourses that consistently ignored it.

But, arguably, in other places, such as Bangalore, no recuperative tricks are necessary. Mysore's status as a princely state afforded Bangalore's psychiatrists a degree of independence to develop a voice and approach that diverged from colonial concerns (Jain and Murthy 2006). In the Indian-led Mysore

Mental Hospital, stuporous patients exhausted by birth and loss, beset by dementia praecox and "confusional reactions," among other diagnoses of the era, were less mysteries than openings to complex understanding. There, the stilled body was not a cultural curiosity but a site of repair, one that in certain instances offers insight into the effects of poverty and illness, among other forces. Such cases did not lack suggestions of trauma, neither did doctors dwell on it. There was more room for the ironies of medicine under colonial rule, of restoring patients to a damaging social order; and there was less room for the moral certitude of cultural pathology that charged Farrer's missionary medicine and medico-legal approaches to imprisoned men's paralyses. Likewise, though trauma was absent from late colonial psychiatry's published writing on afflictions of movement (though, in Europe, it increasingly oriented reckonings of similar symptoms in the wake of World War I), it had a bare and quiet place in less public archives—political records and case files—thanks to diverse record-keepers. People like IMS physician Mrigendralal Mitra, brought in to examine political prisoner Jyotish Chandra Ghosh at the request of his mother and an outraged public, wrote a report that was legible to and recorded by the medical infrastructure, if not released publicly, etiologically shifting the stakes of diagnosis from moral failing to the effects of imprisonment, thereby inscribing connections between freedom, consciousness, and mental well-being into the colonial medical archive.

Fundamentally at stake across readings of immobility is a contemporary critical paradigm, one of our own, which deploys cultural difference in symptoms (as well as diagnostic terminologies) to refute the power dynamics of biomedicine. Such a paradigm too often maps the world in a "west and the rest" division between biomedical knowledge (and its organic/material therapeutics) and meaning-oriented approaches to illness, with the assumption that biologically-oriented imaginations of the body are inherently depoliticizing, violent to the meaning worlds of those imagined as indigenous, and unreceptive to social violences. This is an imaginary that at once maps the world and creates it in its own image. Frozen movement defamiliarizes this arrangement.

Consider this: in Mysore Mental Hospital, the rationale for violent organic therapeutics involved a fundamental recognition of patients' humanity; it accounted for the ways their history and social lives registered in their bodies and acknowledged suffering in the way they represented it. Farrer's psychological efforts and sense of cultural context entailed trickery and saw patients as needing to be conquered; they worked on the psyche by working around patients' subjectivity. Consider, too: the Bengali public, outraged by colonial policing, observing that forms of punishment and the pathogenic conditions of jails fostered "insanity," sought not an alternative to medicine but better medicine and treatment unconnected to punishment. At the same time, Bengali doctors working outside of the Indian Medical Service gendered "fits" and immobility in moral terms that, at the same time, allowed them to question the dangerous effects of European medications. In late colonial India, there were diverse strategies for addressing the ways political conditions live in the body.

I have avoided questions of what may have been "cultural" or "civilizational" precedents for catatonias and stupors, in part because such questions are discussed extensively in an anthropological literature too large to incorporate here. I have taken up some of these issues elsewhere, asking how formulations of grief, trauma, and witnessing are portrayed in classical Hindu portrayals of unconsciousness and speech, and finding diverse articulations of something like trauma-response in South Asian cultural texts (Pinto 2020). The medical archive is a "view on" stillness, not a "view from" it. Yet, its struggles with the impenetrability of nonresponsive persons raise questions of how clinical choreographies *involve* patients rather than simply attending to them. Where bodies pressure medical knowing, is it any wonder that it is *difference*—in shapeshifting forms, methods, and purposes, between heres and theres, us and them, different thems, different us's—that persistently attaches to them? Might it raise the possibility that difference, separation, and removal are not just biopolitical strategies but, in a different key, temporary human goals? So, too, might it suggest ways of sidling up to still and silent bodies that do not require translational readings or other efforts to lay claim?

Catatonia in the archive is less a void to be filled than a highly elaborated site for attaching ethics and politics to immobility and inaction. The still and mute patient draws attention to the stakes of repair—the violence of means, the ethics of returning people to damaged social worlds, the genealogies and implicit cartographies of critical strategies. Understood less as an auratic source of cultural or civilizational meaning than as a point of entry to the stakes of meaning-making, the still moment *opens up*, rather than forecloses, possibilities of making use of the body. It brings into clarity the way political projects are troubled by stillness. The call from the Indian medical archive of stillness is, then, not only to ask what patients are doing or demanding, or how their actions are managed or mistranslated, but to explore what is collectively enacted in the space of immobility. The story of the stuporous, catatonic, and muted patients, those who cannot narrate their own histories yet are narrated by multitudes, are about more than the maps drawn upon them. They are also about the diverse ways—and reasons—people may seek, for a time, to leave the world, and to return to it. The early female cardiazol patient clearly stuck with Govindaswamy—the hysterical woman, catatonic after childbirth, who could only be made to re-enter it by "liv[ing] a cardiazol life"—a life of persistent, repeated, and ever-increasing shock, the chemical summoning to a life from which she so consistently slipped away. As she was treated with ever increasing doses, Jyotish Chandra Ghosh had returned to his revolutionary activities, moving from one place to another, from Bengal to Punjab to Assam, organizing anticolonial activities, rejecting Gandhian nonviolence in favor of more dramatic means, imprisoned, released, and imprisoned, again and again.

Acknowledgments

Research for this paper was funded by the American Institute of Indian Studies, Tufts University, and the American Council of Learned Societies. Aniket De assisted in gathering Bengali materials and translated some materials, and Pratyusa Chakraborty assisted the author in translating Bengali sources. Information about Ellen Farrer, including invaluable archival notes, was generously provided by Lauren Minsky. Access to archived case files of the Mysore Mental Hospital was generously provided by the National Institute of Mental Health and Neurosciences, under the guidance of Sanjeev Jain and Pratima Murthy. Andy McDowell and Benjamin Linder provided helpful comments on drafts of this paper.

References

Banerjea, J.C., and M.N. De. 1941. "Clinical Observations on Landry's Paralysis." *Indian Medical Gazette* 76 (2): 65.

Bayley de Castro, A. 1928. "A Case of Melancholic Atonia or Psychocoma." *Indian Medical Gazette* 55 (8): 132

"Calcutta Medical Society." 1891. ভিষক দর্পণ [*Bhisak Darpan*] (December): 248–52.

"The Case of Babu Jyotish Chandra Ghosh." 1918. *Amrita Bazaar Patrika*, Jaunary 29, 1918.

"The Case of Detenu Jyotish Chandra Ghosh." 1918. *Amrita Bazaar Patrika*, January 26, 1918.

Chevers, Norman. 1886. *A Commentary on the Diseases of India.* London: J. & A. Churchill.

Condos, Mark. 2016. "'Fanaticism' and the Politics of Resistance along the North-West Frontier of British India." *Comparative Studies in Society and History* 58 (3): 717–45.

Dutta, Sailesh Chandra. 1948. "A Case of Spreading Paralysis." *Indian Medical Gazette* 82 (2): 82–83.

Ewens, G.F.W. 1902. "Six Cases of Melancholic Stupor." *Indian Medical Gazette* 37 (10): 381–85.

Ewens, G.F.W. 1908. *Insanity in India: Its Symptoms and Diagnosis: With Reference to the Relation of Crime and insanity.* Calcutta: Thacker, Spink.

Garden, A. 1867. "Notes on Cases of Functional Paralysis in Children." *Indian Medical Gazette* 2 (4): 91–96.

Ghani, Sarah, Pratima Murthy, Sanjeev Jain, and Alok Sarin. 2018. "Syphilis and Psychiatry at the Mysore Government Mental Hospital (NIMHANS) in the Early 20th Century." *Indian Journal of Psychiatry* 60 (Supplement 2): S270–S276.

Government of India Home Department. 1918. "Question and Answer in Council Regarding State Prisoners who have Committed Suicide or Gone Mad or have Otherwise Broken Down in Health." National Archives of India, Digitized Public Records, File No. HOME_POLITICAL_A_1918_MAY_90-103KW, Identifier PR_000003004400 [Digitized Document].

Government of India Home Department. 1920. "Release under the Amnesty Announced in Royal Proclamation of 32 State Prisoners who were Restrained under Regulation III of 1818." National Archives of India, File No. 204-12, Identifier PR_000003004756.

Govindaswamy, Moti Venkatarao. 1939. "Cardiazol Treatment of Schizophrenia and Allied States in Indian Patients." *The Lancet* 233 (6027): 506–8.

Govindaswamy, Moti Venkatarao. 1970. *Dr. M.V. Govindaswamy: Lectures and Writings.* Edited by Saligrama Krishna Ramachandra Rao. Bangalore: Vimala Govindaswamy.

Guarnaccia, Peter J., and Claudia Hausmann-Stabile. 2016. "Acculturation and Its Discontents: A Case for Bringing Anthropology Back into the Conversation." *Sociology and Anthropology* 4 (2): 114–24.

"হিস্টিরিয়া" [*Histiriya*]. 1901. স্বাস্থ্য [*Swasthya*] 5 (6): 174–83.

Hume, T. 1876. "Case of Partial Paralysis Supposed to Have Followed the Injudicious Administration of Arsenic." *Indian Medical Gazette* 11 (4): 103.

Kali, Chandrasekhar, LMS. 1895a. "হিস্টিরিয়া" [*Histiriya*]. চিকিৎসক ও সমালোচক [*Cikitsak o Samalocak*] 8–9 (1): 224–25.

Kali, Chandrasekhar, LMS. 1895b. "হিস্টিরিয়া, cont" [*Histiriya, cont.*] চিকিৎসক ও সমালোচক [*Cikitsak o Samalocak*] 1 (10): 243–47.

Kali, Chandrasekhar, LMS. 1896. "হিস্টিরিয়া, cont" [*Histiriya, cont.*] চিকিৎসক ও সমালোচক [*Cikitsak o Samalocak*] 2 (4): 82–86.

Lal, Rasik Behari. 1931. "Landry's Paralysis in an Infant" *Indian Medical Gazette* 66 (6): 328.

Lucas, Rodney H., and Robert J. Barrett. 1995. "Interpreting Culture and Psychopathology: Primitivist Themes in Cross-Cultural Debate." *Cult. Med. Psychiatry* 19 (3): 287–326

Maddox, R.H. 1899. "A Case of Pseudo-Hypertrophic Muscular Paralysis." *Indian Medical Gazette* 34 (10): 364–65

Marrow, Jocelyn. 2013. "Feminine Power or Feminine Weakness? North Indian Girls' Struggles with Aspirations, Agency, and Psychosomatic Illness." *American Ethnologist* 40 (2): 347–61.

Mazumdar, A.R. 1921. "A Remarkable Case of Infantile Paralysis." *Indian Medical Gazette* 56 (9): 336–37.

Morris, J. 1881. "Paralysis The Result of a Slight Fall." *Indian Medical Gazette* 16 (9): 257.

Moses, O. St. John. 1920. "A Case of Melancholic Stupor (Psychocoma)." *Indian Medical Gazette* 55 (8): 280–81.

Murray, R.D. 1878. "Malarial Paralysis and Apoplexy." *Indian Medical Gazette* 13 (1): 13–14.

Noronha, Frank. 1925. "Observations on Cases of Dementia Praecox." *Indian Medical Gazette* 60 (9): 415–17.

Noronha, Frank. 1926. "Types of Mental Disorder" *Indian Medical Gazette* 61 (11): 540–42.

Panikkar, K.N. 1989. *Against Lord and State: Religion and Peasant Uprisings in Malabar, 1836–1921*. New York: Oxford University Press.

Pearce, J.M.S. 2012. "Brain Disease Leading to Mental Illness: A Concept Initiated by the Discovery of General Paralysis of the Insane." *European Neurology* 67 (5): 272–78.

Pinto, Sarah. 2016. "'The Tools of Your Chants and Spells': Stories of Madwomen and Indian Practical Healing." *Medical Anthropology* 35 (3): 263–77.

Pinto, Sarah. 2020a. "Madness: Recursive Ethnography and the Critical Uses of Psychopathology." *Annual Review of Anthropology* 49: 299–316.

Pinto, Sarah. 2020b. *The Doctor and Mrs A: Ethics and Counter-Ethics in an Indian Dream Analysis*. New York: Fordham University Press.

Redfield, R., R. Linton, and M.J. Herskovits. 1935. "Memorandum for the Study of Acculturation." *Man* 35: 145–48.

Rizvi, K. N. H. 1942. "The Ammonium Chloride Treatment of Schizophrenia." *Journal of Mental Science* 88 (373): 575–77.

Russell, A. J. 1909. "A Case of Acute Ascending (Landry's) Paralysis." *Indian Medical Gazette* 44 (5): 175–76.

Sen, Satadru. 2000. *Disciplining Punishment: Colonialism and Convict Society in the Andaman Islands.* New York: Oxford University Press.

Shah, T.M. 1891. "A Case of Peculiar Paralysis." *Indian Medical Gazette* 26 (12): 369.

"A Sheaf of Internment Cases." 1918. *Amrita Bazar Patrika*, January 23, 1918.

Stoddard, Henry William Butter. 1919. *Mind and Its Disorders: A Text-book for Students and Practitioners.* London: H.K. Lewis.

Thompson, C.M. 1902. "A Case of Landry's Paralysis." *Indian Medical Gazette* 37 (11): 435–36.

Vaughan, Megan. 2007. "Introduction." In *Psychiatry and Empire*, edited by Sloan Mahone and Megan Vaughan. Basingstoke: Palgrave Macmillan.

Viswanathan, R. 1929. "A Case of Acute Ascending (Landry's?) Paralysis." *Indian Medical Gazette* 64 (6): 328.

Yap, Pow Meng. 1951. "Mental Diseases Peculiar to Certain Cultures: A Survey of Comparative Psychiatry." *The Journal of Mental Science* 97 (407): 313–27.

Yap, Pow Meng. 1952. "The Latah reaction: Its Pathodynamics and Nosological Position." *Journal of Mental Science* 98 (413): 515–64.

About the author

Sarah Pinto is Professor of Anthropology at Tufts University. She is author of three books, *Where There Is No Midwife: Birth and Loss in Rural India* (Berghahn, 2008), *Daughters of Parvati: Woman and Madness in Contemporary India* (University of Pennsylvania Press, 2014), and *The Doctor and Mrs. A.: Ethics and Counter-ethics in an Indian Dream Analysis* (Women Unlimited 2019/Fordham University Press, 2020), and numerous articles on gender, medicine, kinship, reproduction, and caste in India.

9 Disability on the Move: Disabled Mobilities in Contemporary India

Michele Friedner and James Staples

> **Abstract:** In this chapter, we explore multiple constellations of disability to challenge the binary opposition drawn between stasis and mobility, and to document the complex ways in which the two are entangled. We draw on multi-sited fieldwork with people affected by leprosy in coastal South India; Indian Sign Language (ISL)-speaking deaf young adults in urban locations across India; and others identified by themselves or others as disabled in Hyderabad, to document the journeys—for treatment, education, work, and activism—taken by disabled people across their life courses. While these movements should not be conflated with progress, we argue, they do create particular creative opportunities for people to transcend identities and life projects and to forge new ones that are not always open to their nondisabled peers.
>
> **Keywords:** disability, identity, medicine and rehabilitation, education, livelihood

> *"Thank goodness I escaped from community-based rehabilitation programs. Otherwise, I would still be in my village picking oranges or something like that."*
> *–25-year-old disabled man, Bangalore, 2009*

Given associations of disability with restrictions in bodily movements and participation in everyday life, exploring the apparent irony that those with restricted personal mobility in India might travel more regularly and more widely than their able-bodied counterparts is a particularly enticing prospect. However, in this chapter our aim is not simply to relish such a paradox, in the way that an earlier generation of anthropologists might have

---

Linder, Benjamin, & Tarini Bedi (eds), *South Asia on the Move: Mobilities, Mobilizations, Maneuvers.*
Amsterdam: Amsterdam University Press 2025
doi: 10.5117/9789463726498_CH09

celebrated the fact that the so-called "primitive" was, on closer inspection, more noble than his or her "civilized" fellow human (Levi-Strauss 1992). Rather, following the new mobilities paradigm (Sheller and Urry 2006), we dig below the surface to investigate both *why* those with atypical bodies might circulate more freely—whether by choice or necessity—and *how* such mobility might in itself reshape the experience of having non-normative embodiment. We argue that analyzing mobility is especially important in the case of disability because disabled people are often considered to be immobile *and* the prescriptive policy framework surrounding disability has focused on community-based rehabilitation (CBR), or on finding ways to rehabilitate people within their own communities. Indeed, there has been a valorization of the local and attempts to fix disabled people in place in international development initiatives (we also see this with the focus on self-help groups in rural environments [Chaudhry 2016]).[1]

In contrast to this privileging of the local, we explore constellations of mobility, or particular patterns of movement, representations of movement, and ways of practicing movement that make sense together, in the context of disability (Cresswell 2010). We argue that a focus on disability mobilities also serves to challenge the tendency within migration studies to privilege certain kinds of movements over others (Glick Schiller and Salazar 2013, 184), and to challenge narratives of movement that portray stasis as the norm and mobility as exceptional (186; Salazar and Smart 2011; Sheller and Urry 2006; cf. Appadurai 1996; Castells 1996; Bauman 2007). Rather, the notion of "disability mobilities" challenges the binary opposition between stasis and mobility to demonstrate the complex ways in which the two are not only interconnected but, in some cases, interdependent (also see Pinto [Chapter 8, this volume] on interactions between stillness and mobility). And, as we demonstrate, while many of our interlocutors are mobile in *attempts* to create upward social and economic mobility, in many cases financial upward mobility does not take place. Rather, what does take place are circulations, departures, and returns, and the inability to transcend or shatter educational or economic barriers.

---

1   This focus on the local is ironic because the local is also situated as a place of lack or as a "disability hell" that must be transformed into a "disability heaven" (Kim 2011). To be sure, Staples (2014a) has observed that cheerleaders for CBR in the leprosy context often have benign intentions, arguing, for example, that treating people at home is less disruptive to those people's everyday lives. What they miss, however, is that with leprosy being predominantly a disease of poverty, maintenance of the *status quo* is not always seen as positive by those concerned. In common with other categories of the disabled poor, change—precipitated through physical movement from one place to another—might well be welcomed in many cases.

We attend to disabled people's journeys within and across India, sometimes to and from natal homes, as well as international journeys. At the same time, we also explore the connections between physical movements across space—from the village to the city in order to seek medical care or education, for example—and less tangible forms of mobility, such as the movement from one social status to another. While "mobility" in the latter instance might be seen as metaphorical, a means of reifying the shift from rural poverty into the urban middle classes, we see the two forms of mobility as intimately linked: social mobility, for many of the people we encountered over two decades of ethnographic fieldwork in India, relates to, and in some cases is dependent upon, physical mobility across space. For many of our interlocutors, social mobility—especially in relation to educational and vocational opportunities—can only happen through leaving one's natal home (even though, as we discuss, people do often return). In thinking through disability mobilities and drawing on Sheller and Urry's (2006, 210) refusal of a "grand narrative of mobility," we are interested in *modest mobilities*, or incremental mobilities aimed at producing more inhabitable worlds for people. In also drawing from work in queer studies on failure (Halberstam 2011), we are interested in the ways that failed mobilities are still productive in terms of creating new political, social, and economic imaginaries. Indeed, disability as a category is attached to specific understandings of modernity, development, and capability (see, e.g., Kohrman 2005; Puar 2017). *Disability as a category is mobile.*

Before we flesh out these arguments, let us first set out the background of the fieldwork from which those examples draw. James Staples, firstly, has a longstanding ethnographic interest in the lives of people affected by leprosy. He has worked with a self-established and self-run leprosy colony in coastal Andhra Pradesh, South India—referred to here as Anandapuram—since the late 1980s, tracking people's movements not only within the colony but as they crisscrossed borders between their community and the local town, their natal villages, and far-flung begging locations across the country. Movements across these boundaries were not only counter to the assumption that leprosy colonies were remote, cut-off locations, separated from mainstream society, but were also vital to the constitution of the leprosy community as a particular kind of place (Staples 2007; 2014a). Since 2005, he has also worked in Hyderabad, India's sixth largest city, with a variety of disabled people and their families, especially parents seeking treatment for children affected by cerebral palsy. His interlocutors in this context were not only relocating to the city from rural villages to access medical treatments, but they were engaged in multiple journeys in search of cure, care and, in many cases, escape from what were perceived to be negative family and community reactions to their conditions. Attendees of a residential school for the blind in the city, with whom he also spent time, had likewise made physical journeys, mostly from the natal villages where the remainder of their families still resided. But in many cases they had also, as will become clear in the following, become mobile in other, less tangible ways.

Michele Friedner has conducted research with Indian Sign Language (ISL)-speaking deaf young adults in Indian cities since 2007, specifically attending to educational and economic mobility practices. Many deaf young adults have life histories that involve leaving natal homes in order to enroll in residential schools in other cities and states. In addition, there are few colleges that provide education in ISL or that are eager to admit deaf students. As such, deaf students travel around India and internationally to attend colleges or vocational programs that specifically cater to deaf people. Furthermore, deaf young adults often travel to Bangalore and Delhi, for example, to receive vocational training and job placements from NGOs, which then place them in employment in multinational corporations or in the hospitality sector. Deaf people are also mobile between NGOs, often circulating between them as they seek out additional training as well as repeat courses that they have already completed elsewhere as a form of "timepass" (Jeffrey 2010; Friedner 2015). In addition, Friedner has also conducted research on the emergence and transformation of "world class" Indian cities, specifically in relation to disability accessibility and the role of disability NGOs, access consultancies, and disability activists in creating so-called accessible infrastructure and public space. In this work, Friedner has attended to the ways that discourses around disability, and around disability as a category in general, have traveled. Understandings about accessibility guidelines and best practices often circulate from elsewhere (Friedner and Osborne 2013; Hartblay 2017). A particularly telling example is an Indian access consultant who often utilized photos of accessible Japanese toilets in her presentations about accessibility in India: here, best practices traveled from Japan to India.

Moving forward, we mobilize (excuse the double pun—they signal how ingrained our assumptions about movement are) ethnographic data from different moments across disabled peoples' life courses in order to attend to diverse disability mobilities. We are cognizant of the fact that we work with different populations in different spaces, and we are not attempting to create a universalizing narrative of Indian disability mobility. Rather, we are interested in identifying and analyzing the different kinds of mobilities that do exist. Deaf peoples' mobilities can be seen as quite different from mobilities of people with locomotor impairments, for example, simply because deaf people are easily mobile in terms of being able to take physically inaccessible public transport and navigate arduous roads and footpaths.[2] This of course makes light of the role of communication barriers. As our examples demonstrate, ways of managing different barriers across impairment categories often articulate surprisingly well with one another. We now turn to specific themes or areas of mobility that we have identified.

Cure and Medicine

What linked the stories told by many of the families with a disabled child that Staples and Friedner worked with in Hyderabad and Bangalore, respectively, was that they were structured by journeys they had taken. Sometimes these journeys were in search of a cure or of care, or for "disability things" (Ott 2014), such as wheelchairs or hearing aids, from other places that they viewed as life-enhancing. In other cases they were to escape the oppressive gaze of smaller communities within which they felt they were blamed for their offspring's bodily conditions. People recounted movements from Ayurvedic treatments in one place to, say, biomedical attention in another, going "wherever we heard from someone there was something that worked." One mother had taken her cerebral palsy-affected daughter with her on a pilgrimage from the suburbs of Hyderabad to a temple in Kolkata—nearly 1,000 miles away—in the hope that conducting *puja* (worship) there would bring the latter some relief. The pair subsequently made numerous similar journeys, of varying distances, from physiotherapists to homeopathic doctors, or from Unani specialists to yoga therapists, in the mother's ongoing quest for a cure. Such movements took their toll: in addition to being physically demanding for all concerned, they often separated the immediate families of disabled children from wider kin support networks. But such journeys also opened up other opportunities and connected people through alternative networks, as well as rendering those who made them field experts on the dizzying range of treatments and therapies available.

Unsurprisingly, given that a neurosurgeon's outpatients' clinic was the place where he had met them, a lot of Staples's interlocutors' stories converged in that particular location, often hundreds of miles from their natal homes. Nageswari, a seven-year-old girl with cerebral palsy, and her family,

---

2   See Kusters (2017) on competition among people with different disabilities on Mumbai commuter trains in order to see who is worthy of a seat in handicapped compartments.

for example, were not alone in having left extended families elsewhere to set up residence, often in modest, one-roomed, rented dwellings in Hyderabad, sometimes to avoid the gaze of village neighbors or the approbation of family members on whom their offspring's disabilities were seen to bring shame, but, more often, to gain closer access to the treatments that were on offer. As Nageswari's mother put it,

> Back at home, some people would tell us, you need to try this or that treatment. Others would complain that we were wasting money and energy in trying to help our child, that we should put her in a hostel. And then others would cast blame: that her condition must be because of me, or my family. "We don't have anything like that in *our* family," one of my husband's relatives would say, "so it must come from you." Since we've shifted here we don't have those problems anymore.

Living in the city not only allowed Nageswari's parents to make their own decisions—about her treatment as well as about how they organized their own day-to-day lives—but it enabled them to establish links with disability organizations, such as the rehabilitation center that Nageswari attended for physiotherapy a few days a week, and to meet with other families of cerebral palsy-affected children across caste and community backgrounds.

In the case of deaf people and their families in Bangalore, many had stories of travelling to the All India Institute of Speech and Hearing (AIISH) in Mysore where they sat in waiting rooms, waiting to see audiologists in order to determine whether their children were deaf. After receiving a diagnosis, this meant more traveling as, depending on the year, there were limited options in terms of rehabilitation and educational services, and families either had to commute across the city in Bangalore to reach an institute offering rehabilitation services and education or send their children to a well-known oral school in Chennai, a journey that could take between five and eight hours, depending on mode of transportation. Finding out that one's child was deaf or hearing impaired was a critical event that served to fracture everyday routines. Families were often urged to send one parent (nearly always the mother) along with their child to Chennai to seek rehabilitation and education at the Little Flower Convent School for the Deaf if they were willing and possessed the financial wherewithal to do so. Otherwise, they traveled with their children to early intervention programs based in Bangalore. In at least three cases, mothers had very fond memories of traveling across the city with their deaf children by auto-rickshaw or bus to attend school together. One mother in particular said that the time she spent in Chennai with her three deaf children was difficult but also very rewarding. While she had to set up her own house in Chennai and to cook, clean, and take three children to school, she was also freer and more independent, as she was removed from the space of her joint family household, and she formed bonds with other mothers who had moved to Chennai as well. Diagnosis thus led to the need to create new everyday routines and these involved mobility as resources were rarely to be found in proximity. As was the case for the families whose lives were changed from a shift to Hyderabad that we discussed above, however, it is important to stress that these mobilities to and from AIISH and early intervention programs were things that parents and not deaf youth themselves discussed. Additionally, they were often discussed ambivalently and usually involved some kind of return to one's natal home, eventually.

In some cases, however, mobility did have a more direct impact on the lives of disabled people themselves. The journeys we have described above, and the reasons for them, closely mirrored those made in the 1950s and 1960s by leprosy-affected people in coastal Andhra Pradesh. They had left natal homes at least in part because of the stigma associated with the disease and the social risks it posed to their families. Siblings, for example, might well have faced difficulties in securing marriage alliances had word got out that their brother or sister was affected by what was referred to locally as *maha rogi* (great disease) or *pedda rogi* (big disease). In some cases, interlocutors also reported that spouses or other members had refused to eat from plates that they had previously eaten from, such was their fear of contagion (see Staples 2007). But they, too, also left in search of treatment and care—or, as many interlocutors put it, with the benefit of hindsight, in search of the *prema* (love) that they found from care takers in some of the mission hospitals and colonies where they eventually received treatment. Movement, as it became clear from countless conversations over the years, was both necessitated by their condition *and* an opportunity that was afforded by it. "How else would I have seen so much of my country?" as one woman expressed it. "Without leprosy I'd have stayed in my village until I got sent to my husband's village after marriage. My life hasn't been easy, but I have seen so many different places, learned so many different things." And through their journeys the former leprosy patients of Anandapuram not only found treatment for their disease, they also radically changed their lives in other ways, too: many converted to Christianity (Staples 2014b), married outside their castes and communities, and—like those we met in Hyderabad and Bangalore years later—acquired knowledge of other places, foods, and languages to which their families back home did not have access.

Movement, then, was about attaining treatment and, with it, other potential advantages, but it also offered the possibility of escape, and for the forms of reinvention which that allowed, both for families of disabled people and for disabled people themselves. So, while Nageswari's mother escaped the negative jibes of her in-laws and developed new connections with the other parents of cerebral palsy-affected children she met at therapy centers, people affected by leprosy in coastal Andhra Pradesh began new lives in leprosy colonies where not only could they avoid the stigma associated with their disease, they could also escape some of the restrictions imposed by caste or community affiliation. It is important to consider the ways that stigma is mobile, too—it moves from individuals to families to communities. Contagion is a form of mobility, after all (Das 2001; Friedner 2018).

Education

Education and training are some of the potential benefits of mobility most welcomed by our interlocutors across locations, even though in some cases there was (initially) ambivalence because educational "opportunities" often took children and young adults far from home. Children who attended a school for the blind in Hyderabad, however, offer a good example of the perceived benefits of disability mobility. Those children were, in certain ways, similar to the children from the leprosy colony who travelled for their education. Many of them, in getting a place at the blind school, were proud to report that they were the only members of their respective families to receive any education at all, in some cases going on to enter more lucrative professions than any of their sighted siblings, the majority of whom worked as agricultural laborers or as daily-waged labor in the city. A class of year nine students, for example, in discussing their aspirations for the future one day, spoke of pursuing careers in law, music, teaching and the civil service. Those considered less academically inclined were offered opportunities to train in physiotherapy. And even if the reality did not always match the aspiration, the fact that such careers were a possibility of thought already distinguished these students from their family members who remained at home.

What was also interesting was that these children, because of the way they had been plucked out of the context of their families and natal homes, came to be differentiated more by their disabled identity—that of "the blind child"—than by that of their caste and community. Indeed, there are many blind and other disabled people who had received superior education to that of other family members because of their disabilities; they were able to leave their natal homes and receive specialized education in residential settings, together with others who were "like them," at least in terms of disability status. While for some this might have been a disadvantage, for others, particularly those at the lower rungs of the social ladder, the privileging of their bodily differences over those of, say, caste, in itself offered a route to social mobility. To be a *blind* lawyer was potentially more impressive, more immediately socially acceptable than, for example, being a *Dalit* lawyer, with the latter located in a far more politicized, contested, and, subsequently, ambivalent space.[3] This speaks to the ambiguous power of certain disabled identities; but—of particular interest to our present purposes—it is a power that can only be fully realized via mobility, by the literal moving away from the anchoring ties of home, extended family, and religious community, and into networks of other connections. On the face of it, then, although the pupils at the school for the blind benefited most from the education they were able to avail for free, and from the occupational opportunities that flowed directly from that, there were other, less tangible social advantages afforded by their mobility. And while socioeconomic disadvantage in one location often follows groups as they travel to new locations, as Ballard (1990) and others have shown, it is also the case that socially disabling identities relating to, for example, caste, even if not eliminated, are certainly diluted by distance. Indeed, movement also results in different kinds of value being attached to disability status in relation to caste or religious status. Many deaf interlocutors similarly engaged in "sameness work," whereby differences in caste, class, religion, and geographic background were ignored or obscured in order to focus on a (presumably) shared sense of deafness.

Mobility also featured widely in many of Friedner's interlocutors' stories about education. For the primary school years, before there were deaf schools in Bangalore, many deaf children traveled to Chennai, where they attended residential schools and lived with other deaf children from around India. In these residential settings, deaf children learned new practices of dress, comportment, and eating from each other. One of Friedner's friends told her about learning to eat (and enjoy) meat for the first time while attending a deaf school in Chennai. When she returned home, she had to adjust to no longer eating meat. Deaf children in these settings also had to learn new

---

3 Disability, unlike caste, religion, and gender, is a form of "feel good" diversity in urban India and is not politicized in the same ways that other categories of difference are (Friedner 2017). Staples noted in his work in schools and NGOs that the ways that sponsors and visitors spoke about blindness, inflecting it with a kind of noble status, was different to how people spoke about Dalits who received care from NGOs (who were much more objects of abject pity).

ways of communicating with each other—orally and/or in ISL—and they met deaf children from all over India with whom they remained friends. Indeed, Friedner attended an alumni function at Little Flower Convent in 2009, where she met deaf adults from all over India who had returned to the school to socialize and learn about new developments (as well as to protest about the school's continued oral focus).

Deaf young adults in Bangalore who did not attend residential schools often spoke about how their commute to and from school offered opportunities to meet other deaf children along the way—on buses—and how they would speak ISL with each other during these journeys. In addition, traveling to and from deaf schools in Bangalore provided opportunities to meet other deaf people such as Christian missionaries or older deaf role models—with whom they signed. The importance of mobility for creating social connections was foregrounded in a discussion with two deaf young adults who did not attend deaf churches, unlike many of their peers. When asked why they did not go to church, they said it was because when they were growing up, they lived close to their school and walked to school and home—they were not mobile throughout the city in the same way that their peers were and therefore they did not have opportunities to interact with diverse deaf people. What is interesting is how vitally important commuting is. While conducting research with young adults in vocational training programs, Friedner observed that there were deaf missionaries who would meet deaf young adults leaving these programs, accompany them on their bus rides home, and use every available moment for teaching and/or spreading the word of God. The commute was not just an interlude between point A and point B, but it was time for learning, sharing, and, possibly, for salvation.

Deaf young adults also traveled some distance to attend higher education programs, since programs accessible to deaf students were few and far between. Deaf students from all over India came together in Mysore to attend the JSS Polytechnic Institute for the Deaf, in Chennai to attend the St. Louis School for the Deaf, and previously, in Delhi to attend a BA Program in Applied Sign Language Linguistics. The BA program, while it was open, attracted deaf students from all over the world. There were students from Burundi, India, Nepal, Uganda, China, and Mexico, among other countries, studying together in Delhi in what appeared to be a feat of deaf international education coalescing in the Indian capital. Indeed, to be educated as a deaf person in India, as to be educated as a blind person, one often had to go elsewhere.[4] Deaf

---

4   The United Nations Convention on the Rights of Persons with Disabilities has called for inclusive education, and there have been debates around the value of separate schools for deaf

interlocutors also spoke about Gallaudet University, which was seen as a deaf "Mecca" (Lane, Hoffmeister, and Bahan 1996), which they aspired to attend.

Mobile Livelihoods

Movements across space did not stop once disabled people found treatment, shelter, and/or education. With the proliferation of both nongovernmental organizations offering vocational training and multinational corporations offering employment in major metro cities such as Bangalore, Delhi, Pune, and Chennai, many deaf young adults have flocked to these cities in search of both training and job placement services, as well as hopefully and eventually employment. Deaf young adults have been mobile between vocational training programs—moving back and forth between them and repeating the same trainings—as they wait for employment and seek out additional skill development and training. During the fifteen months that Friedner spent in Bangalore between 2008 and 2009, she saw the same students enroll and repeat the same or similar basic computer skills class at multiple NGOs. Or, as they waited for employment, they returned to NGOs to practice their typing skills.

Deaf young adults, and other disabled people in general, working in multinational corporations or in India's new hospitality outlets, were simultaneously mobile and immobile. They were mobile in that they traveled to new cities to seek out additional training and livelihood. However, often, once they were hired, they were largely immobile. According to rhetoric espoused by NGOs and diversity organizations (Diversity and Equal Opportunity Centre 2009), disabled workers tend to attrite less than non-disabled workers. Take the case, for example, of one deaf woman who worked at a coffee café chain in Bangalore and who had been there longer than any of her (hearing) coworkers. Newer coworkers came to her to ask for advice or direction on how to do tasks at the café because she knew how to do most things, although she had never been promoted to manager.

Eventually, however, this café worker left her job to go to work as a missionary or Bible outreach worker for a Christian organization. Many of Friedner's friends and interlocutors from Bangalore went to work for this

---

and blind children in particular, with deaf communities around the world arguing for the continued existence of separate deaf schools. It will be interesting to see how inclusive already existing schools become and whether there is as much of a need for traveling elsewhere to attend schools.

organization as Bible translators or, more attractively, as outreach workers. There was a sense that one had more freedom as an outreach worker—one could traverse the city looking for other deaf people, manage one's own time, and also move beyond state and potentially national boundaries. Some of the missionaries had been sent to Kenya to work at a Bible translation center to create DVDs of Indian Sign Language Bibles. And missionaries and pastors crossed state lines to attend marriages of members of their flock—or to arrange such marriages.

Those same kinds of national and international movements had also been made possible for leprosy-affected people in Anandapuram, likewise through missionary and NGO connections established over the course of seeking treatment. For a rather larger number of them, however, a key source of income—particularly in the early years after settlement—had been from begging. In Anandapuram, a number of people continued to travel long distances to beg for alms: the journey to Mumbai, for instance, the most popular location for begging, entailed a train journey of nearly 700 miles. Although some of the older members of the community preferred to keep their begging local, returning to the relative comfort of their own huts each evening, those with the most notable deformities were often very willing to travel long distances, because for the latter it was the most lucrative (see Staples 2007). These people were not cosmopolitan in the same way as the educated, upper-middle-class city dwellers—or even as evangelical pastors, whose lifestyles drew on international rather than local tropes (see, e.g., Mazzarella 2003)—but they were nevertheless noticeably different from the often monolingual, uneducated peasant farmers and local traders who occupied the neighboring hamlets and small towns of the region.

These differences were not only to do with their status as "lepers," either. Their greater and more protracted movements across space gave them a set of knowledges that also, in certain contexts, afforded them certain advantages. Knowledge of other regional languages, foods, and cultural styles meant they were more at ease in other places than those they characterized as their "simpler" neighbors. They were also able to shift between alternative identities as they moved between these locations—from a vagrant begging persona in the city, for example, to one of urbane respectability in the provincial town (see, e.g., Staples 2003). As such, they saw and experienced themselves as different from those whose movements and encounters were more limited. For example, food offered by visiting philanthropists in the begging settlement set up by Anandapuram residents in Mumbai was sometimes disparaged as "the kind of food they eat in poor villages" (see Staples 2008); different, as they saw it, to the more sophisticated preparations that their movements through space had attuned their palettes to. In addition, they were also able to use movement to counter the stresses of everyday life. Like the movements of nineteenth-century, working-class French sufferers of fugue who Ian Hacking documents so vividly in his book *Mad Travelers* (1998), going begging, or undertaking the other journeys for education or treatment that we have described, offered a sense of relief that was not achievable by staying put. It was not coincidental, as Staples has argued elsewhere (2012, 2015), that those in Anandapuram who attempted suicide or self-harm were not those who went begging but those whose lives felt more firmly anchored *within* the village.

In addition to various forms of social capital (Bourdieu 1986), their mobility, forced as in many cases it had been, also gave the residents of Anandapuram a wide network of contacts across the country on which they could rely when, for example, seeking college placement for their own children, medical treatments, employment opportunities, and/or marital alliances. The fact that many more of their children were educated and accommodated in geographically distant hostels than were the children of local farmers, for example, was not just made possible by their disease status, but because their range of contacts had been widened by the movements that their leprosy had precipitated.[5] In common with the rural-to-urban labor migration that David Mosse, Sanjeev Gupta, and Vidya Shah (2007) describe, it was not so much that village life was destroyed through migration but that the maintenance (and sometimes transformation) of rural lifestyles was, in many cases, *only* possible because of the inward flows of remittances (and information) that labor migration provided.

Deaf young adults also adopted the trappings of "middle class" (Mazzarella 2003) lifestyles as they worked for Information Technology Enabled Services (ITES) companies or in India's hospitality sector. These young adults preferred to wear branded jeans and other clothing and to frequent restaurants and cafés such as McDonalds and Café Coffee Day. There was a gendered dimension to this in that deaf young men often lived together in rented rooms and apartments away from their families and had freedom that young women typically lacked. Many female interlocutors, for example, were not able to work night shifts, and there were many more men than women involved in

---

5   Because leprosy-affected parents who begged in Mumbai had been able to bring the kinds of consumer goods into the village that, until recently, were not available locally, their movements also changed the lives of many of those left behind in the village. Anandapuram's young men, for example, could be distinguished from the sons of local farm laborers by their sartorial styles: duplicate Levi's jeans, branded sweatshirts, and trainers, in which they moved with confidence, were in contrast to the trousers and shirts stitched by local tailors.

computer training courses focused on ITES employment. Overall, however, these urban dwellers developed new tastes and modes of self-fashioning. They also developed new language practices in that they interacted with other deaf people from elsewhere in India and learned new varieties of ISL as well as new discourses about what it means to be a deaf Indian.

Recreational Practices and Social and Cultural Organizing

Many of Friedner's interlocutors in Bangalore spoke to her about how much they enjoyed *goomna,* or roaming, with other deaf people. By this, they meant going out, exploring, wandering, and generally engaging in "timepass" (Jeffrey 2010) with deaf friends. *Goomna* is a social practice among urban Indians, and it has come to have an important valence in deaf worlds in India. Deaf young adults often discussed a strong desire to go out roaming with their deaf friends because staying at home—being immobile—was a source of boredom, poor communication, and missed opportunity for growth and development. Deaf young adults often complained that they did not understand anything at home and that their families did not know ISL and so could not communicate adequately (Friedner 2015). *Goomna*, in contrast, was not just idle wandering around but was being with other deaf people and being open to the possibilities such sociality might bring. It was also the unexpected pleasure of running into other deaf people in bus stations or on the street, for example.

There are also organized recreation opportunities through deaf sporting and cultural associations which sponsor sporting matches and cultural events—including beauty pageants and cricket matches—around India. Traveling by train or bus with other deaf people (and chatting away for the entire duration of the trip) from Delhi to Calcutta is not uncommon. Staples (2003, 308–9) witnessed similar recognition between leprosy-affected people traveling by train to World Leprosy Day marches held in Chennai, where he observed leprosy-disabled people intuitively offering support to—and engaging in conversation with—those they recognized as having been affected by the same condition as they were. In the case of older deaf people attending the gatherings described above, it is also possible that they might know each other from attending residential schools together as children in Chennai. Leprosy-affected people, similarly, had often met before in mission hospitals. Pan-Indian disability worlds were not just imagined (cf. Anderson 1983); they are also materially made up of people with shared histories.

In addition to being active within India, deaf people are also quite mobile through involvement in international deaf sporting events in the Deaflympics,[6] and in cultural and educational programming through the World Federation of the Deaf (WFD) and its Youth Section Camp. Deaf Indians have traveled to the WFD congresses, which are held around the world every four years, and they also participate in Asia-Pacific-related WFD events as well. Friedner heard stories from deaf Indians who attended the 2011 WFD congress in Durban, South Africa, about their experiences traveling to South Africa and interacting with international deaf people.

To be clear, this international participation is not tied only to deafness. Since the 1980s, there has been an internationalization of disability achieved through the UN-declared "Decade of Disabled Persons (1983–1992)" and through disability activists and professionals traveling to attend training courses, workshops, and informational meetings. India is no exception, with a host of accessibility consultants that have been set up, particularly in Delhi, as part of the nation's attempt to constitute metro cities as "world class." Disability access and the seamless movement of disabled people through public space have become ways to index and promote this "world class" status. Disability mobility becomes a way of showcasing modernity, whether it be through highlighting the existence of accessible buses, elevators for the Delhi metro system, or tactile guidepaths.

Discussion

Conducting work with disabled interlocutors requires that anthropologists be mobile, too. In writing his biography of Das, an interlocutor and friend, Staples (2014) traveled with him across India by train, and followed other interlocutors back and forth on trains, buses, and rickshaws as they traversed the country to go begging, seek treatments, attend marches, or visit family in their natal homes. Friedner traveled by train from Bangalore to other Indian cities with deaf people who were members of multilevel marketing programs, and she also traveled within cities with her interlocutors, weaving through buses at crowded bus stands and hopping from bus to bus in order to take the quickest route on Bangalore's increasingly crowded roads. And while traveling with friends who are wheelchair users or with other mobility disabilities, there were

---

6 In 2017, deaf Indian athletes won four medals at the Deaflympics in Samsun, Turkey. There was much criticism of the Indian state because these athletes' accomplishments were not recognized or supported by the state. See *Hindustan Times* 2017.

arguments with auto-rickshaw drivers about whether wheelchairs were a form of luggage. More recently, there have been new taxi companies with accessible vehicles designed to transport disabled and aged passengers in air-conditioned comfort. To be sure, we do not espouse or advocate for anthropologists or other researchers to engage in disability simulations (which are regrettably quite popular in NGO and charitable circles), yet, like Sheller and Urry (2006), we are interested in considering how being mobile with our interlocutors enables certain kinds of intimacies and embodied knowledge to come to the fore, both through shared experiences and through narrating those experiences.

We also want to stress that none of the above examples are meant to suggest that movement unequivocally relates to progress, an assumption Salazar and Smart (2011) challenge in their overview of anthropological approaches to mobility. Begging, for example, in common with other forms of labor migration, is often far more physically and socially challenging than staying put at home, however necessary such movements might be for bare survival. Rather, we recognize the tensions inherent in the kinds of movements, across spaces and between social categories, that disabled people in India are engaged in. And for every disabled person able to benefit from moving, it is also worth pointing out, there are likely considerably more who, like members of the older generation of cerebral palsy-affected people that Staples occasionally caught glimpses of in Hyderabad, were hidden away in back rooms at home rather than accompanied to specialist centers or on pilgrimages. For some, disability created particular kinds of immobility.

Nevertheless, as our examples indicate, contemporary mobilities have also opened up the worlds of our interlocutors in a range of interesting, albeit often ambivalent, ways. In the past, as neurosurgeons told Staples in Hyderabad, adults with cerebral palsy and other conditions might have ended up strapped to their beds, never to leave the house, let alone the village or the neighborhood. But the explosion of information afforded by globalization since the economic liberalization of the 1990s has led subsequent generations, across income groups, to chase treatments wherever they might be. Such movements—even when they do not lead to the long hoped-for cure—create opportunities of their own: for families to ditch routines once enforced by the gaze of their local communities and to try out their own, for example, or to forge new—sometimes cross-caste and cross-community—connections with others on the basis of shared bodily differences. Movement for work opened up similar possibilities, even as disabled people struggled to get promoted, and so to move within their working lives, once they had filled the places reserved for them. Indeed, while disabled people often covet government employment, earned through a quota system, this system does not allow for advancement or promotion; once someone gets a government job, the job is "fixed" in place.

And with all these physical movements also came the chance (or sometimes compulsion) for social mobility: to transcend identities imposed by, for example, caste, and to redefine oneself (or be redefined) in relation to one's bodily impairment. Here, too, movements were of ambivalent value: a deaf or a blind professional might rank their disability identity higher than a Dalit identity, for example, but associations with leprosy were harder to present in a positive light. Nonetheless, what is important here to recognize is the *creative* potential that disability might offer in relation to social identity: having a body that did not fit pre-existing blueprints, for all the potential discrimination that engendered, offered spaces for mobility and reinvention that were not always open within mainstream society.

We want to end by thinking about mobility, marriage, and love. Many deaf interlocutors pursued love marriages with other deaf people across caste and religious lines, as did the older generation of leprosy-affected people in Anandapuram, where more than half of all marriages were intercaste. In some cases, marriage occurred across geographic boundaries as well. One of Friedner's deaf friends from Kerala married a Punjabi man from North India, while another person from Bangalore met his future Russian wife through an online Jehovah's Witness community. Such relationships serve as a platform for social, cultural, and economic (re)production, and ultimately for future mobility. Note that we did not devote time and space in this essay to discussing online communication and the kinds of mobility afforded through participating in online chat groups and support networks, and through finding other deaf and disabled people on Facebook and on other social media sites. Indeed, online communication and social media offer up possibilities for disability mobility to develop in new and interesting ways (Boellstorff 2012; Hartblay 2015). While we make no claims, then, to have provided an exhaustive account of the ways in which disabled people in India are mobile, what we have offered are some illustrative glimpses into the everyday and imaginative work of disabled people, the state, and NGOs in relation to disability mobilities.

References

Anderson, Benedict. 1983. *Imagined Communities: Reflections on the Origins and Spread of Nationalism*. New York: Verso.

Appadurai, Arjun. 1996. *Modernity at Large: Cultural Dimensions of Globalization*. Minneapolis: University of Minnesota Press.

Ballard, Roger. 1990. "Migration and Kinship: The Differential Effect of Marriage Rules on the Processes of Punjabi Migration to Britain." In *South Asian Overseas: Migration and Ethnicity*, edited by Colin Clarke, Ceri Peach, and Steven Vertovec, 219–49. Cambridge: Cambridge University Press.

Bauman, Zygmunt. 2007. *Liquid Times: Living in an Age of Uncertainty.* Cambridge: Polity Press.

Boellstorff, Tom. 2015. *Coming of Age in Second Life: An Anthropologist Explores the Virtually Human*. Princeton: Princeton University Press.

Bourdieu, Pierre. 1986. "The Forms of Capital." In *Handbook of Theory and Research for the Sociology of Education,* edited by John G. Richardson, 241–58. Westport: Greenwood.

Castells, Manuel. 1996. *The Rise of the Network Society.* Cambridge: Blackwell.

Chaudhry, Vandana. 2015. "Neoliberal Disorientations: Changing Landscapes of Disability and Governance in India." *Disability & Society* 30 (8): 1158–73.

Cresswell, Tim. 2010. "Towards a Politics of Mobility." *Environment and Planning D: Society and Space* 28 (1): 17–31.

Das, Veena. 2001. "Stigma, Contagion, Defect: Issues in the Anthropology of Public Health." Paper Presented at Stigma and Global Health: Developing a Research Agenda, Bethesda, September 5–7.

Diversity and Equal Opportunity Centre. 2009. *A Values Route to Business Success: The Why and How of Employing Persons with Disability*. Bangalore: Confederation of Indian Industries.

Friedner, Michele. 2015. *Valuing Deaf Worlds in Urban India*. New Brunswick: Rutgers University Press.

Friedner, Michele. 2017. "How the Disabled Body Unites the Body of the Nation: Disability as 'Feel Good' Diversity in Urban India." *Contemporary South Asia* 25 (4): 347–63.

Friedner, Michele. 2018. "(Sign) Language as Virus: Stigma and Relationality in Urban India." *Medical Anthropology* 37 (5): 359–72.

Friedner, Michele, and Osborne, Jamie. 2013. "Audit Bodies: Embodied Participation, Disability Universalism, and Accessibility in India." *Antipode: A Radical Journal of Geography* 45 (1): 43–60.

Glick Schiller, Nina, and Noel Salazar. 2013. "Regimes of Mobility Across the Globe." *Journal of Ethnic and Migration Studies* 39 (2): 183–200. DOI: 10.1080/1369183X.2013.723253.

Hacking, Ian. 1998. *Mad Travelers: Reflections on the Reality of Transient Mental Illnesses.* Cambridge: Harvard University Press.

Halberstam, Jack. 2011. *The Queer Art of Failure*. Durham: Duke University Press.

Hartblay, Cassandra. 2015. "Pixelization in Crip Time: Disability, Online Sociality, and Self-Making in Russian Apartments." *Somatosphere*, July 13, 2015. Accessed on July 6, 2018. http://somatosphere.net/2015/07/pixelization-in-crip-time-disability-online-sociality-and-self-making-in-russian-apartments.html.

Hartblay, Cassandra. 2017. "Good Ramps, Bad Ramps: Centralized Design Standards and Disability Access in Urban Russian Infrastructure." *American Ethnologist* 44 (1): 1–14.

Hindustan Times. 2017. "India at 70: Virender Singh Brought India 3 Golds but Can't Afford a House." Accessed on July 6, 2018. https://www.hindustantimes.com/india-news/india-at-70-virender-singh-brought-india-3-olympic-golds-but-can-t-afford-a-house/story-jafD4dRIGIFAXLHdH1IacJ.html.

Ingstad, Benedict. 1995. "Public Discourses on Rehabilitation: From Norway to Botswana." In *Disability and Culture*, edited by Benedict Ingstad and Susan Reynolds Whyte, 174–95. Berkeley: University of California Press.

Ingstad, Benedict. 1997. *Community-Based Rehabilitation in Botswana: The Myth of the Hidden Disabled*. Lewiston: Edwin Mellen.

Jeffrey, Craig. 2010. "Timepass: Youth, Class, and Time among Unemployed Young Men in India." *American Ethnologist* 7 (3): 465–81.

Kohrman, Matthew. 2005. *Bodies of Difference: Experiences of Disability and Institutional Advocacy in the Making of Modern China*. Berkeley: University of California Press.

Kim, Eunjung. 2011. "'Heaven for Disabled People': Nationalism and International Human Rights Imagery." *Disability and Society* 26 (1): 93–106.

Kusters, Annelies. 2017. "Autogestion and Competing Hierarchies: Deaf and Other Perspectives on Diversity and the Right to Occupy Space in the Mumbai Suburban Trains." *Social & Cultural Geography* 18 (2): 201–23.

Lane, Harlan, Robert Hoffmeister, and Ben Bahan. 1996. *A Journey into the Deaf-World*. San Diego: Dawn Sign Press.

Levi-Strauss, Claude. 1992. *Tristes Tropiques*, translated by John Weightman and Doreen Weightman. New York: Penguin Books.

Mazzarella, William. 2003. *Shoveling Smoke: Advertising and Globalization in Contemporary India*. Durham: Duke University Press.

Mosse, David, with Sanjeev Gupta and Vidya Shah. 2007. "Vulnerable in the City: *Adivasi* Seasonal Labour Migrants in Wesern India." In *Livelihoods at the Margins: Surviving the City*, edited by James Staples, 187–214. Walnut Creek: Left Coast Press.

Puar, Jasbir. 2017. *The Right to Maim*. Durham: Duke University Press.

Salazar, Noel B., and Alan Smart. 2011. "Introduction: Anthropological Takes on (Im)Mobility." *Identities: Global Studies in Culture and Power* 18: i–ix.

Sheller, Mimi and John Urry. "The New Mobilities Paradigm." *Environment and Planning A* 38 (2): 207–26.

Staples, James. 2003. "Disguise, Revelation and Copyright: Disassembling the South Indian Leper." *Journal of the Royal Anthropological Institute* 9 (2): 295–315.

Staples, James. 2007. *Peculiar People, Amazing Lives: Leprosy, Social Exclusion and Community Making in South India*. New Delhi: Orient Longman.

Staples, James. 2012. "The Suicide Niche: Accounting for Self-Harm in a South Indian Leprosy Colony." *Contributions to Indian Sociology* 46 (1–2): 117–44.

Staples, James. 2014a. "Communities of the Afflicted: Constituting Leprosy through Place in South India." *Medical Anthropology* 33 (1): 6–20.

Staples, James. 2014b. "Putting Indian Christianities into Context: Biographies of Christian Conversion in a Leprosy Colony." *Modern Asian Studies* 48 (4): 1134–59.

Staples, James. 2015. "Personhood, Agency and Suicide in a Neo-Liberalising South India." In *Suicide and Agency: Anthropological Perspectives on Self-Destruction, Personhood and Power*, edited by Ludek Broz and Daniel Muenster, 27–45. Farnham: Ashgate.

Whyte, Susan Reynolds, and Benedict Ingstad. 1995. "Disability and Culture: An Overview." In *Disability and Culture*, edited by Benedict Ingstad and Susan Reynolds Whyte, 3–32. Berkeley: University of California Press.

About the authors

Michele Friedner is a professor in the Department of Comparative Human Development at the University of Chicago and the author of *Valuing Deaf Worlds in Urban India* (Rutgers University Press, 2015) and *Sensory Futures: Deafness and Cochlear Implant Infrastructures in India* (University of Minnesota Press, 2022), among other publications.

James Staples is a professor of Anthropology at Brunel University London, and the author of multiple publications including *Peculiar People, Amazing Lives: Leprosy, Social Exclusion, and Community Making in South India* (Orient Longsman, 2007), *Leprosy and a Life in South India: Journeys with a Tamil Brahmin* (Lexington Books, 2014), and *Sacred Cows and Chicken Manchurian: The Everyday Politics of Eating Meat in India* (University of Washington Press, 2020). He is also co-host of the podcast The Migration Menu (www.themigrationmenu.com).

10 Conclusion: Thinking Theory, Pedagogy, Method

Tarini Bedi

Abstract: This conclusion reflects on the overall development of this volume, on our engagements with the writings of our contributors, and on the living, emergent shifts from our initial introduction to the mobilities turn as anthropologists and South Asianists. It also reflects on how to bring a mobilities orientation into a classroom and into fieldwork in South Asia and beyond. I provide some concrete ways that mobilities scholars could translate paradigmatic thinking into a pedagogical and methodological toolbox. These pedagogical examples come from my work with both graduate and undergraduate students at three universities and in three distinct disciplinary/interdisciplinary programs. It centers on how to get our students to grasp the range of theory over the last fifteen years of the mobilities turn, and on how to translate motional theory into *doing* mobilities teaching and research. I hope it provides some guidance to Anthropology students on how to embark on their ethnographic work while keeping movement in mind.

Keywords: mobile methods; pedagogy; ethnography; mobilities

Ben Linder's introduction to the vast and still richly developing mobilities turn provides an important analytical history of this turn. What Linder clearly shows us and what all our contributors address so vividly is that a South Asian perspective on mobility, rooted in fine-grained ethnographic work, can both unsettle paradigmatic claims at the same time that it amplifies the importance of paying attention to the grounded practices, categories, and ideologies that the mobilities paradigm has provoked over the last fifteen years. As Linder says, indeed South Asia is on the move. Thinking with mobilities through and from South Asia allows us to *move*

Linder, Benjamin, & Tarini Bedi (eds), *South Asia on the Move: Mobilities, Mobilizations, Maneuvers*. Amsterdam: Amsterdam University Press 2025
doi: 10.5117/9789463726498_CH10

the mobilities paradigm out of the Euro-American contexts in which it was produced—provincialize it, as Linder argues in our introduction. However, contributors, using their rich ethnographic work, do not simply take the mobilities paradigm to South Asia. Rather, they bring South Asia into mobilities thinking. This attunement to motion and movement, located in South Asian linguistic, political, and social categories, was something we felt had the capacity to South-Asianize the paradigm itself. As our introduction outlines, this is certainly what primarily drives the analytical ambitions of this volume. We were very fortunate that our contributors rose magnificently and thought provokingly and capaciously to meet this ambition. We think of this capacious thinking as vital to illustrating what mobilities approaches can do—what Linder's introduction points to as the patchwork, heterogenous hallmark of what has come to be called the mobilities turn.

At the same time, collaborative volumes do not only begin in one place; instead, they begin in various places and through different orientations to a field of study. This one began squarely in the context of pedagogy, and therefore we felt it apt to end this volume with some reflections on the pedagogical and methodological impacts of our analytical ambitions. This conclusion shows what happened over the course of the development of this volume, our engagements with the writings of our contributors and the living, emergent shifts from our initial introduction to the mobilities turn as anthropologists and South Asianists. Additionally, we also provide some reflections on bringing a mobilities orientation into a classroom and into fieldwork in South Asia and beyond. These pedagogical examples come from my work with both graduate and undergraduate students at three universities and in three distinct disciplinary/interdisciplinary domains; the department of Anthropology at the University of Illinois at Chicago (where I have my academic appointment and teach courses on ethnographic methods), the department of Comparative Human Development at the University of Chicago (where I co-taught a class on Mobilities with Dr. Michele Friedner, who is also a contributor to this volume); and the department of Transcultural Studies at the University of Heidelberg (where I did several guest lectures and designed some exercises in a class on mobilities taught by Dr. Christiane Brosius).[1]

There is a reason that I have become particularly invested in the possibilities of pedagogical relations that I now know can sharpen both analytical and methodological domains. Several years ago, in an independent study

---

1   To protect student confidentiality and because I do not have permission to share student projects, I will only discuss the general exercises designed for the classroom.

course, Ben Linder (who was a doctoral student in our Anthropology department at the time) and I (a member of his dissertation committee) began to read various strands of what was emerging in the field of cultural and critical geography as the mobilities turn. Linder outlines a broader genealogy of this literature in the introductory chapter of this volume. As he points out, the mobilities turn owed its intellectual debts to some key clusters of institutional and publication outlets, largely, though not exclusively, in the United Kingdom and Europe. At the time, Linder was working on a dissertation on the connections between changing urban neighborhoods and cultural transformation in Nepal and between Nepal, London, and Hong Kong (Linder 2022). Meanwhile, I was researching mobile labor and automobilities between India and Singapore (Bedi 2016). This was a relatively new area for me, as it was for Linder. We found this work provocative. However, as Linder's introduction to this volume discusses in some detail, this was where we first grappled with how a mobilities approach could help us think with and from South Asia as a "region" with both shared and divergent relationships to the rest of the world; through South Asian experiences as material sites for ethnographic practice; and of South Asia a linguistic, social, and cultural amalgam. This was 2014. Indeed, the expansion of this early thinking into nuanced analytical arenas—and the nudges and pushes that have been given to authors by Ben Linder—is the exemplar of how early pedagogical experiences can have long-lasting scholarly and analytical impacts. Pedagogy has blossomed into serious scholarly attention!

As our early pedagogical debates have developed over the years, we have often asked ourselves how scholarship located in South Asia and across its multiple diasporas might trouble and expand a scholarly paradigm that is undergirded by "Western" experiences and governed by Western regimes of movement. What has been the greatest strength of the mobilities turn is that it has remained open to regional and cross-regional debate; much of the writing in the journals most dedicated to mobility studies has kept to the "unsettled" spirit of the turn. The mobilities paradigm has never claimed geographical universality. It has invited into its debates some of the widest net of scholars and practitioners. In many ways, the initial claim of a "paradigm" has landed in more humble but also more generative places. In the foregoing essays, thinking with mobilities from South Asia suggests thinking with an interdisciplinary, analytical, and methodological toolbox rather than with a settled paradigm. As Linder importantly argues in his introduction to this volume, the mobilities turn encourages a singularly transdisciplinary mode of analysis. It crosses disciplines but it also encompasses an astonishingly vast range of topical areas. It seems only fit that many of our contributors to this volume have grappled with their own intellectual place within the mobilities paradigm and have developed their writing and thinking on mobilities through reading the work of their co-contributors and through suggestions and nudges from the editors. This is where the mobilities paradigm is most generative—it does not require one to fully commit to the turn but allows one to dip into the toolbox as one needs.

Anthropologists of mobility will often find themselves in a room with engineers, artists, dancers, disability studies scholars, transportation planners, environmental studies scholars, migration scholars, communications scholars, and epidemiologists, just to name a few. South Asianists of mobility will often find themselves in conversation with Africanists, Latin Americanists, and East Asianists. Therefore, this also has the capacity to open up one's intellectual communities. While scholars who work in these other regions of the world are actively expanding the field from their own geographic and linguistic contexts, the essays in this volume aim to contribute from South Asia. Additionally, as our thinking developed, we recognized that South Asian contexts and experiences provided us a way to think about mobilities in terms of movements but also in terms of maneuvers[2], which is a marriage of analytics that probably resonates in several other regions of the world. Many scholars working across these regions are explicitly invested in thinking with the concept of mobilities and its politics (Bruner 2005; Chu 2010; Hart 2016; Kotef 2015; Koyagi 2021; Mavhunga 2018; Monroe 2016; Pratt 1992; Premawardhana 2018; Small 2018; Sopranzetti 2017; Velasco 2022). Others have centered the practices of maneuver, and the navigation of movement and aspirations without necessarily tying themselves as explicitly to specific terms or concepts (Fortuna 2018; Gowayed 2022; Kleinman 2019; Piot 2019; Salazar 2010; Schielke 2020).[3]

The authors in this volume provoke us to think empirically about South Asia, South Asians, and South Asian experiences. This regional provocation from South Asia does not take the region as a settled "site" or object in the geographical sense. Rather, the diverse contributions focus on the material contexts of social relations (Sadana, Liechty, Friedner and Staples); on labor, intimate, and diasporic relations across borders (Sur, Nelson); on relational forms of *modest* mobility of disabled bodies (Friedner and Staples); on the

---

2   See Simone 2019
3   Note that for those looking to adopt material for courses and would like a quick introduction to the works, many of the monographs here have featured interviews with authors on the New Books Network (https://newbooksnetwork.com).

digital and imaginative forms that social relations take in contexts of racial hierarchies (Putcha); on the place of money, kinship, and temporal logics in moving and traveling (Liechty, Sur); on legal, medical, and embodied realities of movement in crisis (Pinto); and on policing as a regime of urban mobility (dillon). As the authors in this volume have shown so well, nothing in the world "moves" by accident, and mobilities are fundamentally relational, social, and political.[4] Therefore, in our classrooms, it becomes important to orient students not just to singular practices of movement, stillness, or redirection, but also to the relations between them. When one thinks about mobilities from and with South Asian experiences, South Asia itself becomes a moving object of knowledge, at the same time that it actually allows for an orientation to different objects of knowledge.

While we have attempted to highlight experiences from as many parts of the subcontinent, we also know that this does not represent a full coverage of every country in the region. Instead, we encourage readers to use the essays here in a classroom to speculate a bit on whether the boundaries of what South Asia is are stable at all. We also ask our readers to pay attention to the specifics of South Asian categories, practices, and worldly relations both within and outside the region that shape the possibilities and limits of movement. For example, in Rashmi Sadana's essay on the Love Commandos, Sadana makes clear that this particular social and political relation emerges at the interstices of kinship, generation, South Asian caste, and transit infrastructures. Sarah Pinto shows us how colonial science and medicine took on very specific forms in South Asia that shaped various categories of illness through their relation to mobility—frozen bodies, catatonia, head waggles, paralysis. But these are intertwined with gender, caste, and religious categories both extant and emergent in South Asia. Michele Friedner and James Staples argue against many of the dominant approaches that inform disability studies in the Western world, and they demonstrate that thinking from South Asia can unsettle the category of disability itself. Therefore, engaging with mobilities thinking with and from South Asia has the capacity to shift our knowledge of various dominant categories.

The study of the South Asian region—at least in the social sciences—has a deep history of being viewed through other paradigms, such as security paradigms, ethnicity and nationalism paradigms, democracy approaches, circulation, etc. However, as so many of the papers in this volume show, attending to a "mobilities" paradigm allows us to attend to the socialities of what these other modes elide—via things like migration, borders,

---

4 See Cresswell (2010) on the "politics" of mobility.

colonial archives, disabled bodies, tourism, migration and consumption, labor dynamics, class and caste mobility, the mobility of imaginations, etc. Undoubtedly, these are shaped by other paradigms of geopolitics, democracy, and security, but for ethnographers, a mobilities approach allows for a more intimate social science, both analytically and methodologically.

How does one translate this to carry this paradigmatic thinking into a pedagogical and methodological toolbox? In other words, once our students have grasped the last fifteen years of the mobilities turn, how can one translate motional theory into *doing* mobilities teaching and research? How can we get our students to do their ethnographic work keeping movement in mind? How do we move away not just from sedentarist analysis, but also from sedentarist pedagogy and ethnography. Anthropologists are by their trade, mobile people; curiously, until recently, our own mobile experiences and how these intertwine with those we work with in various parts of the world remain largely hidden from our ethnographic writing and remain tangential rather than central to the ways in which we interpret and analyze our ethnographic material. I have learned that it seems important to incorporate this recognition into early pedagogy so that we encourage our students not just to move away from sedantarist theory but also to unsettle our sedentarist practice and pedagogy. Ethnography, as I will often say in my classroom, is a method that trains one's attention to mundane and everyday things. Tuning one's attention to motion (and to what cannot or does not move), can make us pay attention in different ways and to different things. Of course, as Linder points out in our introduction, the sedentary and the mobile are co-constitutive, and turning attention to both provides richer ethnographic analysis. By encouraging ourselves and our students to pay attention to movement in South Asian studies, we aim to provoke different discussions that would not be possible if movement were elided or ignored.

Mobilities Resources for the Classroom

For those looking to bring mobilities-related material into their regional studies courses (or the other way around), a number of digital resources dedicated to these engagements are now available. Mobilities scholars have been particularly open to engaging transnationally and through new modes of communication. Some examples are:

- Cosmobilities Network (http://www.cosmobilities.net/)
- The Mobility, Technology, and Well-Being Lab or MoLab (https://www.eth.mpg.de/molab-inventory/introduction)

- The Mobilities and Methods Lab (MML) (https://mobilities.lab.uic.edu)
- The Center for Mobilities Research (CeMore) (https://www.lancaster.ac.uk/cemore/)
- Mobility Lab (https://mobilitylab.org/what-is-mobility-lab/)
- Mobilities and Methods on the New Books Network (https://newbooksnetwork.com/category/academic-partners/mobilities-and-methods)
- Roadsides (https://roadsides.net/)
- ReRoot Project (rerootproject.eu)

Bringing Mobile Questions into the Ethnographic Mix

In the hope that this volume also orients us pedagogically, methodologically, and regionally, I would like to direct readers to the important claim by Büscher and Urry, two important voices in the shaping of the mobilities turn. The contributions these authors make to the mobilities turn is discussed at some length by Linder in his introduction. Büscher and Urry argue that thinking with and from places of movement and stillness allows for a social science that attunes to the empirical in different ways (Büscher and Urry 2009). They provoke us to think about mobilities as both an analytical and a methodological lens. This attunement is particularly valuable for ethnographers, for whom critical thinking and ethnographic practice land in specific material and empirical contexts that encompass people, objects, laws, documents, social relations, infrastructures, imaginations, memories, and much more.

Drawing from Büscher and Urry's (2009) claim, in empirical terms, a mobility approach can orient our fieldwork in important ways, ensuring that different objects and social relations become apparent. This approach encourages us to take stock of, observe, and interrogate the following in our ethnographic fieldwork and, in turn, to think critically of the social relations and of the social actors behind them.[5]

1. What and who is "forced" to stay in place? (prisoners, a booted car, a poster)
2. What is temporarily stationary (a bus at a bus stop; a car at the petrol pump; someone in queue in a line)
3. What cannot move on its own but is portable (a baby, a suitcase, an Amazon package)

---

5   This orientation to various empirical contexts is adapted from Büscher and Urry (2009).

4. What allows or restricts mobile bodies (passports, visas, airline boarding passes)
5. What makes up parts of what John Urry (2004) calls a system of mobility systems (drivers, toll-booth operators, security at the airport)

Mobility Journals: Teaching Mobile Thinking/Feeling/Sensing/Observing:

Inspired by many of the expanding conversations in mobilities studies, Michele Friedner (see Friedner and Staples, this volume) and I decided to co-teach a cross-institutional course called Mobilities in the spring of 2019. We felt right from the start that a mobilities syllabus could be open and experimental. We ended up arranging the roadmap of the course along the lines of the following thematic areas. I list them here in the order that students encountered them and to signal how the study of mobilities can be as vast or as focused as one chooses. I also list them here to illustrate that in this experimentation, there were also several points where students looked for a coherence that is more typical of graduate seminars. We wanted to capture the openness of the field and the capaciousness of the category of "mobilities," though in our next iteration we do see the need for additional coherence. A regional framing around South Asia could be beneficial in this regard. We also dedicated the last five weeks of the class for students to develop written or alternative media projects that integrated their own interests with a mobilities lens.

- Introduction: Approaching Mobilities, Key Concepts, Keywords
- Mobilities/Circulations: Historical and Transcultural Approaches
- Mobile People
- Immobilities/Boredom/Waiting/Politics
- Bodies/Metabolic Ruptures/Absorption
- Automobilities
- Mobile Deaf
- Movements of Caste, Class, Race, Religion and Queer Mobilities
- Vital Capital Mobilities
- Cosmologies and Linkages
- Migrations/Workers/Bodies

Our two campuses—the University of Illinois at Chicago and the University of Chicago—are about 8.5 miles apart, and students from our two universities traveled to one or the other campus each week for our seminars. The *moving* nature of the class was appropriate to the subject matter, and I am so grateful to the twenty students who were along for the ride! They came with many disciplinary and interdisciplinary interests ranging from anthropology, sociology, disability studies, dance studies, science and technology studies, and urban planning. About one-third were planning to work, or already were working, somewhere in South Asia, while the rest were planning projects in various other parts of the world. Several were working in our own city of Chicago. While Michele Friedner and I both conduct our own scholarly research in various parts of India, our class did not focus explicitly on South Asian topics, though some of the readings we assigned were on South Asia. An earlier published version of Rashmi Sadana's essay in this volume was on our reading list (Sadana 2018). It provoked a great deal of discussion about how to think about the emotive and the mobile together, or how love and mobility are so closely intertwined. This was an entry into asking students what kinds of "vehicles" we might focus on that move people and their social relations around. This search for the material expressions of these *vehicles* can support where and what we look for when we are doing fieldwork. For instance, while Mark Liechty's essay in this volume illustrates the importance of the vehicles of aviation in producing the differently classed experiences of tourism, Sadana illuminates the ways that forbidden love is enabled by the presence of railway lines. Andrew Nelson's essay illustrates how labor relations are both the object and the relations that travel with diasporas, showing that these dynamics also mediate the social and professional relations between different migrant communities in the United States.

In our mobilities class, one of the key assignments that we asked students to focus on throughout the semester was the production of what we called "mobility journals." These were intended both as low-stakes reflections on the experience of movement and on its limits and as practice for ethnographers to get into the habit of notetaking. Many of our students took this exercise into their fieldwork, where they also added their reflections on and observations about stillness, rhythms, blockages, jams, and other crises of movement, as both Pinto and Sur help us see in their essays in this volume.

Mobility Journal Exercise

Assignment: As part of the course, we will all keep a journal in which we write about our experiences of commuting to and from campus as well as other kinds of commutes, we've taken during the week. During Week 7, we will ask each of you to reflect upon your journal, what you've written, and the kinds of insights within it. As part of this, we invite everyone to read a sample entry aloud and to share how experiences of and thinking about mobility, as part of your commute or otherwise, have changed or not.

We do not expect polished write-ups for every week. Rather, we expect you to get into a practice or to experiment with different practices of documentation. You might jot something, you might talk into your phone and then have it auto-entered into text, you might take a photo, etc. At least two of these entries though should take the format of the traditional "field note"—this will give you and us an opportunity to practice with this genre. While the "field" in these field notes might center your experiences of travel outside your homes in your everyday lives, you are not bound to make "field notes" of travel/transit experiences only. Other experiences of movement both at home and outside your homes that many of you mentioned in class such as cooking, walking, dancing, skating, crocheting, Facetimeing, etc. could also be included as notes in your mobility journals.

For your presentation for week seven, we expect the following:
- An oral reflection on your experience of writing or keeping the mobility journal
- The sharing of a sample entry with the class
- Turn in to us a document: either a fieldnote entry (that is typed up in the words or diagrams/schematics you used to write it and a reflection on this entry), an image with a typed up analysis/overview/reflection, a sound recording with a typed up analysis/overview/reflection, etc. This document should be no more than 500–600 words (approximately two double spaced pages)

We found this exercise a useful way to ground our theoretical and methodological goals for the class. The structure of the class project above allowed us to orient our students in two important arenas. The first was to get them habituated to the regular practice of writing fieldnotes. Because commuting and journaling did not ask students to do things that required too much extra commitment, it was a low stakes way to bring them into this practice. Second, while the journals began as personal notes and experiences, over the course of the term we saw that students began to pay close attention to the intersections between the sensory and the spatial; they also began to attune to the movements of other people and things they encountered and to the obstacles to movement that were so taken for granted that they did not otherwise rise to conscious articulations. The final two-page document allowed students to bring their readings and ethnographic observations together. Certainly, this kind of method is possible in a wide range of classes. However, because mobility and its limits are mundane and everyday experiences, I have found that it was easier to combine the pedagogy of theory and method into the same classroom. The mobility journals also took a lot of the burden off students to find a "place" or a "site" for research. Instead, it allowed them to shed the presumptions of settled places to collect material as they traversed the city. Many of our authors point to how this different form of attention and relationship to moving spaces and people can yield rich insights.

Algorithmic Walks: Contingent and Socially Produced Movement

I have spent almost two decades conducting research in South Asia. While digital maps via the ubiquitous mobile phone have come to occupy an important place in South Asian life, the realities of South Asian landscapes and the social understandings of space, time, and distance mean that patterns and possibilities of mobility rely on socially produced algorithmic decisions rather than entirely on technologically dictated ones. A mobile method that scholars have loosely called an Algorithmic walk (Ziewitz 2017) is an interesting way to introduce students to the uncertainties and contingent decision-making that occurs when traveling outside the dictates of a point-to-point digital map where people must attend instead to the social and cultural contexts within which mobility takes place. Below is a version of the exercise adapted from Ziewitz (2017) that I have used in my classrooms both at the University of Illinois at Chicago (UIC) and at the University of Heidelberg. In the case of the former, students conducted this exercise in and around the urban UIC campus in the city of Chicago, located just west of the downtown area. In the case of the latter, the students conducted the exercise around one of the three University of Heidelberg campuses located very close to the city's main Altstadt/downtown location and to its major, central transit hub at Bismarkplatz. In both cases students moved in groups of between two and five classmates. In the case of the University of Illinois students, the exercise took place in the early weeks of a semester-long class on ethnographic methods. These students were entirely unfamiliar with the mobilities paradigm but engaged with the method as part of several other methods in ethnographic research. In the case of the University of Heidelberg, the exercise took place several weeks into a class specifically on mobilities, where students had read a significant amount of the key literature on the mobilities paradigm but had until then had no exposure to hands-on ethnographic experiences in the world outside the classroom.

University of Illinois:
In this class, we will do an exercise to help us learn how to approach our ethnographic projects with an openness that is not predetermined. While most of the time, we have all become accustomed to following "maps" that already predetermine our way through the world, this exercise will open us up to making our own "algorithms" and decisions for where we will go. This exercise draws on scholars who work on questions of logistics, movement, and Science, Technology, and Society Studies to trace how and why people make certain decisions on how to approach a problem of logistics.

We will all meet outside the UIC Pavilion (and not in the classroom). I will divide students into groups of four to five. Each group will take about five minutes to decide amongst themselves how they will make their way back to the classroom in Lincoln Hall. No one can use google maps. There are four rules you must follow:

1. Each group must procure a CTA ticket from a vending machine at either the Racine or the Halsted Station. Decide amongst yourselves how you will pay for it/who will pay for it and how?
2. Each group must take at least two right turns and at least one left turn along the routes they choose to get back to the classroom.
3. Each group must stop ONE person they see and ask for directions to Lincoln Hall. Make note of what responses you get. You may or may not take the person's advice.
4. In order to get credit for this assignment, you all have to be back in the classroom no later than 5:35pm.

University of Heidelberg:
In this class we will do an exercise to help us learn how to approach our ethnographic projects with an openness that is not predetermined. While most of the time, we have all become accustomed to following "maps" that already predetermine our way through the world, this exercise will open us up to making our own "algorithms" and decisions for where we will go. This exercise draws on scholars who work on questions of logistics, movement, and Science, Technology, and Society Studies to trace how and why people make certain decisions on how to approach problems of getting from one place to another.

We will all meet in the courtyard outside HCTS (please arrive a bit early as though you have to catch a train that leaves at 11:07 sharp. We will divide students into groups of four to five; and we will leave the building at 11:07 sharp.

If you miss the train, you must sit on the bench outside the building and make notes of all the things that you did that morning that prevented you from joining the exercise. No one can use google maps or communicate with each other via text or phone.

There are six rules you must follow:
1. Each group must purchase ONE bottle of water from somewhere along the route you take. Decide amongst yourselves where you will buy this, and how you will pay for it/who will pay for it and how?
2. Each group must take at least two right turns and at least one left turn along the routes they choose to get back to the classroom (each person must individually record either in a notebook or on your phones where you took these turns and how and who decided where to turn). Remember you can't lose each other—you have to stay together.
3. Each group must stop at at least one restaurant, coffeeshop, or shop along the way and stop there to look at the menu or to take a picture of an item or commodity that you think has traveled from somewhere else to Heidelberg. You can decide amongst yourselves what this will be, but it has to be just one that you can all agree on.
4. For about five to ten minutes of the walk, each group must experiment with tempo and flow—i.e., walk very slowly or very fast, or stop against the conventional route of the flow; notice what happens for example when you stand still in the walking or biking lane or when you walk backwards. Note what others around you do to either accommodate or avoid you.
5. Each group must also stop ONE person they see and ask for directions to the HCTS building. Make note of what responses you get, what languages you use; note why you chose to ask that person and not someone else. You may or may not take the person's advice on direction.
6. You all have to be back in the classroom no later than 12:07. We will begin the discussion promptly at 12:07.

In both cases the attunement to mobility and movement, like it did in the previous exercise using mobility journals, allowed us to encourage students to straddle theory and method. In both cases students were asked to reflect both in the classroom and in fieldnotes on their experience with the algorithmic walk. They were asked to pay particular attention to the obstacles that their walk encountered. They were asked to draw diagrams/maps/photos of the route they took. They reflected on who or what they think was responsible for their obstacles. They were asked to pay attention to the languages they heard or needed to use in asking directions. Who did they see along the way and how did they make decisions along the way? What happened when they changed tempo? How did the social/infrastructural contexts affect the ways they moved individually and as a group? How does moving here differ from moving in other places? In both cases the exercise generated vigorous conversation, analysis, speculation, and not a little discomfort.

In conclusion, as Linder's provocation that opens this volume says, we invite you into what we hope will be a shared and expanding conversation. This is a conversation that grapples with what we mean when we speak of South Asian mobilities and what South Asian ethnographic and analytical categories can do to expand mobilities approaches elsewhere. We also invite you to think with us about how we can materially and ethically do mobilities research and teach our students how to center movement and mobility as key ethnographic modes of inquiry.

We very much hope that this volume will provide our readers with a capacious and creative understanding of how to think about the mobilities turn in all its various aspects—first as a regional approach from and with South Asian categories, linguistic navigations, and experiences. We also hope that in the classroom it will encourage students to consider the different objects that mediate mobility practices. We invite our readers who are South Asianists to expand these categories from different regions of South Asia, as we always intended this to be an emergent rather than a closed or definitive volume. We also hope that it will inspire collections from other regions of the world. Most importantly, we truly hope that this volume provokes its readers to read each of this volume's essays in conceptual, pedagogical, and methodological terms.

References

Bedi, Tarini. 2016. "Taxi Drivers, Infrastructures and Urban Change in Globalizing Mumbai." *City and Society* 28 (3): 387–410.

Bruner, Edward M. 2005. *Culture on Tour: Ethnographies of Travel*. Chicago: University of Chicago Press.

Büscher, Monika, and John Urry. 2009. "Mobile Methods and the Empirical." *European Journal of Social Theory* 12 (1): 99–116.

Chu, Julie. 2010. *Cosmologies of Credit: Transnational Mobility and the Politics of Destination in China*. Durham: Duke University Press.

Cresswell, Tim. 2010. "Towards a Politics of Mobility." *Environment and Planning D: Society and Space* 28 (1): 17–31.

Fortuna, Victoria. 2018. *Moving Otherwise: Dance, Violence and Memory in Buenos Aires*. Oxford: Oxford University Press.

Gowayed, Heba. 2022. *Refuge: How the State Shapes Human Potential.* Princeton: Princeton University Press.

Hart, Jennifer Anne. 2016. *Ghana on the Go: African Mobility in the Age of Motor Transportation*. Bloomington: Indiana University Press.

Kleinman, Julie. 2019. *Adventure Capital: Migration and the Making of an African Hub in Paris*. Oakland: University of California Press.

Kotef, Hagar. 2015. *Movement and the Ordering of Freedom: On Liberal Governances of Mobility*. Durham: Duke University Press.

Koyagi, Mikiya. 2021. *Iran in Motion: Mobility, Space, and the Trans-Iranian Railway*. Stanford: Stanford University Press.

Linder, Benjamin. 2022. "Placing Practice in Thamel, Kathmandu." *American Ethnologist* 49 (3): 427–41.

Mavhunga, Clapperton Chakanetsa. 2018. *The Mobile Workshop: The Tsetse Fly and African Knowledge Production*. Cambridge: MIT Press.

Monroe, Kristin. 2016. *The Insecure City: Space, Power, and Mobility in Beirut*. Rutgers: Rutgers University Press.

Piot, Charles. 2019. *The Fixer: Visa Lottery Chronicles*. Durham and London: Duke University Press.

Pratt, Mary Louise. 1992. *Imperial Eyes: Travel Writing and Transculturation*. New York: Routledge.

Premawardhana, Devaka. 2018. *Faith in Flux: Pentecostalism and Mobility in Rural Mozambique*. Philadelphia: University of Pennsylvania Press.

Sadana, Rashmi. 2018. "At the "Love Commandos": Narratives of Mobility Among Intercaste Couples in a Delhi Safe House." *Anthropology and Humanism* 43 (1): 39–57.

Salazar, Noel. 2010. *Envisioning Eden: Mobilizing Imaginaries in Tourism and Beyond*. New York: Berghahn Books.

Schielke, Samuli. 2020. *Migrant Dreams: Egyptian Workers in the Gulf States*. Cairo: American University in Cairo Press.

Simone, AbdouMaliq. 2019. *Improvised Lives: Rhythms of Endurance in an Urban Global South*. Cambridge; Medford: Polity Press.

Small, Ivan V. 2018. *Currencies of Imagination: Channeling Money and Chasing Mobility in Vietnam*. Ithaca: Cornell University Press.

Sopranzetti, Claudio. 2017. *Owners of the Map: Motorcycle Taxi Drivers, Mobility and Politics in Bangkok*. Berkeley: University of California Press.

Urry, John. 2004. "The 'System' of Automobility." *Theory, Culture and Society* 21 (4/5): 25–39.

Velasco, Soledad Alvarez. 2022. "Deportees in Transit Between Ecuador and the US: A Historical and Ethnographic Approach to Migrant Disobedience and its Spatial Impacts." *Antipode* 54 (2): 333–56.

Zietwitz, Malte. 2017. "A Not-Quite Random Walk: Experimenting with the Ethnomethods of the Algorithm." *Big Data and Society* (July–December 2017): 1–13.

About the author

Tarini Bedi is Professor of Anthropology in the Department of Anthropology at the University of Illinois at Chicago and Program Director for Cultural Anthropology at the National Science Foundation (USA). Her research and teaching interests lie at the intersection of urban, political, and economic anthropology, environment and ecology, anthropology of infrastructure and mobilities, cultural geography, science and technology studies, and gender studies. She is the author of two published books, *The Dashing Ladies of Shiv Sena: Political Matronage in Urbanizing India* (SUNY Press, 2016) and *Mumbai Taximen: Autobiographies and Automobilities in India* (University of Washington Press, 2022).

Index

accessibility 17, 21, 182–183, 193
Adey, Peter 11, 25, 87
aspiration 17, 18, 38–39, 54–56, 62, 64, 130–131, 135, 143–144, 186, 189, 202
algorithmic walks 209–211
Aragalaya 73–74
archive 23, 151–152, 154, 170–174
asylum 153–155, 158, 160
automobilities 17, 87, 201, 206,
aviation 16, 102, 207

Bangladesh 8, 15, 16, 21, 35–37, 39–40, 42–44, 47, 77, 131, 135
begging 181, 190–191, 193–194
Bihar 60–61, 64
blindness 182, 186–189, 195
borderlands 15–16, 35–40, 42–43, 46–47
borders 10, 14–16, 22, 35–45, 46–47, 59, 61, 77–78, 113, 137, 181, 202–203
buses 19, 47, 59, 70–71, 98–100, 103–104, 184, 188, 192–193, 205

call centers 60–62
Cardiazol 168–170, 174
caste 24, 51–54, 56–58, 60–65, 67, 70, 86, 124, 184, 186–187, 194–195, 203–204, 206
catatonia 152–154, 156, 158, 161, 163, 165–171, 173–174, 203
cell phones 58, 61, 209
Chamar (lower schedule caste group) 60
Chau, John 111–113, 116–117, 120–125
chemical shock therapy 168–170
classroom(s) 199–200, 203–204, 209–212
colonialism/coloniality 111, 113–117, 120–121, 123–125, 131, 137, 139, 151–156, 158–160, 163, 165, 170–174
community-based rehabilitation 179–180
cosmopolitanism 17, 123, 190
Cresswell, Tim 8–9, 203
cross-ethnic solidarity 133, 139, 144
cure 118, 153–154, 160–165, 167–168, 170, 181, 183, 194

Dalits 52, 54, 187, 195
Dallas-Fort Worth metroplex (DFW) 130–133, 139, 141–143
deafness 18, 179, 182–185, 187–193, 195–198
Delhi 14, 17, 51–52, 54–56, 59, 63, 102, 118, 130, 161, 182, 188–189, 192–193
Delhi Metro 17, 52, 54, 59, 193
diaspora 7–8, 14, 21–22, 24, 36, 78, 91, 123, 129, 131, 138–140, 144–146, 201–202, 207
  pan-ethnic diaspora 137–140
disability 23, 152, 179–189, 192–195, 202–204, 207
driving 17–18, 67–72, 74, 77–87, 100, 194, 206

Eat, Pray, Love 20, 111–113, 117
employment 18, 36, 129, 131, 138, 140, 182, 189, 191–192, 194
ethnography 12, 17, 54, 56, 79, 111, 133, 138, 204

family 35, 41, 43–46, 51, 53–64, 73, 132, 135, 139–140, 155, 162, 166, 182–187, 193
  expectations 45, 54, 56
  violence 53, 62–63
feminism 69, 72, 111, 113, 118
fieldnotes 208, 211
freedom 18, 53, 62, 84, 86–87, 154, 160, 172, 190–191
friction 7, 11

gas stations 22, 129–144
gender 16, 21, 24, 35–38, 46, 51, 63, 70, 111–112, 121–122, 131–132, 140, 151–152, 161, 163–165, 173, 187, 191, 203
geographical universality 201
geopolitics 15, 22–23, 108, 111, 204
Goondas (thugs) 62, 77, 85
government colleges 64
Gurgaon 60, 62

Haryana 55, 57, 59, 61, 62, 64
Himalayas 7, 16, 95, 108
honor killings 51–52
hysteria 151–153, 157, 161–166, 169

immobilities 7–8, 10–12, 14, 18, 20, 23–25, 37, 39, 42, 44, 47, 56, 59, 63–64, 86, 151–156, 164, 171–173, 194, 206
India 8, 15–17, 21–23, 35–37, 39–55, 61, 64, 72, 77, 78, 96, 99, 101, 107, 109, 113, 114–139, 144, 151–161, 166–167, 170–173, 179, 181–182, 187–195, 201, 207
individualism 51, 53–54, 63–64
inequality 16–17, 20–22, 86, 139
infrastructure 11–12, 16–17, 19–21, 24, 70, 93–95, 97, 99, 101, 106–108, 129, 151, 153, 171–172, 182, 203, 205, 212
intercaste relationships 9, 17, 51–57, 63, 195

Kathmandu 18–19, 57, 96–100, 102–105, 108, 130–131, 135–136, 138
kin/kinship 42, 63, 163, 177, 203

labor 17–18, 21, 37, 73, 77, 129–135, 137–144
leprosy 179–181, 185–186, 190–192, 195
love 52–59, 62–64, 185, 195, 207
  as aspiration 54–56, 62, 64
  as ideology 57
  politics of 53, 56, 63, 119
Love Commandos 17, 51–59, 62–63, 203

maneuvers 202
maps 43, 156, 206, 209–211
marriage 16, 35–47, 51–58, 60–66, 117, 121, 162–163, 185, 190, 195, 202
   arranged 42–43, 56, 62–63
   intercaste 53–55, 57, 195
   love 53, 55
media 15, 18, 20–21, 52, 54, 93–94, 115–117, 131, 206
melancholia 46, 155, 158
method/methodology 8, 10, 13, 24, 38, 54, 113, 115, 133, 173, 199–201, 204–205, 208–209, 211–212
migrants 8, 20–22, 44, 129–140, 142, 144, 207
migration 9–10, 14–15, 18, 20–22, 36–40, 42, 44–45, 85–86, 129–135, 137–139, 159, 180, 191, 196, 198, 202–204, 206
militarization 15, 18, 42, 67–74, 78, 80, 86
mobilities 7–16, 18–25, 37–39, 43, 53, 56, 65, 67, 69, 85, 93–94, 109, 112, 144, 170–171, 179–183, 185, 194–195, 199–207, 209, 212
   embodied 14, 63, 194, 203
   narratives 51, 53–54
   social 17–18, 43, 56, 61, 64, 130, 131, 181, 187, 195
   spatial 17, 20, 56, 112, 181
Mobilities (journal) 9, 11–12
mobilities resources 204–205
mobility journals 207–209
mobility regimes 18, 70, 83, 84, 144
mobility trajectory 64, 129, 134
momos 142–143
moorings 11, 16
morality 41–42, 55, 57, 63, 80–82, 85–86, 153, 159, 163–165, 172–173

National Geographic 96, 114–115
Nepal 8, 18–19, 20–22, 93–109, 135–137, 141–144, 188, 201
Nepali migration 14, 21–22, 129–132, 134–147
New Age music 118–119
"new mobilities paradigm" 7–8, 10, 23, 180

occupational niche 22, 129, 133
Orientalism 13, 20, 111–120, 122, 124–125

Pakistan 8, 15, 40–41
paralysis 23, 152, 156–157, 162–166, 171, 203
Partition 8, 40–41
Pedagogy 24, 199–201, 204–205, 209, 212
photography 19, 46, 112, 115–117, 126
pilgrimage 24, 183, 194
policing 18, 39, 67, 69–70, 72, 74–77, 79–81, 84–87, 171, 173, 203
postcolonialism/postcoloniality 7–8, 13, 16, 19, 68, 72, 80, 135, 137–138
psychiatry 151, 158, 166–168, 170–172
pyar (love) 58

Rajasthan 55, 64, 114
refugees 8, 14, 18, 21, 43, 86, 140–142
resettlement 41, 43–44, 141, 157
rickshaws 7, 12, 14, 17, 67, 70, 72, 74, 77–79, 81–86, 184, 193–194

safe houses 17, 51, 53–57, 59, 63–64, 213
scale 7, 9–10, 14–16, 19, 22–23, 36–37, 39, 46, 52, 104, 107
secularity/secularism 55, 57, 132
sensory 10, 13, 113, 155, 208
service labor 129, 131, 140, 144
sign language 179, 182, 188, 190, 192
social media 112, 116, 195
South Asia 7–9, 12–17, 19–20, 22–25, 38, 94, 98, 104, 112–115, 125, 199–203, 206–207, 209, 212
Sri Lanka 8, 13, 15, 17–19, 21–22, 36, 37, 67–69, 72–73, 78, 80, 85
status 18, 37, 44, 53–57, 62, 64, 82, 159, 181, 187, 193
stillness 11–12, 23, 151–152, 154, 159, 168, 173, 180, 203, 205, 207
students 312, 135, 143, 169, 200–201

taxis 17, 194, 212, 213
technology 10, 16, 19, 93–95, 108, 191, 204, 207
territory/territoriality 7–8, 10, 14–16, 25, 35, 37–41, 43, 47, 71, 98, 111
timepass 82, 182, 192
toolbox for teaching 199–202, 204–212
tourism 9–10, 18–20, 73, 76, 84, 93–109, 111–114, 116–118, 120–125, 204, 207
trains 59, 62, 82, 190, 192–193, 210–211
Transfers (journal) 12
transit 17, 203, 208–209
transport 10–11, 17–19, 56, 70–71, 77, 93–94, 98–99, 102, 106–108, 183–184, 194, 202
trekking 14, 18, 94, 101–107

urban networks 17, 54
urban planning 15, 207
urbanism 17, 51, 53–56, 64, 192
Urry, John 9, 194, 205–206
US immigration policy 131, 135, 139

visas 42, 44, 124, 138, 206
visas (United States)
   business (B-1) 139
   Diversity Visa 132, 135–137, 140, 144
   employment-based visas (H-1) 130, 140
   student visas (F-1) 130, 140
   Temporary Protected Status (TPS) 130, 140

yoga 7, 112–115, 117–120, 122–125

Publications / Global Asia

Matthias Maass (ed.): *Foreign Policies and Diplomacies in Asia. Changes in Practice, Concepts, and Thinking in a Rising Region*
2014, ISBN 978 90 8964 540 1

Volker Gottowik (ed.): *Dynamics of Religion in Southeast Asia. Magic and Modernity*
2014, ISBN 978 90 8964 424 4

Frédéric Bourdier, Maxime Boutry, Jacques Ivanoff, and Olivier Ferrari: *From Padi States to Commercial States. Reflections on Identity and the Social Construction of Space in the Borderlands of Cambodia, Vietnam, Thailand and Myanmar*
2015, ISBN 978 90 8964 659 0

Michiel Baas (ed.): *Transnational Migration and Asia. The Question of Return*
2015, ISBN 978 90 8964 658 3

Kees van Dijk: *Pacific Strife. The Great Powers and Their Political and Economic Rivalries in Asia and the Western Pacific 1870-1914*
2015, ISBN 978 90 8964 420 6

Juliet Pietsch and Marshall Clark (eds): *Migration and Integration in Europe, Southeast Asia, and Australia. A Comparative Perspective*
2015, ISBN 978 90 8964 538 8

Arndt Graf and Azirah Hashim (eds): *African-Asian Encounters. New Cooperations and New Dependencies*
2017, ISBN 978 94 6298 428 8

Wendy Smith, Hirochika Nakamaki, Louella Matsunaga, and Tamasin Ramsay (eds): *Globalizing Asian Religions. Management and Marketing*
2018, ISBN 978 94 6298 144 7

Ngok Ma and Edmund W. Cheng (eds): *The Umbrella Movement. Civil Resistance and Contentious Space in Hong Kong*
2019, ISBN 978 94 6298 456 1

Emilia Roza Sulek: *Trading Caterpillar Fungus in Tibet. When Economic Boom Hits Rural Area*
2019, ISBN 978 94 6298 526 1

Eva P.W. Hung and Tak-Wing Ngo (eds): *Shadow Exchanges along the New Silk Roads*
2020, ISBN 978 94 6298 893 4

Tamas Wells: *Narrating Democracy in Myanmar. The Struggle Between Activists, Democratic Leaders and Aid Workers*
2021, ISBN 978 94 6372 615 3

Ishihama Yumiko and Alex McKay (eds): *The Early 20th Century Resurgence of the Tibetan Buddhist World. Studies in Central Asian Buddhism*
2022, ISBN 978 94 6372 864 5

Birgit Abels: *Music Worlding in Palau. Chanting, Atmospheres, and Meaningfulness*
2022, ISBN 978 94 6372 512 5

Carola E. Lorea and Rosalind I. J. Hackett (eds): *Religious Sounds Beyond the Global North. Senses, Media and Power*
2024, ISBN 978 94 6372 616 0